Masculinity and Film Performance

Masculinity and Film Performance

Male Angst in Contemporary American Cinema

Donna Peberdy

First published 2011
Paperback edition 2013 by
PALGRAVE MACMILLAN

Palgrave Macmillan in the UK is an imprint of Macmillan Publishers Limited, registered in England, company number 785998, of Houndmills, Basingstoke, Hampshire RG21 6XS.

Palgrave Macmillan in the US is a division of St Martin's Press LLC, 175 Fifth Avenue, New York, NY 10010.

Palgrave Macmillan is the global academic imprint of the above companies and has companies and representatives throughout the world.

Palgrave® and Macmillan® are registered trademarks in the United States, the United Kingdom, Europe and other countries.

ISBN 978–0–230–28378–7   hardback
ISBN 978–1–137–33772–6   paperback

This book is printed on paper suitable for recycling and made from fully managed and sustained forest sources. Logging, pulping and manufacturing processes are expected to conform to the environmental regulations of the country of origin.

A catalogue record for this book is available from the British Library.

A catalog record for this book is available from the Library of Congress.

10   9   8   7   6   5   4   3   2   1
22   21   20   19   18   17   16   15   14   13

Printed and bound in Great Britain by
CPI Antony Rowe, Chippenham and Eastbourne

Contents

List of Illustrations

Acknowledgements

This book started out as a PhD project undertaken at the University of Nottingham and I am indebted to the Institute of Film and Television and School of American and Canadian Studies who made this project both possible and pleasurable. I am eternally grateful to my supervisors, Paul Grainge and Sharon Monteith, for their immensely valuable and unwavering encouragement, guidance and friendship. I could not have asked for better supervisors. I am extremely grateful to Jake Smith for priceless feedback on my work while at Nottingham and since. My thanks also go to Jude Davies, Mark Gallagher, Roberta Pearson, Gianluca Sergi, Julian Stringer and Peter Urquhart for their advice and comments and to Jim Burton, Fran Eames, Fran Fuentes, SooJeong Ahn, Nandana Bose, Serena Formica, Kerry Gough, Anthony McKenna, Jack Newsinger, Iain Robert Smith and the rest of the wonderful postgraduate community at Nottingham who proved that doing a PhD need not be an isolating experience. Many thanks to Roger Bromley for those conversations with me about *Fight Club* during my undergraduate degree at Nottingham Trent University that helped sow the seeds for this project. At Palgrave Macmillan, my thanks go to Catherine Mitchell, Felicity Plester and Cristabel Scaife for their support and enthusiasm for the project. I am also grateful to the fantastic Film and Television Studies team at Southampton Solent University where I have been lucky enough to teach since 2007. The opportunity to take my research into the classroom proved invaluable in making the final revisions to the book. Finally, this book would not have been possible without the unconditional love and support of my parents. I dedicate this book to them.

A version of Chapter 3 appeared as 'From Wimps to Wild Men: Bipolar Masculinity and the Paradoxical Performances of Tom Cruise' in *Men & Masculinities* 13 (2), December 2010: 231–54. Parts of Chapter 2 have been published in extended form as 'Tongue-tied: Film and Theatre Voices in David Mamet's *Oleanna*', *Screening the Past*, special issue: Cinema/Theatre/Adaptation, Spring/Summer, 2007 and 'Michael Douglas: An Ordinary Man' in Anna Everett (ed.) *Pretty People: Movie Stars of the 1990s* (Rutgers University Press, 2012).

Introduction: Being a Man

Two men sit at their desks in an office that was burgled the previous night; their future as salesmen rests in the hands of the policeman in the adjacent room. 'I swear it's not a world of men', Ricky Roma (Al Pacino) states matter-of-factly, 'It's a world of clock watchers, bureaucrats, office holders. We're the members of a dying breed. That's why we gotta stick together.' Shelley 'The Machine' Levene (Jack Lemmon) nods but is less confident than his colleague. Praising him on his performance that day, Roma continues: 'I thought: "The Machine, there's a man I would work with". That stuff you pulled. That was admirable. It was the old stuff. The things I could learn from you.' A nervous half-hearted smile crosses Levene's face: he cannot contain his pride at being complimented by the best salesman in the office but, at the same time, he knows he does not deserve such an honour for he is the man who has stolen the Glengarry leads. As Roma makes a sales call, the camera stays on Levene. The actor takes his clasped hands to his face, presses his index fingers to the bridge of his nose and slowly draws his fingers down, outlining his nose until they rest against his lips (see Figure 1.1). He chokes slightly. With a resigned laugh and sad smile, he sighs and drops his still-clasped hands to his lap. When the policeman calls his name, the camera closes in on Lemmon's face as he nods wearily. Glancing over at Roma, Levene tries to catch his eye to say sorry for letting him down, or to explain he is no longer the salesman of his younger years and needed the money, or that his daughter's mounting hospital bills left him with no choice. But confident and assertive Roma is mid-pitch and watery-eyed Levene cannot find the words.

1

Figure 1.1   Male angst performed via hand gestures in *Glengarry Glen Ross* (New Line, 1992)

The brief sequence and the film in which it appears provide a fitting allegory for the relationship between masculinity, angst and performance in contemporary American cinema. Released in 1992, a film adaptation of David Mamet's Pulitzer prize-winning 1984 stage play, *Glengarry Glen Ross* is explicitly concerned with defining male identity and what it means to 'be a man', particularly in the context of the workplace. Not only is *Glengarry Glen Ross* concerned with masculinity and male social roles but it is also a significant case study of male performance as an ensemble film. The ensemble cast offers multiple examples of male performers and performance, different presentations of angst and different enactments of male social roles. While the workers may share a similar template for the 'salesman', their performances indicate no single image exists. The film showcases an array of performances of masculinity: the aging Levene and Aaronow (Alan Arkin), who are past their prime and struggling to compete with younger colleagues; self-assured yet volatile Roma; boorish Moss (Ed Harris), who repeatedly threatens to leave his authoritarian job but has nowhere else to go; duplicitous office manager and 'company man' Williamson (Kevin Spacey); Roma's client, the hen-pecked husband James Lingk (Jonathan Price); and egotistical browbeat Blake (Alec Baldwin), the downtown rep who is called in to give the salesmen a 'pep' talk. The portrayal of this aging, cynical group of men, threatened by downsizing and bankruptcy, is a clear departure from the optimistic youth and individualism on display in 1980s films *Wall Street* (1987), *The Secret of My Succe$s* (1987) and *Big* (1988), exemplified respectively by Bud Fox (Charlie Sheen), Brantley Foster/Carlton Whitfield (Michael J. Fox) and Josh Baskin (Tom Hanks).

Although the film is an adaptation of a 1980s play, a review in *The Washington Times* (aptly entitled '*Glengarry* hits the screen with the joys of male angst') suggested that the film was 'at its prime in the recessionary 90s' in its depiction of struggling salesmen, authoritarian bosses and job insecurity.[1] As salesmen, the main characters define their masculinity in relation to the plots of land they sell, the commissions they make, the higher up the board their names appear. Placards hanging on the office walls serve as a constant reminder that 'A man only hits what he aims for' and 'Salesmen are born not made.' Despite Roma's declaration, the world of *Glengarry Glen Ross is* a world of men; the only woman seen in the film is a coatroom attendant with a single line of dialogue. For Roma, and the film more broadly, 'man' refers not to a biological sex but an identity; 'man' and 'men' are loaded terms, defined in differing ways by the members of the ensemble cast. Highlighting the precarious position of men, Roma defines masculinity in terms of honour, male unity and a strong work ethic. 'Man' is a threat used to undermine ('Whoever told you that *you* could work with men?') and incite ('Are you man enough to take it?'). Masculinity is something to have or to lack: 'You don't have the balls to run this office', Levene spits at Williamson; 'It takes brass balls to sell real estate', booms Blake; 'My balls feel like concrete', Roma bluntly declares.

Not only does the film foreground that to 'be a man' is a performance – something to be proved and acted out – it also points to the varying ways male identity is defined and performed. On the one hand, an eruption of expletives, a gesture (cupping the groin) or a prop (brass balls) unequivocally call attention to the methods and strategies used to reassert manliness.

In Lemmon's facial expressions and hand movements, on the other hand, performance is revealed for all its subtle complexity; the effect hinges on the audience knowing more than Pacino's character does but not enough to guess precisely what Levene is thinking during the final few minutes of the closing scene. Lemmon's actions and gestures – fingers to his lips, slight choke, lingering glance, defeated sigh and watery eyes – underscore the notion of masculinity as performance; just below the surface of the mask of arrogance and self-confidence that he wears as a salesman lingers a profound sense of melancholy and regret.

Masculinity and Film Performance understands masculinity as an image to be performed or acted out and explores instances where performances of what I refer to as 'male angst' are particularly visible: discursively and as representations. While the two should certainly not be confused, discourse and representation come together via the performance of male social roles, roles that are constructed and maintained by a multitude of cultural and media forms that are then taken up in screen enactments. In the main, *Glengarry Glen Ross* focuses on the salesman and the struggle to live up to all the role evokes. This is not a single identity, however, as most of the salesmen are also fathers and husbands: male social roles that compete with the image of the salesman they strive to be. *Glengarry Glen Ross* highlights the historically determined nature of male social roles in speaking to both the recessionary 1990s and the Reagan-era 1980s and, in turn, encapsulates the three core themes of this book: masculinity as performance, the actor as performer, and the relationship between cinema and socio-cultural discourses affecting men. These themes coalesce in the imaging of male angst, or the figure commonly referred to as 'the man in crisis'.

Western mass media, in the form of men's and women's magazines, newspaper headlines and editorials, novels, self-help books, advertising campaigns, music, television and film, have collectively formed an expressive field through which images of male angst have been disseminated and in which they have been played out. The positioning and interrogation of men as a 'problem' is nowhere more evident than in the burgeoning discourse around the contemporary 'crisis of masculinity' that featured heavily in popular and critical forums in the 1990s and early 2000s. 'Masculinity crisis' became a ubiquitous buzz-phrase in media and critical discourse, habitually cast to encompass virtually any moment where definitions of maleness were contested, renegotiated, or simply made visible. Quests for definition dominated academic studies of the so-called crisis, leading feminists such as Tania Modleski and Abigail Solomon-Godeau to suggest that crises of masculinity are a 'recurring theme' and that male power continually operates through 'cycles of crisis and resolution'.[2] Social historians such as Michael Kimmel have attempted to locate crises of masculinity historically, quantifying them schematically according to dominant social positions such as 'profeminist, antifeminist, and promale'.[3] Kimmel defines crises of masculinity as cultural and historical 'moments of gender confusion [that] assume a prominent position in the public consciousness', offering examples in Restoration England (1688–1714) and the US in the years 1880 to 1914. Yet the plethora of positions evident in the 1990s renders this schematic approach impossible because it does not allow for those readings that occupy or cross a number of social positions.

Backlash: The Undeclared War Against Women (1991) and *Stiffed: The Betrayal of the Modern Man* (1999), by feminist Susan Faludi, provide a benchmark for the 1990s crisis debate, demonstrating how perceptions of gender relations shifted during this period and how the contemporary discourse of crisis was framed in popular accounts in the 1990s. In *Backlash*, Faludi argued that 'so-called female crises' – such as the 'infertility epidemic' or the 'man shortage' – are constructed by the mass media, popular culture and advertising, becoming an 'endless feedback loop that perpetuates and exaggerates its own false images of womanhood'.[4] Faludi argued that media sensationalism creates the notion that women are in an unstable predicament and feminism becomes the scapegoat onto which this backlash is projected. Faludi noted that any backlash against feminist progress is not a new phenomenon, however, as such instances of revolt emerge every time women take steps towards equality.

Eight years later, in *Stiffed*, Faludi argued that a female crisis in the US had been replaced by a cultural crisis besetting men. Highlighting the cultural impact of the crisis debate, here Faludi presents the 'crisis of masculinity' as a catastrophic epochal moment, a trademark for the contemporary period. Again, she blames the mass media for their part in creating and inflating the crisis of masculinity. The man in control of his environment, argues Faludi, is the 'prevailing American image of masculinity' – an image reinforced by the 'visual avalanche of

Marlboro Men and Dirty Harrys and Rambos'.[5] These popular cultural forms produce what Faludi refers to as an 'ornamental culture' where the qualities previously aligned with manhood, 'surefootedness, inner strength, confidence or purpose', have become objects to display on the body's exterior 'by posture and swagger and "props," by the curled lip and petulant sulk and flexed biceps' rather than innate characteristics.[6] Despite acknowledging the crucial role played by the mass media in the creation and circulation of masculine myths that contribute to anxieties about male instability, Faludi's romantic, and somewhat utopian, resolution calls for men to confront such myths and unite with women to create a 'new paradigm ... that will open doors for both sexes'.[7] Her agenda shift emphasises the instability of gender in the contemporary period and suggests that responses to such moments in history cannot be easily categorised or grouped together under simple headings.[8] Yet Faludi's suggestion that the performance of masculinity is unique to the 1990s ornamental culture she describes is misleading, particularly when considering that the three icons of masculinity she calls on – Malboro Men, Dirty Harrys and Rambos – are categorically defined in relation to their 'posture, swagger and props'. While blaming media images of masculinity for the 'condition' of men in the 1990s, Faludi sidesteps the question of what such images *do* to generate such a powerful hold on definitions of gender, focusing her argument, instead, on all the reasons men appear to be 'in crisis'.

In *Marked Men: White Masculinity in Crisis*, Sally Robinson suggests that what is crisis ridden is not 'masculinity' itself, but rather the conception of a 'normative' masculinity. As the title of Robinson's study implies, the white male was at the centre of critical debates around masculinity crisis and identity politics in the 1990s, developing alongside a burgeoning field of whiteness studies.[9] The normativity of white masculinity, Robinson argues, is consistently produced and reproduced by various cultural media, and crisis occurs when it is called into question. As a result, a 'master narrative of white male decline' has developed in American culture as the cultural stability of the white male 'spokesman for unmarked normativity' has become increasingly threatened. The same cultural media then take up what she calls the 'rhetoric of crisis', which similarly functions to situate white masculinity at the cultural centre of attention, leading Robinson to suggest that the normative in American culture 'has vested interests in *both* invisibility and visibility'.[10]

Although Robinson proposes that the rhetoric of crisis is performative, labelling a crisis as that which 'puts into play a set of discursive conventions and tropes that condition the meanings that event will have', she does not call attention to the performative nature of normative white masculinity.[11] Crucially, since what constitutes 'masculinity' is always already constructed, normative masculinity is itself an image; only *conceptions* or representations of normative masculinity exist. It is important to note, however, that while the white male may appear to be the dominant image of male instability in American culture, since he represents normative masculinity, he does not occupy this position exclusively. As the following chapters demonstrate, African American actors such as Denzel Washington, Will Smith, Don Cheadle and Morgan Freeman also interact with discourses of male angst in culturally suggestive ways. Nonetheless, Robinson's work highlights the centrality of race and whiteness to the cultural positioning of men as crisis-ridden.

While I agree with Robinson that 'the question of whether dominant masculinity is "really" in crisis is ... moot', it is impossible to deny the instability of the male *image* evident in the overwhelming permeation of a discourse of masculinity crisis during the 1990s and 2000s. My concern in this book, therefore, is not with defining male crisis or arguing its existence, but with considering the *image* of instability that is projected and portrayed, for the most part by movie-made men and, to a lesser extent, by male icons and public figures in the mass media and politics. Through them I examine how angst is performed on the screen, the ways in which such performances have been read in popular culture and how particular actors may be read as embodying or epitomising male angst through their enactments.

Before considering film performances, it is first necessary to address the problem of terminology that inevitably arises when discussing male 'crisis'. The word generates a myriad set of complications to do with the ubiquity of the term in the mass media. 'Crisis' presupposes a number of connotations and stereotypes, largely applied to instances of upheaval, instability and critical junctures. 'Crisis' is often used to describe moments or situations where such instances and changes are particularly prominent or visible. The term does not tell us anything about those involved in that crisis, however; indeed, it tells us little about the critical juncture itself, apart from the perception that there is a critical juncture. Perhaps understandably then, many discussions of 'masculinity crisis' have been overly concerned with defining what the crisis actually is, locating the cause of the perceived crisis, and determining a solution by which to solve the crisis. By using the term 'angst', it is my intention to call attention to the semantic indeterminacy of 'crisis' in order to move past definitions and solutions and examine representations and what is at stake in those representations. The term 'crisis', then, is often used to speak about moments of male insecurity, instability and uncertainty in a broad sense, while 'angst' more usefully refers to the specific manifestations, performances and presentations of masculinity.

Some discussion of 'angst' has taken place in the disciplines of philosophy and psychoanalysis, where the term has been appropriated from the German word *Angst* to mean anxiety (often incorrectly defined as fear, for which *Furcht* is the appropriate translation).[12] While I do not wish to get caught up in philosophical debates around angst and anxiety, it is worth briefly mentioning how the term has been defined. For philosophers such as Martin Heidegger and Søren Kierkegaard, angst describes a specifically human emotion that does not necessarily have a definable origin. Summarising the work of such philosophers, Charles Bellinger notes:

> Angst is that uneasiness that results from the individual's awareness that he could possibly be different than he is currently.... There is a possibility that is open to him, which could become an actuality. But what would be the consequence of this actuality? He does not know and is thus anxious. He is drawn to the possibility, but at the same time he is made uncomfortable by it.[13]

Angst in this case refers to an emotion – something that comes from the individual – rather than an actual, definable moment; it is 'not the thought of specific events (real or potential) but the very nature of the human condition'.[14] Angst is clearly distinguished from both fear and crisis in referring to human emotion; while fear and crisis are predominantly defined by external factors, and crisis is a collectively received moment, angst is internal and individual.

I use 'angst' in the following chapters in order to move away from the broad ambiguity of 'crisis' but also to focus on the emotion and individuality of the term as it relates to performance. In many cases, the performance of angst is internally motivated. However, the term can also be employed to usefully describe those performances that react to or engage with the socially and culturally constructed male 'norm', which is both internal and external. 'Crisis' is the stereotype whereas 'angst' is a more constructive term to explore the nuances of performance rather than only the concept. This book examines the mechanics of masculine performances, the specific 'sign vehicles' that comprise those performances, and the ways in which these sign vehicles have been read in popular culture. The emphasis is on 'performing masculinity', which refers to men performing angst and actors performing an emotion according to codes and conventions; but it also refers to men performing codes of masculinity: an inability to convincingly present 'normative' masculinity while, at the same time, demonstrating the performative nature of the normative. *Masculinity and Film Performance* considers not only on-screen performances by US film actors, but also their off-screen performances as contributing to the construction of their screen personas. I contextualise both in a wider cultural framework by considering the notion of masculinity as performance as it is constructed in socio-cultural discourse.

Very little published work has specifically addressed the relationship between masculinity and film performance. Two key book length studies include Steven Cohan's *Masked Men: Masculinity and the Movies in the Fifties* and Dennis Bingham's *Acting Male: Masculinities in the Films of James Stewart, Jack Nicholson and Clint Eastwood*. *Acting Male* is closer to a 'star study' of three actor case studies (Robert Sklar's *City Boys: Cagney, Bogart, Garfield* is similar in this regard).[15] The approach taken in *Masculinity and Film Performance* of considering the performance of masculinity not just as screen enactment but as social performance is comparable to that taken by Cohan. However, Cohan's study is limited to the 1950s, and neither Cohan nor Bingham significantly engage with the concept of performance and its relevance to reading screen masculinities. In terms of performance, this book is indebted to James Naremore's *Acting in the Cinema* yet, while Naremore's study focuses on the specific performances of particular actors, it is less concerned with thinking about those performances in relation to gender or social context.

In more recent publications, a number of scholars have written about the contemporary crisis of masculinity or masculinity on screen, usually in terms of a specific genre. Such titles include: Brenton Malin's *American Masculinity under Clinton: Popular Media and the Nineties Crisis of Masculinity*, Philippa Gates's *Detecting Men: Masculinity and the Hollywood Detective Film*, Phil Powrie, Ann Davis, Bruce Babington's edited collection *The Trouble with Men: Masculinities in European and Hollywood Cinema*, and Peter Lehman's collection of essays *Masculinity: Bodies, Movies, Culture*. While such examples focus on masculinity, they are mostly concerned with representation and the implications of representation (that is, 'doing masculinity') rather than *how* masculinity is performed or reading such performances in relation to their social and historical context. *Masculinity and Film Performance* should also be considered alongside the growing field of star studies and smaller body of work on performance in film such as Andrew Klevan's introductory 'short cut' *Film Performance: From Achievement to Appreciation*. A number of studies of stardom have been concerned with the ideological and social significance of stars – although mostly focusing on the star as 'symbol' than examining their importance regarding gender more broadly. A recent study that has specifically examined performance and gender on screen is Karen Hollinger's *The Actress: Hollywood Acting and the Female Star*. As the title suggest, the focus is on the female actor and star and, again, while Hollinger's study considers the relationship between femininity and acting through her actress case studies, it is less concerned with examining such performances in relation to wider social implications of performing gender or the specific socio-historical period.[16]

This book seeks to combine all three approaches: an examination of the representation of masculinity on screen; specific analysis of the performance of masculinity on screen; and reading performances and representations in relation to their specific social and historical contexts. In other words, *Masculinity and Film Performance* examines the relationship *between* the performance of masculinity on screen (playing a character) and the performance of masculinity off screen (social roles, gender discourse, and popular culture).

The book is therefore divided into two distinct yet complementary parts. Part I – 'Performance and Performers' – introduces the concept of 'performance' and examines its usefulness as a term in considering masculinity as a social and cinematic construct. It does this first by bringing together definitions and understandings of performance from different disciplines and, second, by examining specific performances in film: that is, how actors perform masculinity and male angst and the mechanisms of performance. Part I situates performance in relation to cinema, performance in relation to masculinity, and masculinity in relation to the screen. 'Performance' is a wide-ranging and thorny concept that this section seeks to unpack, first, by examining the concept of performance broadly as it has been studied across numerous disciplines and, second, by providing a structure by which to study masculinity and men on screen. The chapters demonstrate how performance is a concept that should not be taken for granted or considered as only acting; 'acting' is only one of the many components of performance, and performance involves more than what happens on the screen. Part II considers the social, cultural and historical context in which performances take place and how a number of contemporary American films engage with and respond to the changing social positioning of men and masculinity.

Chapter 1 establishes a vocabulary with which to describe performance, and provides a framework for how to consider performance styles. It assesses the significance of the concept of performance, for a study of representations of masculinity and its relationship to male identity inevitably introduces a number of complex and contradictory issues. How useful, for example, are established critical theories of performance to the study of cinematic masculinities? Performance has been variously understood, by sociologists and anthropologists such as Erving Goffman and Victor Turner, by feminist and post-structuralist scholars such as Judith Butler, and by film scholars such as Barry King and James Naremore. What does each approach bring to the study of screen masculinity and film performance? Where are the similarities and contradictions? The chapter explores the concept of performance by mapping critical appropriations of the term as they relate to notions of gender construction. In doing so, I return to *Glengarry Glen Ross* as a way of making sense of the correlation between performance and masculinity.

In considering masculinity as an identity and a social role, Chapter 2 strips a number of screen performances right down to the 'sign vehicles' that comprise them, examining facial expressions, bodily gestures, and speech patterns and asking what it means to perform masculinity in these ways. Building on concepts of performance and of acting as evaluated in Chapter 1, Chapter 2 extends the study of performance, masculinity and cinema through detailed exploration of three representative actors aligned with male angst in the 1990s and 2000s. The chapter considers the male body in and as performance, examining the methods used in the creation of character in order to reveal the multiplicity of performance styles and methods for enacting male angst. The close analysis of actor case studies offers a framework for reading specific performances of masculinity. At the same time, the chapter further examines the relationship between performance, masculinity and the cinema in highlighting auxiliary factors that impact or affect performance and how it is read, such as cinematography, film technology, costume, the star persona, the director, subjectivity, and historical context.

The chapter begins by addressing Michael Douglas's associations with the 'zeitgeist', exploring the actor's agency in the construction of 'white man in crisis', particularly in *Falling Down* (1993) and *Wonder Boys* (2000). In addition to considering Douglas's presentation of character in the films as a whole, the section focuses on specific sequences in order to determine what the actor *does* to portray male angst. The second and third case studies address parts of the body and areas of performance that have received very little scholarly attention yet provide particularly powerful images of male angst. Examining the face as site of performance, I explore the gestures and 'given-ness', to borrow from Barry King, that have aligned Bill Murray with notions of 'midlife crisis'.[17] Finally, the chapter considers the role of the voice in constructing angst, examining an actor's vocal performances but also the role played by the director and screenwriter in controlling the voice. This is achieved through a close reading of William H. Macy's performance in David Mamet's *Oleanna* (1994).

Not only does the chapter focus on the actor as performer but it also assesses the impact of other factors in the construction of male angst, such as the role of the director and the difficulties of separating actorly performance from technological intervention. While it is possible to determine a repertoire of performance signs in the enactment of angst, the case studies reveal the difficulties in determining such a repertoire and, indeed, the impossibility of determining a *fixed* repertoire of performance signs. Although the chapter's main objective is to focus on the ways angst is performed and to provide a framework for reading performance *on the screen*, the case studies also reveal the cultural specificity of performing angst and highlight the importance of situating performances in their social and cultural contexts: the aim of the second part of the book.

Part II – 'Roles and Representations' – locates performances of male angst within their specific social and historical contexts. Victor Turner has noted that, 'when we act in everyday life we do not merely re-act to indicative stimuli, we act in frames we have wrested from the genres of cultural performance'.[18] The chapters in Part II consider the correlation between on-screen and off-screen performances, assessing socio-cultural moments or events affecting definitions of male identity, the impact of such moments on film performance and the effect of film performance on such moments. The male social roles introduced in Part I – father, son, husband, worker, old man – are examined in more detail through film and actor case studies. Chapter 3 is concerned with the relationship between two key tropes of male instability made evident in different cultural forms in the 1990s: the Wild Man and the Wimp. The chapter problematises stud-ies that consider masculinity according to radical shifts in identity, such as Susan Jeffords' reading of 'hard bodies' and sensitive men and Robert Bly's 'deep' and 'soft' masculinity, arguing instead that images of male identity are inherently 'bipolar' and often simulta-neously exhibit seemingly opposing traits. As an actor who, it has been argued, straddles 'hard' and 'soft' modes of masculinity, the chapter goes on to investigate Tom Cruise's bipolar performance as estranged son and self-help celebrity in *Magnolia* (1999) alongside his public performances on *The Oprah Winfrey Show* and, subsequently, YouTube.[19]

The 'fatherhood crisis' of the late 1990s is the focus of Chapter 4, which examines the problematic image of traditional fatherhood as it featured in socio-political discourse around family values and four representative films from the period. Considering President Bill Clinton's shifting political commentary on American fatherhood, the 'deadbeat dad' and issues around race and racism, the chapter challenges the assumption that normative fatherhood is equated with whiteness by analysing the father figures in *Pleasantville* (1998) and *Far from Heaven* (2002) and the performances of 'responsible fatherhood' by Denzel Washington and Will Smith in *John Q.* (2002) and *The Pursuit of Happyness* (2006).

In focusing on the figure of the aging male, the final chapter chal-lenges traditional notions of masculinity that are defined in relation to youth. I suggest that two 'events' in the late 1990s and early 2000s – the introduction of Viagra onto the marketplace and the mass retirement of the 'baby boom' – brought the aging male to the fore and called for a reassessment of what it means to be 'old' and a man. Considering Jack Nicholson as a 'boomer icon', Chapter 5 examines the cultural impact of *About Schmidt* (2002) and *Something's Gotta Give* (2003), exploring how the actor addresses fears of aging through his performances of old age and youthful screen persona.

By analysing these representations of masculinity and examining the specific signs that comprise such performances, I ask what it means to perform 'male angst'. This book does not limit itself to a consideration of performances in film, but also examines off-screen enactments of masculinity, exploring the circulation of discourses around male identity in American culture as a way of making sense of the performances of screen actors. In the following chapters I consider how film performances are culturally received both in film reviews and news items, assessing how performance is described and how meaning is ascribed through film roles. In Part II in particular, I consider film performances alongside the socio-cultural moments in which they take place and are consumed, in other words, considering performance as a 'socially-embedded experience' and a 'social and rhetorical event' not just a series of actions performed in isolation.[20] Contextualising film performances in this way is all the more important in a period in which the boundaries between fiction and reality are apparently blurring. In *Life the Movie*, for example, Neil Gabler argues that life and art have become impossible to differentiate, evident in what he terms 'lifies' or 'movies written in the medium of life, projected on the screen of life, and exhibited in the multiplexes of the traditional media, which are increasingly dependent upon the life medium'.[21] My consideration of performance in this book is not only concerned with looking at specific performances in film, that is, how male actors perform or the mechanisms of performance, but also the social, cultural and historical contexts in which the performances take place. Reading performances in relation to the wider culture enables a more objective reading and reveals more about those enactments than simply an in-depth examination of signs.

Masculinity and Film Performance ultimately considers the performance of masculinity and male angst as more than just a display but as a series of social roles comprised of a wide variety of mechanisms or sign vehicles. According to James Naremore, 'By analyzing the paradoxes of performance in film, by showing how roles, star personae, and individual "texts" can be broken down into various expressive attributes and ideological functions, we inevitably reflect upon the pervasive theatricality of society itself.'[22] This book foregrounds the link between the paradoxes of performance in film and the pervasive theatricality of society itself by considering not just the film texts and performances found within them, but the contexts in which such performances circulate. In its focus on 'contemporary' American cinema, *Masculinity and Film Performance* examines what I argue are the increasingly explicit, increasingly self-conscious performances of the last two decades that not only demonstrate the multiple ways of performing 'male angst' but, in doing so, present the male 'norm' as cultural and cinematic construct. Ultimately, by bringing together film, performance and masculinity, I shall argue that cinematic performances of male angst, and male identity in general, are intricately and intimately connected to performances of male social roles in everyday life.

Part I
Performance and Performers

1
Performance and Masculinity

The term 'performance' has been adopted in a variety of ways by numerous disciplines, from literary and theatre studies, to the social sciences and education, spanning both theory and practice. Marvin Carlson has called attention to the 'essential contestedness' of performance, arguing that different appropriations of the term are so disparate that 'a complete survey of them is hardly possible'.[1] It is not my intention in this chapter to attempt such a survey. However, there is a great deal to gain in bringing together differently inflected understandings of the concept; while effectively offering distinct and discrete interpretations, differing approaches do share key themes that are more complementary than contradictory. This chapter explores some of the central tenets of performance across disciplinary boundaries and assesses their usefulness in analysing cinematic performances of masculinity.

What, precisely, is meant by 'performance'? It may refer to the actor's actions and enactments on screen, that is, what physically takes place. But how should such performances be measured and described? And what of performances that are less visible, less obvious? If performance is understood as 'all human activity ... at least all activity carried out with a consciousness of itself' as Carlson observes, what is there to gain by considering screen masculinity in this way?[2] This chapter seeks to approach a greater understanding of the relationship between masculinity and performance, both in terms of gender as an act and social construction, and the role played by film actors in the construction and circulation of gendered acts and male social roles. The chapter begins by broadly locating performance, assessing ways in which the term has been considered in performance theory, particularly in the work of sociologist Erving Goffman, since the 1950s. Building on Goffman's analysis, I consider the ways 'performance' has since been appropriated to describe gendered identities. These include feminist scholar Judith Butler's notion of 'performativity', and Steven Cohan's 'masked' men, which bridges the gap between performance, gender and film. Drawing from film scholars such as James Naremore, Roberta Pearson and Andrew Higson, I finally map theories of performance and gender onto film performance and acting, setting up the theoretical parameters that will inform the case studies of the following chapters. I return to *Glengarry Glen Ross* throughout the chapter, extending the reading of male performers and performances of masculinity started in the Introduction, to elucidate the complex relationship between masculinity, performance and film that is central to this book.

What is performance?

In his 1977 publication, *Verbal Art as Performance*, anthropologist Richard Bauman defines performance as a term that conveys 'a dual sense of artistic *action* ... and artistic *event*' with the event comprising 'performer, art form, audience, and setting'.[3] In Bauman's terms, performance not only involves what the performer does (action) but also where and when the performance takes place (space, place and time). Crucially, in order for the performance to become an event, the performance action must take place in front of an audience; the action is watched and understood as an action by persons other than the performer. Similarly considering performance as action and event, Henry Bial has categorised performance in three main ways. The first and most common deployment of the term, he notes, is as a 'tangible, bounded event that involves the presentation of rehearsed artistic actions'. Second, Bial suggests that performance can be used more broadly to refer to *any* action or activity involving the presentation of rehearsed or 'pre-established sequences' of words or actions. Finally, performance should be understood as 'a concept, a way of understanding all types of phenomenon'. For Bial, then, performance is a conscious action (rehearsed, pre-established) and event that involves both 'a performer (someone doing something) and a spectator (someone observing something)'.[4] The task of relating male angst to performance is immediately complicated by the breadth and comprehensiveness of the term 'performance', underscored by Bial's purposefully imprecise terminology. Yet this flexibility also invites the question as to why the issue of performance has received so little extended consideration in film studies, particularly when performance is so central to the discipline both in terms of acting and off-screen performances. I will return to the possible reasons for eschewing this approach in film studies later in the chapter, but it is important to note the extensive discussion of 'performance' that has been taking place for some time in the interdisciplinary field of performance studies. This discussion usefully sets up key debates and terminology that can be further investigated via the film medium.

While performance studies is a relatively new discipline, it comprises what Richard Schechner describes as a 'broad spectrum approach', and is critically underpinned by theories of performance from academic fields as diverse as anthropology (Bauman, Victor Turner), linguistics (Ferdinand de Saussure, J. L. Austin), sociology (Erving Goffman, Pierre Bourdieu), and feminism and gender studies (Simone de Beauvoir, Eve Kosofsky Sedgwick, Judith Butler).[5] Goffman's *The Presentation of Self in Everyday Life*, first published in 1959, is a key antecedent for performance studies and his work is particularly useful in establishing terminology and approaches that can be applied to film performance. Drawing examples from the theatre to read performances in everyday life, rather than simply those performances that are acted out in the theatre or the cinema, Goffman argues:

> A status, a position, a social place is not a material thing, to be possessed and then displayed; it is a pattern of appropriate conduct, coherent, embellished, and well articulated. Performed with ease or clumsiness, awareness or not, guile or good faith, it is none the less something that must be realized.[6]

In Goffman's analysis, performance refers to 'all the activity of an individual which occurs during a period marked by his continuous presence before a particular set of observers which has some influence on the observers'.[7] As with the definitions offered by Bauman and Bial, a performance is something that is performed *to* someone; without an audience, an action cannot be considered a performance, and so performances are something to be watched. Goffman's definition also introduces the possibility of an unintentional performance; while the audience is necessary for an act to become a performance, the performer need not be aware of their presentation. The issue of intentionality is particularly important in the performance and playing out of social roles whereby the performer may be acting out a male role, in accordance with socially-determined 'appropriate conduct', but not actively aware that he is doing so.

Goffman uses the term 'front' to describe those activities in society that are 'intentionally or unwittingly' presented to an audience. The front involves a setting that often must be established before the performance can take place, such as the hospital for a doctor or the school for a teacher. In addition to the social front, the 'personal front' refers to specific 'items of expressive equipment' or 'sign vehicles' that are identified with the performer, including 'insignia of office or rank; clothing; sex, age, and racial characteristics; size and looks; posture; speech patterns; facial expressions; bodily gestures'. For Goffman, consistency between appearance, manner and setting is essential for the performer to convey 'an impression that is compatible and consistent with the overall definition of the situation being fostered'.[8] Without this 'expressive coherence', as he terms it, a performance can be undermined. For example, a surgeon is expected to wear a medical gown and mask when carrying out an operation. If the surgeon wears a Stetson and a fringed jacket, his performance as a doctor would be seen as inauthentic in the very least.

To a certain extent, the social actor can choose whether he will adhere to the accepted norm or reject it, and yet Goffman complicates this by suggesting that in taking on a particular social role, the actor usually:

> finds that a particular front has already been established for it.... If he attempts to change the light in which his task is viewed, he is likely to find that there are already several well-established fronts among which he must choose.[9]

The implication is that social actors are rarely afforded opportunities to change an established front; conventions in any given culture dictate how people should behave or 'act' thus determining the 'appropriate conduct' for a particular role or person. Departures from established conventions are then labelled as irregular, inappropriate or deviant. The notion of appropriate conduct and established fronts clearly links to ideas of stereotype and social typing whereby social roles generate types in accordance with social expectations.[10] If we understand old age as a front, a well-established role with its boundaries determined by society, the individual performing the role of old man is already restricted by the established associations of that role. The front of old age in Western society, for example, may consist of slowness, weakness, dementia, forgetfulness, impotency, tiredness, and retirement. An 80-year-old man would be expected to have grey or white hair with receding hair line or baldness, a more rounded and drooping frame, wrinkles and sagging skin; a person with a full-head of dark hair, no wrinkles and well-defined muscle tone would go against the front of old age. At the same time, it is likely that the 80-year-old may have other social roles to enact: father, grandfather, son, husband, breadwinner, or worker. As Bauman notes, 'performance genres, acts, events, and roles cannot occur in isolation, but are mutually interactive and independent'.[11] Each role should be considered alongside the other roles, working with, and often against, the front of old age, or whichever the dominant social role may be (see Chapter 5).

It is clear to see how the notion of fronts might apply to screen performance. Film actors, like social actors, have a limited number of fronts available to them when enacting a role. A film actor playing the part of a doctor would face similar decisions about setting, appearance and manner as a doctor in everyday life and would face similar obstacles when attempting to alter or adapt the established front. In *Glengarry Glen Ross*, the sales office front is indicated by large desks, swivel chairs, a chalkboard displaying 'sales to date', desk lamps, filing cabinets, an open briefcase propped on a desk, and 'Premiere Properties' etched on the door. The actors' personal fronts reinforce what is presented by the setting to create an image of salesmen: they are all white males, in their thirties to early sixties; they wear grey suits, a plain shirt and tie, and carry briefcases to denote their white-collar status. The front is further reinforced by dialogue and intonation: the use of sales jargon such as 'leads', 'targets', and 'pitch' or an animated and assertive tone adopted for a telephone call to a client. However, film narrative often foregrounds the instability of fronts and, indeed, depends on such instabilities as a mode of entertainment and interest. In his discussion of the failure to maintain expressive coherence in film, James Naremore speculates:

> Perhaps Hollywood movies give us pleasure and a sense of identification simply because they enable us to adapt to the 'acted' quality of everyday life: they place us safely outside dramatic events, a position from which we can observe people lying, concealing emotions, or staging performances for one another.[12]

The implication is that Hollywood films offer audiences pleasure not only when they are able to witness the playing out of social roles, but also when those roles are played out in ways that depart from social norms. Fronts may be deterministic but film demonstrates that they are not fixed or wholly stable.

The actor's screen persona can also be considered in terms of a front that is established as a result of their previous roles. This is certainly the case for many character actors who adopt similar roles from film to film or actors who have supposedly been typecast as a result of their film choices; the closer an actor is to earlier characters, the more 'coherent' the characterisation is deemed to be.[13] Although Al Pacino's Ricky Roma is a white-collar worker rather than a gangster, he is an extension of his characters in *The Godfather* films (1972, 1974, 1990) and *Scarface* (1983), with verbal invectives replacing the gun as an outlet for his rage. Jack Lemmon's Shelley Levene comes across as an older and angrier Harry Stoner, the disillusioned character he played in *Save the Tiger* (1973), still attempting to fight back at the powers that be. In his movement between weak and strong, Kevin Spacey's John Williamson is a forerunner of the actor's characterisations in *Swimming with Sharks* (1994), *The Usual Suspects* (1995) and *American Beauty* (1999). For an actor to 'act against type' he must try to change his social front (role) by changing his personal front (attributes); Pacino's performance of homosexuality by adopting effeminate mannerisms and vocal inflections in *Cruising* (1980) is a case in point.[14]

Developing the idea of coherence, Goffman distinguishes between a 'real, sincere, or honest performance' and false or 'contrived performances', noting that:

> We tend to see real performances as something not purposely put together at all, being an unintentional product of the individual's

unselfconscious response to the facts in his situation. And contrived performances we tend to see as something painstakingly pasted together, one false item on another.[15]

In the 'contrived' performance, the performance itself is explicit whereas the 'real' performance is more seamless, subtle to the point of not seeming to be a performance at all. In delineating between real and contrived, Goffman introduces a key problem in determining the boundaries between what is and is not performance. This boundary has been a central concern in performance studies, exacerbated by the implication that what is 'real' cannot also be a performance. Richard Schechner, for example, distinguishes 'make-believe' from 'make-belief' performances. Make-believe performances 'maintain a clearly marked boundary between the world of the performance and everyday reality', and these performances are quite obviously acted out with no confusion as to whether the act is real or not. Film performances, according to Schechner, fall into this category, with the line between real life and performance clearly demarcated by the cinema screen and rows of seating. Make-belief performances, on the other hand, 'intentionally blur or sabotage' the boundary between performance and everyday reality so it is unclear what is performed and what may be real. 'Today's American presidency – at least its public face', Schechner notes, 'is a totally scripted performance', from the speech writers employed to write the presidential address, to the props and settings that construct the political 'world' in which he resides, such as the presidential seal and the American flag.[16]

While giving the impression of being make-believe, film performances, as with performances in everyday life, are informed by actual events whether they choose to replicate, revise or ignore them, thus problematising Schechner's distinction. As anthropologist Victor Turner has noted, 'When we act in everyday life we do not merely re-act to indicative stimuli, we act in frames we have wrested from the genres of cultural performance.'[17] The relationship between film and 'real life' is most evident in films that are 'based on a true story', such as *The Pursuit of Happyness* examined in Chapter 4; but it can also be seen in the presentation of social types, like those depicted in *Glengarry Glen Ross*, that build on cultural stereotypes as well as self-consciously referencing earlier presentations of social types found in literature, film and theatre. In this case, *Glengarry Glen Ross* alludes to earlier images of struggling salesmen depicted in the play, novel and films *Death of a Salesman* (1951, 1985) and *The Man in the Gray Flannel Suit* (1956).

In distinguishing between real and contrived performances, Goffman suggests that there is a strict divide between two extremes yet his separation does not expand on what a real or contrived performance looks like, defining the concepts more in terms of how they are received than how they are presented. It is useful to consider the distinction between the two as a sliding scale rather than as opposites, as drama scholar Michael Kirby has suggested is the case with 'acting' and 'not-acting'. In his article, Kirby proposes an 'acting/not-acting continuum' ranging from the performer 'doing nothing to feign, simulate, impersonate' to 'behaviour of the type that defines acting appears in abundance'. The continuum thus includes varying degrees of performance from 'non-matrixed performing' (indicated by costume rather than action) to 'received acting' (commonsense) to 'complex acting' (multiple performance codes presented simultaneously).[18] Rarely is an action firmly rooted at either extreme of the sliding scale; it is more likely to operate between the two. However, Goffman's distinction does highlight the cultural importance of performance, arguing that performances are ultimately socially determined and therefore must be read as products of the social or historical moments in which they take place.

As well as distinguishing between real and contrived performances, Goffman divides the 'sign vehicles' used to create the personal front into the 'relatively fixed' (Goffman offers the examples of race and gender) and the 'relatively mobile and transitory' such as facial expressions.[19] The notion of 'fixed' sign vehicles is increasingly problematic, however. Scholars such as Judith Butler and David Buchbinder strictly oppose such a reading in their claims that sex and gender are performative; and theories of 'passing' increasingly question the fixity of race and gender.[20] While there is a greater potential for manipulation and contortion of the face, voice and body, it is also important to take into account an actor's natural qualities that cannot be as easily disguised or manipulated, such as the shape of a nose or a vocal lisp. Before evaluating the ways performance has been understood in film studies, the following section examines in more detail the notion of gender as performance.

Performance and gender

In conceiving of gender as an act rather than a fixed or innate characteristic directly related to an individual's sex, Judith Butler's study of the performative nature of gender provides a basis from which to understand film performances of masculinity. Elaborating on J. L. Austin's definition of performativity as 'performative utterances', Butler examines gender as an intentional 'corporeal style ... manufactured and sustained through corporeal signs and other discursive means'.[21] According to Butler, because gender is performed – that is, made up of a series of acts and rituals that are consistently repeated – it not only questions the naturalness of gender, but also calls into question the existence of a 'true' gender to begin with:

> Because there is neither an 'essence' that gender expresses or externalizes nor an objective ideal to which gender aspires, and because gender is not a fact, the various acts of gender create the idea of gender, and without those acts, there would be no gender at all. Gender is, thus, a construction that regularly conceals its genesis.[22]

The body becomes an ideological site of 'naturalized knowledge' whereby what is taken to be the norm or ideal is utilised in order to naturalise and hence disavow its very existence.[23]

For Butler, discourses of gender 'perform, produce, and sustain discrete and polar genders', which then enter into the public consciousness to become the cultural or 'regulatory fiction'.[24] Gender as performance in the theatrical sense is, therefore, distinguished from gender as performative; while the former refers to something easily put on and taken off, the latter is 'a forced reiteration of norms' that are culturally imposed and maintained.[25] Gender is thus ideological, created and fuelled by public and social discourse in order to normalise what is conceived to be 'masculine' or 'feminine' at any given time. The ideological aim of gender norms is to maintain the physical and emotional binary oppositions that set masculinity and femininity apart, for example: strong/weak, rational/irrational, macho/gentle, active/passive, and hard/soft. Contesting such gendered binaries, Butler's theory of performativity asserts that gender is fluid and subject to change. Ultimately, when the categories that one takes for granted as the *markers* of one gender or another become uncertain or unstable, then the 'reality of gender' is put into 'crisis'. The boundaries between the real and the unreal become blurred and it is no longer clear what constitutes the binaries of gender. The 'naturalized differences' are then revealed as a 'changeable and revisable reality'.[26]

Butler's suggestion that gender norms are 'phantasmatic,' that is, unreal or illusory, complements Tania Modleski's assertion that masculinity is *always* in a state of crisis because what defines it is constantly fluid and malleable; the boundaries of masculinity are then repeatedly tested and challenged.[27] Butler's theory of performativity concurs with the ideas put forward by Modleski through her persistent emphasis on the construction and maintenance of gender norms. By discussing this construction and maintenance as a strategy or 'regulatory fiction' and pointing out how performativity conceals or disavows the very existence of gender, Butler proposes that the performance of gender ultimately seeks to reinforce 'masculinist domination and compulsory heterosexuality'.[28] In this way, Butler's suggestion follows the same line of thought as Modleski's assertion that masculinity operates according to cycles of crisis and resolution; ultimately, the aim is to restore men and masculinity to their dominant societal position: to reassert patriarchy. If 'crisis' occurs when the gendered binaries between masculinity and femininity break down, the threat posed by femininity must be suppressed and the gendered binaries re-established in order for male dominance to be restored (or, at least, the illusion of dominance).

That there is no such thing as a 'true' gender is central to understanding masculinity as a performance. While a 'true' gender does not exist, images of a 'true' or normative gender are constructed and perpetuated by Western culture and particularly by the mass media via men's and women's magazines, on television, in popular films and via a multitude of other media platforms. The power of such images should not be underrated; the image of a 'true' gender is omnipotent, projected onto key words such as 'traditional' and 'natural' that help to mask their construction. Images of masculinity that go against the idea of a masculine norm thus become all the more intriguing. Butler's theory of performativity is useful to the extent that it considers *all* masculinity to be a performance and yet there is a problem in seeing each and every performance of masculinity as an attempt to reinforce patriarchal dominance. The distinction appears to lie in the difference between those performances that attempt to perpetuate the myth of 'true' masculinity by masking performance and those performances that highlight and call attention to the construction of masculinity rather than concealing it.

The ideological power of male performance has been discussed by David Buchbinder in *Performance Anxieties: Re-Producing Masculinity*, in which he concurs with Butler that 'representations of men not only often reproduce dominant notions of masculinity – in the sense that a painting may be reproduced – but also re-produce these notions, inviting men to "recognise" themselves and other men in such representations'. In this way, the 'dominant masculine' is re-produced as 'both a reflection of a particular social reality and as a model on which men in the culture may pattern themselves'.[29] The character of Blake (Baldwin) in *Glengarry Glen Ross*, for example, functions as a salesman prototype with his executive suit, BMW, designer watch and professional idioms. His character is offered as the dominant masculine, the ideal salesman who embodies success and ruthlessness. In Buchbinder's analysis, male performance is intricately linked to socio-cultural change, borrowing from the discourse and feeding back into it. But the reproduction is also carried out in ways that keep the very mechanisms of its production hidden. Masculinity thus operates via a system of cultural beliefs and practices that function to mask its construction:

> The representation of men and masculinity in the culture is not merely accidental ... such representation works to enable men to 'recognise' themselves and each other within the relevant culture and social class, and hence to approve male behaviour in terms of ideological correctness. In such a representation, therefore, is encoded a system of *prescriptions* ('Men shall be thus and thus') and *proscriptions* ('Men shall not be thus and thus').[30]

The all-male office environment of *Glengarry Glen Ross*, for example, is littered with masculine prescriptions and proscriptions: to be a man is to close a sale; those failing to close are 'losers' and 'fucking faggots'. As Levene (Lemmon) shouts at Williamson (Spacey): 'A man *is* his job, and you are fucked at yours.' Men are under pressure,

Buchbinder notes, to 'perform masculinity as flawlessly as possible, lest he suffer the withdrawal of power available (notionally, anyway) to all men in the culture, and the consequence of the displeasure, and possibly ridicule, of other men'. Again, these prescriptions and proscriptions are performative, since their presentation or enactment draws from culturally determined gender norms and social expectations, ensuring their 'ideological correctness'. Buchbinder develops Butler's notion of citation – the performativity of gender – to include what he calls the 'ex-citation and in-citation of gender'.[31] The ex-citation is the naturalisation of performativity; the process of making that which is performed appear unquestionable, not unlike Goffman's definition of 'real' performance that masks the processes of construction. In-citation refers to those features that comprise masculinity, the markers that are then taken up through performance. Performance is reliant on a system of signs or connotations when it reproduces the dominant masculine which, like Butler's 'true' gender and Goffman's 'real' performance, is a complete fabrication despite passing itself off as natural. Buchbinder's proscriptions and prescriptions ultimately present masculinity as a 'front' that is performed and presented according to socially established conventions and any deviation from that front is seen to go against traditional conceptions of male identity.

While I would certainly agree that there is much ideological power in the construction of 'true' masculinity or the dominant masculine, focusing on this power ignores the fact that notions of masculinity can also have a damaging effect on men and male identity. Indeed, what is at stake in men representing themselves as crisis-ridden? What about the constraining effect of male gender roles on men? The various roles that comprise masculinity, such as fatherhood, each have their own conventions defined by the wider culture and constructed, determined and perpetuated by the mass media, invariably informing an actor's decision to perform a role in a particular way. The 'social front' of fatherhood, as Chapter 4 demonstrates, involves a set of restricting prescriptions and proscriptions that limit the range of acceptable performances associated with the role. Retirement and aging, the subject of Chapter 5, have boundaries for acceptable and unacceptable, normal and abnormal behaviour. Crucially, as I discussed earlier in the chapter in reference to Goffman, male social roles do not operate independently but work alongside other roles and identities. In *Glengarry Glen Ross*, for example, Levene's role as salesman and breadwinner competes with his role as father; he needs to earn enough money to support his family but, in doing so, is distanced from his home life as a result of the long hours he works selling real estate. While there may be 'much symbolic power to be reaped from occupying the social and discursive position of subject in crisis', as Sally Robinson argues, this fails to account for instances where men are under pressure to fulfil the social obligations of masculinity presented *to* them, not necessarily *by* them.[32]

Steven Cohan's work on depictions of 1950s screen masculinity effectively bridges the gap between theories of gender performance and film performance. In *Masked Men*, Cohan examines the restrictive nature of male social roles and traditional notions of masculinity as perpetuated by American popular culture in the 1950s. Taking the fundamentals of Butler's theory of performativity and applying them to popular representations of masculinity in American films, Cohan also recontextualises these performances by considering the various discourses around masculinity that circulated during the decade. He proposes that a normative masculinity – encapsulated by the ubiquitous fifties figure of The Man in the Gray Flannel Suit – functioned to 'mask the social differences that stratified US society' in the period.[33] At the same time, this 'logo of the age' was challenged by films and characters who presented various masquerades of masculinity, contradicting this supposed norm. Characters such as the conflicted 'tough guy' epitomised by Humphrey Bogart in *Dead Reckoning* (1947) and *In a Lonely Place* (1950) or Rock Hudson's bachelor playboy in *Pillow Talk* (1959), presented a 'masculinity in crisis' that contested the naturalness of gender norms and questioned what constituted 'masculinity' in the first place.

Taking Cary Grant's characterisation of Roger O. Thornhill in *North by Northwest* (1959) as the definitive emblem of The Man in the Gray Flannel Suit, Cohan demonstrates how Grant performs masculinity, first in a performance of normative masculinity that conforms to the social and cultural masculine ideals of the time, but also through a performance of various other masculinities that calls the masculine ideal into question. *North by Northwest* serves as a particularly pertinent example of male masquerade through its plot, which is based on mistaken identity: Grant's Thornhill is presumed to be an American spy named George Kaplan, and he spends the film attempting to assert his real self. Grant's character takes on numerous 'masculine personae' including the Madison Avenue executive, kidnap victim, alcoholic, momma's boy, murderer, fugitive, lover, and Red Cap.[34] Each guise, in turn, is taken up by Grant in order to reconstruct his identity according to the cultural associations that each persona evokes. Not only does the film narrative indicate the fluidity of male identity and the possibility of endless re-creation and adaptation, but it questions the very essence of masculinity, for it is uncertain, after each recurring transformation, which persona may be the original or 'true' identity. Consequently, *North by Northwest* corroborates Butler's assertion that not only is the fixity of gender questionable but the notion of a true or original gender is a myth or 'an imitation without an origin'.[35] This is reinforced by Thornhill's repeated reiteration to his captors (fronted by James Mason) that he is not who they think he is although he is incapable of proving his 'true' identity. *North by Northwest* thus calls into question whether masculinity 'can *ever* be assumed to be a coherent and singular, not to say authentic, condition in culture'.[36] Thornhill ultimately realises that it is easier for him to become someone who never existed in the first place (the fantasy figure Kaplan) than to be his 'real' self.

For Cohan, 'masculinity crisis' as a term is employed to describe instances in 1950s films whereby the male protagonist is in an uncertain or unstable position, precisely because masculinity is presented as a construction and performance. In the contemporary narratives of male angst examined in the following chapters, masculinity is a performance according to which cultural expectations are continuously employed and recycled. Where these narratives differ is in the mechanisms of performance and the ways in which 'crisis' is constructed in the film. Male instability is not subtly hidden behind various masks, as in the case of *North by Northwest*, but is obvious, explicit and self-consciously aware of itself. In contrast to Cohan's 'masked' men, the men of many of the case studies in this book are 'unmasked,' their performances exposed, their male identities vulnerable and open to attack. Rather than conforming to Modleski's cycles of crisis and resolution, where the ultimate goal is to reinforce hegemonic masculinity, the performances examined in the chapters that follow emphasise the crisis not the resolution, foregrounding angst over stability. *Glengarry Glen Ross* for example, ends with Levene about to be questioned by the police detective; the issue remains unresolved, suspending the angst-ridden male, salesman, husband and father in a permanent state of insecurity.

While Cohan's study is useful in bringing together masculinity as performance and film, what the actor *does* to perform masculinity, that is, the mechanics of performance, is only given limited consideration. What does Grant *do* to depict or imply 'masculinity crisis'? How does he perform the momma's boy or lover? In other words, what codes and conventions are enacted to present male angst? In *Acting in the Cinema*, James Naremore sets out to reveal 'buried, paradoxical assumptions about society and the self' by analysing codes and conventions of film performance, or what he refers to as the 'theatrical quality of movies'. Perceiving a connection between screen performances that are passed off as 'natural' in order to be believed and the function of ideology to appear natural and commonplace, Naremore concludes that 'the very technique of film acting has ideological importance'.[37] Naremore's statement suggests that not only is it important to analyse performance gestures or signs to determine how they create meaning but that the study of performance is much more than the study of signs that comprise them and should be considered within the wider matrix of identity formation in society. In the final section of this chapter, I examine the significance of performance signs and consider the role played by performance in constructing meaning, particularly addressing those problems inevitably raised when studying screen performances of angst. This extended consideration of acting and performance will introduce some of the main ideas which will be further developed in the following chapters, via close performance analysis of three actor case studies (Chapter 2) and contextual readings of the cinematic performance of male social roles (Chapters 3, 4 and 5).

Performance and film

Existing scholarship on film and performance is limited. As Philip Drake has noted, 'The broad discussion of performance that has taken place in performance studies is yet to materialize in film studies.'[38] In the 1980s and early 1990s, notable attempts to establish a framework in which to consider film performance were made by film scholars such as Barry King, Andrew Higson, James Naremore, Roberta Pearson and Virginia Wright Wexman. More recently, collections such as *Screen Acting* and *More Than a Method* have set out to correct the critical insufficiency in film studies, yet studies of film performance remain few and far between.[39] One explanation that has been proposed for the small body of work addressing film performance is the dominance of star studies. Peter Krämer and Alan Lovell suggest two main reasons: first, star studies considers stars as unique and distinct from the 'everyday' film actor and is tied to the assumption that 'stars can't act'. As such, the study of acting is auxiliary at best in this context. Second, star studies is predominantly concerned with the ideological function of stars, aligning the ideology of the star's films with the star persona. Consequently, attention has been directed at the role played by publicity and advertising rather than performance.[40] Yet the conflict between stardom and performance in film studies is confusing; are stars not also performers and does this mean that actors who are not 'stars' do not operate ideologically?

Christine Geraghty has suggested that the parameters of what we understand as 'stardom' should be extended in the contemporary period to usefully make sense of the ways meaning is ascribed to stars. Rather than limiting the study to stars *as* stars, Geraghty argues that the ways stars should be considered are three-fold: as celebrity (private identity that becomes public, constructed largely outside film texts), as professional (public persona is indistinguishable from private persona), and as performer (the public 'work' of the star on screen). 'The different modes of stardom', Geraghty states, 'require different kinds of knowledge from audiences and although some film stars do operate as celebrities, knowledge of this is not essential to understanding their film appearances'.[41] Offering the example of Johnny Depp, she proposes that the extratextual information about the actor's alleged bad behaviour is 'largely irrelevant' when considering Depp as a performer, which 'comes instead from textual knowledge of the performance itself'.[42] While this extends the idea of star as icon and demonstrates the inseparability of stardom from performance, there is an assumption that the star as 'performer' operates outside the other two categories, discounting the fact that 'celebrity' and 'professional' are also performances enacted according to specific codes and rituals. Furthermore, while Depp's film performances can be read without taking into account the actor's off-screen behaviour, extratextual knowledge shapes audience perceptions of actors and performances, leading me to disagree with Geraghty and suggest that this knowledge *is* essential to understanding film performance. My analysis of the cultural impact of Tom Cruise's television appearances in Chapter 3, or of Jack Nicholson's 'great seducer' persona in Chapter 5, further underscore the importance of considering on-screen performances alongside off-screen acts. What Geraghty's study does highlight is the increasingly blurry line between what constitutes a star, a celebrity, or an actor in the contemporary period. Definitions of stardom change according to the culture and historical decade, yet all actors are performers by their very nature. It is, therefore, more useful to consider actors as performers rather than stars, not only examining *what* they represent but what they *do* to represent it.

In *Stars*, Richard Dyer provides a basic definition of film performance as 'what the performer does in addition to the actions/functions s/he performs in the plot and the lines s/he is given to say. Performance is how the action/function is done, how the lines are said'.[43] Determining what the performer does, how the action is carried out, how the lines are said, is by no means a straightforward task. In the first instance: how is an actor's performance separated from those other elements inevitably affecting performance, such as technology or the role of the director, cinematographer or editor? As Pamela Robertson Wojcik has posed, 'Where is acting and where is technology? Where and how can we distinguish them?'[44]

Indeed, the relationship between screen performance and technology has been considered by a number of film scholars, particularly in response to what is widely known as the 'Kuleshov effect'. After carrying out a series of film experiments between 1910 and 1920, Russian filmmaker Lev Kuleshov contended that it is the editing together of shots and images that creates meaning in film rather than the performance of actors. Juxtaposing images of an actor with shots of a bowl of soup, a coffin and a young girl to create a montage, Kuleshov's audience praised the actor's complex acting apparently enthusing about 'the actor's sensitive projection of hunger, grief, and paternal joy, his subtle shifts of emotion depending on what he was looking at'.[45] Yet the image of the actor was the same, merely repeated to create the illusion of acting in response to the other shots. Kuleshov's findings suggest that editing and the order of shots creates performance rather than the result of an actor's agency. Attempts to replicate the Kuleshov experiments since, however, have been largely unsuccessful. In the early 1990s, for example, Stephen

Prince and Wayne Hensley found that 'even if the Kuleshov effect did once exist, that effect seems not to be a factor in the same way for the modern audience', adding that the experiments should ultimately be 'recognized as myth and not mis-identified as fact'.[46] Rather than seeing actorly performance as something that is created by, or cannot be isolated from, film technology, I agree with Cynthia Baron that 'the selection and combination of actors' movements, gestures, and expressions can have a *mutually interactive relationship* with the selection and combination of shots, editing patterns, design elements, and audio choices'.[47] Screen performance is inseparable from other cinematic elements and while this complicates the study of performance, it by no means invalidates it. I address the 'problem' of reading performance in relation to film technology further in Chapter 2, by considering Michael Douglas's performances in *Falling Down* and *Wonder Boys* and William H. Macy's vocal performance in *Oleanna*.

Once the role of the actor is determined, how can performance be located? And once located, what vocabulary should be used to describe that performance, particularly when considering Dyer's observation that 'any attempt to analyse performance runs up against the extreme complexity and ambiguity of performance signs'?[48] For Lesley Stern and George Kouvaros:

> It is not just a question of asking: What is cinematic performance? How does it take place? What are the pertinent taxonomic categories? How are they to be culturally and historically differentiated? It is a question of how to *describe* performance in film, and this question is enmeshed with (yet also needs to be differentiated from) the difficulty of how to describe those filmic moments/ scenes/sequences that one is analysing.[49]

Stern and Kouvaros's questions introduce a further problem of subjectivity since *describing* a performance is a matter of individual interpretation. Certainly, as Paul McDonald has stressed, the study of acting and performance will 'never become a precise semiotic science'. He goes on to argue, however, that it is 'only in brief and fleeting moments that the actor's voice or body may present something of significance. ... They are instances that can only be detected in the minutest details of the actor's vocal and physical actions'.[50] Similarly in *Film Performance: From Achievement to Appreciation*, Andrew Klevan employs a 'moment-by-moment' approach to screen acting in order to locate 'the "intricacies" and "richness" of the performance'.[51] How, then, can meaning and significance be established without affecting the potential validity of such meanings through subjective interpretation? If Foster Hirsch is correct in his assertion that 'acting *should* elicit a personal response', to what extent can the analysis of screen performance be carried out objectivity?[52] This is one of the overriding problems in performance analysis.

John O. Thompson's reworking of the 'commutation test' used in structural linguistics is one technique that has been utilised in an attempt to consider film performance in an objective manner. By making hypothetical substitutions within films, replacing Cary Grant with Gary Cooper for example, Thompson suggests a 'more methodological and reflexive discourse' is achieved.[53] Not only is it possible to commute actor for actor, Thompson proposes that there is also much to gain from substituting features, such as a smile. Ultimately, the commutation test is purely hypothetical and still largely based on subjective opinion yet a more tangible version of the test has been taken up by film scholars and applied in particular to the remake. Roberta Pearson, for example, has compared Fredric Marsh and James Mason's performances of Norman Maine in *A Star is Born* (1937 and 1954), while Paul McDonald has evaluated the small but significant differences between Janet Leigh's Marion Crane in *Psycho* (1960) and Anne Heche's performance in Gus Van Sant's 1998 'shot-for-shot remake'.[54] Despite the director's claims of replication in the case of the latter example, the film remake will always be a translation of the original and, as McDonald notes, this is particularly apparent when considering film performance: 'use of shot scale, editing patterns, camera movement, and script all appear to *roughly* approximate the original. Where Van Sant's remake really struggles to create an exact imitation is with its performers and their performances'. Correspondingly, while Pearson finds that factors separate from performance, such as cinematography and editing, help to create the two different Norman Maines, it is the 'actor's delivery of his dialogue, together with his facial expressions, gestures, and posture that most vividly endow a cinematic character with life'.[55]

The remake provides an excellent model for locating what an actor does and demonstrates how different actors create different meaning through their actions. Unfortunately, however, only a small percentage of performances can be analysed comparatively and diachronically via the remake. An alternative might be to consider instances where a different actor plays the same character, such as the varied performances of Bob Dylan by Cate Blanchett, Christian Bale, Richard Gere, Heath Ledger, Ben Whishaw and Marcus Carl Franklin in Todd Haynes's *I'm Not There* (2007) or the replacement of Heath Ledger with Johnny Depp, Jude Law and Colin Farrell in Terry Gilliam's *The Imaginarium of Doctor Parnassus* (2009) following Ledger's death mid-production. A comparison of the various actors who have played the fictional characters of James Bond, Doctor Who, and the Joker, or historical figures in biopics such as Richard Nixon and James Dean, might also offer a more tangible approach to film performance analysis. Any conclusions drawn from making substitutions across a film, such as switching Al Pacino and Jack Lemmon, or Lemmon and Alan Arkin, or Pacino and Alec Baldwin in *Glengarry Glen Ross*, would remain largely hypothetical and would lack the specificity that can be achieved by comparing actors in remakes. The discussion of Michael Douglas and Bill Murray in the following chapter employs a commutation of sorts by considering the same actor in two different roles, observing how their expressions and gestures alter from role to role. This technique can only provide limited conclusions since the actors are playing different characters, yet it does demonstrate various ways that male angst can be presented and the practices involved in the creation of character.

   The task of locating and describing screen performances of male angst is further complicated by the fact that 'angst' refers to an emotion or an interior feeling. In *Creating the Couple*, Virginia Wright Wexman encapsulates the problem of analysing emotion:

> How are commentators to distinguish between an actor's portrayal of emotion and the emotion of a person who is actually experiencing a given state? Although actors may express pain in performance, their emotion has a different status from the feelings of a person who is genuinely in pain.[56]

Rather than study the 'interior life of the actor', Wexman suggests a more useful approach would be to consider 'technique over feeling', to analyse the specific ways emotion is performed by the actor. The analysis of acting technique, as Roberta Pearson points out in her study of performances styles in the Griffith Biograph films, is much more straightforward when the actions are exaggerated and histrionic than restrained and verisimilar. 'Because the verisimilar code was intended to mimic reality and create individual characterizations', Pearson notes, 'one cannot turn to mechanical formulations and prescriptions'.[57] Despite this difficulty, there are certain methods that are used in the cinema to draw attention to an actor's interiority, such as the close-up and the voice-over, techniques that are particularly associated with film noir, a film form predominantly concerned with the instabilities of the male psyche.[58] In the closing sequence in *Glengarry Glen Ross*, Roma's speech may dominate the soundscape but the camera stays on Levene, indicating that it is his actions rather than Roma's words that are the more significant. Roma's dialogue becomes background noise as the audience are forced to watch Levene's subtly changing expression: his angst becomes the focal point. Elsewhere in the film, Levene is often framed in tight and overcrowded spaces – a telephone booth, a car, a toilet cubicle – accentuating Levene's increasing frustrations and the oppressive nature of his work.

Once again, the study of film performance presents a paradox, which Barry King succinctly identified in 1985:

> While film increases the centrality of the actor in the process of signification, the formative capacity of the medium can equally confine the actor more and more to being a bearer of effects that he or she does not or cannot originate.[59]

While more restrained, 'real' performances are more difficult to pin down, they are performances nonetheless, and while technology and editing work to create meaning, they extend what is already presented by the actor. A close-up, for example, draws attention to the actor as locus of emotion, it does not create that emotion. Without the close-up, emotion may not be as evident because the performances signs and gestures are less visible but without the actor, the close-up is meaningless. As King notes, 'film poses limits on the representation of interiority', it does not replace or destroy it completely (see Chapter 2).[60]

Andrew Higson's discussion of 'externalising emotion', while acknowledging the 'tensions' between actor and camera, provides a number of avenues through which to assess what the actor does to create meaning. Although acting techniques such as The Method or the Stanislavsky System call for an actor to internalise a role, Higson suggests it is more important to analyse what is visibly presented on the actor's exterior – 'the production of visual and aural signs' – than what takes place emotionally, that is, seeing 'the body, its physical characteristics and the economy of movement, as a field of discourse'. Higson proposes that acting can be more usefully assessed through anti-naturalist means, even with those performances that strive to create an impression of naturalism; 'What is important, in the final analysis,' he notes, 'is not the inner feelings of the actor, but how the image of actor-as-character and the performed gestures look on the screen'.[61] On the one hand, the economy of movement may be presented clearly via a 'highly conventionalised cultural coding of movement', such as those found in the Peking opera or Delsarte's melodrama. On the other hand, Higson states, performances can be comprised of 'a much more ambiguous though still readable cultural codification of "everyday" gestures'.[62] Commenting on Lemmon and Pacino's approaches to acting in *Glengarry Glen Ross*, for example, director James Foley notes:

> Jack is very verbal and enjoys discussing emotions in a very open way. With Al, certain things are not uttered in front of him ... he operates in a very unconscious, spiritual, nonverbal way. You don't use full, declarative sentences around Al. Give him fragments of ideas and let him go with it, find the emotional reality.[63]

As with Wexman, Higson's approach suggests that the tactics and techniques actors use to create character should not be confused with the result of those techniques. The emphasis is on the outcome and the process, not the actor's perception of the process. An awareness of Pacino and Lemmon's approach to acting determines how their performances are informed, but it is not necessary to observe the effects of that process.

The differing economies of movement suggested by Higson are well illustrated by a collection of photographs by Howard Schatz in *In Character: Actors Acting* (2006) and published in *Vanity Fair*.[64] Actors including Michael Douglas, James Earl Jones, Don Cheadle, Chevy Chase and Christopher Lloyd were asked to 'act out' a series of scenarios using their face and hands. Douglas's three scenarios consisted of: a father whose daughter has been missing for two months called in by the police to identify the body of a young murder victim. The sheet is pulled back and the victim is not his daughter; a boy at a carnival, watching a pierced performer eat live cockroaches; and a 14-year-old girl who walks in on her 18-year-old sister having sex with her boyfriend.

Although limited to gestures of the face and hands, the collection of photographs stresses outcome over the process of performance. The scenarios suggest the image that should be created but do not tell us anything about what Douglas is thinking in establishing these expressions; in order to present an image of a grief-stricken father, Douglas may have drawn on his own experiences of grief or recalled a time when he was worried about his own children, or he may have tried to imagine what he would feel like in that situation. What *is* clear are the gestures and the expressions and the differences across the three images. For the first scenario, Douglas presses his right hand to the back of his neck, forcing his chin towards his chest. His eyes are tightly closed and his eyebrows pinched together, creating frown lines between the eyes and across the brow. A vein visibly protrudes from his forehead. The actor's lips are pursed to form a half smile, accentuated by slight smile lines around the corners of the mouth. The overall image is one of anguish, grief, and relief. In contrast to the subtle, reserved image of the grieving father, the subsequent poses are exaggerated and animated, reflecting the younger age of the characters. As the boy at the carnival, Douglas screws up his facial features, retracting his head into his neck and recoiling his lips to depict revulsion and horror. As the 14-year-old girl, Douglas's hands clutch his temples, his mouth is wide and his eyes are fixed open in startled amazement.[65]

The photographs of Don Cheadle included in the collection also offer economies of movement according to open and closed gestures. For his first scenario ('You are a man at a bar, overhearing another man telling his friend about your wife'), anger is depicted via a stone-faced expression with the mouth tightly shut and with his head tilted to one side in a confrontational stance. This contrasts the broad, toothy grin with head tipped back in laughter and eyes closed for the second scenario ('You are the same man, realising the conversation is actually about your sister-in-law').[66] However, with

Cheadle's closed eyes in the second image implying amusement rather than the sadness and revulsion presented by Douglas as grieving father and disgusted boy, the five poses by the two actors already signal the complexity of performance signs.

Without the scenarios, Douglas and Cheadle's expressions would lack the specificity that their inclusion generates, functioning in a similar way to a film script. The scenario or script may be the 'site of coherence', as Higson describes it, but the scenario only states the outcome and it is the responsibility of the actor to determine the process by which to achieve it. While the photographs of Douglas and Cheadle capture the outcome, they cannot elucidate the process undertaken. The photographs of Cheadle may hint at the process by showing a change of expression by the same character, yet they indicate a distinct shift or transformation rather than the development of gesture. The close analysis of performance sequences is an approach especially favoured by Andrew Klevan who notes: 'Continuous attention to sequences brings out the relationship between appreciating a performance and understanding a film's meaning as it *develops* – the unfolding of an interpretation'.[67] Film, unlike the static image framed in a photograph, is concerned with both the process and the outcome, that is, the repertoire of sign vehicles and the transition from one gesture to another. A still of Jack Lemmon holding his clasped hands to his face may imply that his character is sad or deep in thought, but it barely alludes to the complexity of Levene's guilt, fear, melancholy, disappointment and shame presented in the larger sequence (see Introduction and Figure 1.1).

While the above discussion goes some way towards establishing a vocabulary through which to describe performance and sets a framework for how to consider performance styles, the images of Douglas and Cheadle and Lemmon's performance of Levene highlight the necessity for considering performances in social and cultural terms, acknowledging what Pearson has referred to as the 'cultural and historical specificity of performance codes'.[68] As Erving Goffman and Victor Turner each stress, social acts are influenced by the cultural moment in which they take place but this also works in reverse. 'Life itself now becomes a mirror held up to art', Turner observes, 'and the living now *perform* their lives'.[69] In presenting anguish, for example, Douglas draws from an accepted repertoire of actions to create meaning, taking into account Western cultural codes for expressing sadness, anxiety, fear and relief. It is impossible, then, to divorce the mechanics of film performance from the performances found in everyday life for, as Stanley Cavell has noted, 'the creation of a (screen) performer is also the creation of a character ... the kind that certain real people are: a type'.[70] Douglas and Cheadle's performances are informed by received ideas about what a particular emotion looks like but they must take into account the performative nature of male identity and male social roles that are also enacted according to cultural codes. In this case, Douglas and Cheadle's scenarios require knowledge of the 'fronts' of fatherhood and marriage; Douglas and Cheadle are not just 'men' expressing anguish but 'a father' and 'a husband' and such identities have their own socially, culturally and historically determined codes of enactment.

Before examining the performance of male identities in Chapter 3 (the Wimp and the Wild Man), Chapter 4 (fatherhood and breadwinning) and Chapter 5 (old age), Chapter 2 develops the theoretical discussion of film performance presented here via three actor case studies. The following chapter strips a number of screen performances right down to the sign vehicles that comprise them, examining the facial expressions, bodily gestures, and speech patterns and asking what it means to perform angst-ridden masculinity in these ways. Specifically, the chapter addresses the 'problem' of locating actorly performance in cinema and establishes a vocabulary for reading film performances of male angst.

2
Performing Angst

In the previous chapter, I considered the concept of 'performance,' assessing its usefulness in analysing the cinematic construction of masculinity and male angst. While the second part of the book will specifically examine a number of discursive moments affecting definitions of male identity that took place in the 1990s and 2000s, this chapter will examine, more explicitly, the role of the performer in the construction of such discursive moments. Through case studies of Michael Douglas, Bill Murray and William H. Macy, I examine the mechanics of performance employed by actors to portray angst, considering the specific methods used, how such performances have been read in popular culture and how certain actors have been aligned with 'male crisis' as a result of their on-screen performances.

There has been a propensity in critical discussions of 'masculinity crisis' to collapse ideas of masculinity onto notions of the 'zeitgeist,' assuming the crisis is particular to the 1990s period. There has also been a tendency to rely on one or two actors or films as archetypal embodiments of 'crisis,' or to view the man-in-crisis as a definitive, unchanging type. The actors considered here have been repeatedly aligned with male instability or 'crisis' as a result of the films in which they have been cast. While the films they have appeared in could certainly be described as narratives of male angst in their foregrounding of the instability of male identity, I am more concerned with what the actors *do* in these films than particular plots and storylines. The three performers demonstrate various and disparate ways angst can be performed – ranging from subtle, nuanced gestures to more pronounced and animated movements – questioning discussions of acting that see 'masculinity crisis' as the territory of one or two actors who perform it in the same way. I have purposely narrowed the framework for considering performances of male angst in this chapter by limiting the case studies to white, middle-aged and middle-class actors since it is their expression of male angst that has been most evident in mainstream cinema. It is my intention here to reveal the multiplicity of performance styles and methods for enacting male angst even from within such a select field. Not only will an exploration of these performances serve to reject the notion of an archetypal 'man-in-crisis' but it will also emphasise the multiple ways that angst can and has been performed and the significance of such performances within cultural and critical discourse.

According to Andrew Klevan, 'Interpretations unfold and complicate with our moment-by-moment experience of viewing the performer's activity.' Rather than read an actor's performance across a whole film, or across a number of films, Klevan argues that it is only by studying the moment-by-moment movements found in select sequences that the 'presentness of performance' is revealed. Borrowing from Charles Affron, Klevan suggests that focusing on sequences allows the viewer to '"savor the delight of their rhythms and rhymes, the flow of their contours" [which] also enhances our understanding of film characterisation'.[1] Although he does not provide a rationale for his selection of sequences, Klevan organises his readings thematically, considering what he deems to be particularly momentous scenes that foreground the relationship between performance, 'position and perspective', place and plot. The implication is that any number of scenes or sequences could have been chosen to illustrate the three themes of his book.

I do not dispute the idea that attention to 'moment-by-moment movements' is crucial to an understanding of film performance and characterisation. Yet certain scenes and sequences 'stand out' in regards to performance as more powerful or meaningful than others, demanding increased attention from the viewer, and such sequences are not limited to one per film. Paul McDonald's position regarding the selection of performance moments is worth quoting at length. He argues:

> the work of analyzing performance need not require reading a performance for the totality of its actions but only in key selected

parts. Those parts are unlikely to involve the analysis of even a whole scene, for it is frequently only in brief and fleeting moments that the actor's voice or body may present something of significance. Although only transitory, those moments are nevertheless disproportionate in their impact. They are instances that can only be detected in the minutest details of the actor's vocal and physical actions. At these moments, the voice and body produce micro-meanings, the significance of which affects a film as a whole.[2]

The sequences discussed in this chapter were chosen for their impact in terms of the performance of angst, either due to their explicitness or performances that foreground and raise questions about male identity. Key performance moments may be brief, fleeting and transitory, as McDonald describes, or may be extended in longer sequences, as Klevan suggests. However, I believe there is also much to gain by considering key performance moments across a whole film, or by the same actors across a number of films, either as the repetition of performance traits (what James Naremore refers to as a performer's 'idiolect'[3]) or key moments of departure, development and transition. Departing from Klevan, then, this chapter considers numerous moments across the same film, as well as performances across a number of films by the same actor, in order to understand the codes and conventions for performing male angst.

In providing close readings of three actors, the chapter will also address a number of the issues regarding performance introduced in the previous chapter, such as the role and function of cinema technologies in the presentation and analysis of performance, locating what the actor 'does', and strategies of locating and reading minimalist 'interiority'. While the emphasis here is on male performance *on the screen*, the chapter inevitably introduces the significance of context to the study of film performance, setting up an examination of the performance of male social roles that takes place in the following chapters.

Performing the zeitgeist: Michael Douglas

Michael Douglas is considered by many to be the quintessential 1990s man-in-crisis. Linda Ruth Williams calls Douglas '*the* representation of flawed, crisis-ridden masculinity and the concomitant decline of male cultural and social authority'. Michael Kimmel argues that Douglas 'offers an allegory of the besieged middle-class white male in today's society'. Celestino Deleyto adamantly asserts that Douglas is 'the paradigm of the male in crisis. ... Of course'.[4] Whether portraying men threatened by a dominant female (*Fatal Attraction* 1987, *Basic Instinct* 1992, *Disclosure* 1994), or threatened by society (*Falling Down* 1993), Douglas's screen persona has consistently been read as the epitome of contemporary renderings of masculinity crisis. The actor's films have predominantly been examined in relation to feminist film criticism and whiteness studies, with discussions concerned with Douglas's 'whiteness' and how dominant female characters continually threaten his masculinity.[5] While these ideological readings highlight the socio-cultural implications of Douglas's films and how such representations react to or fuel particular moments in the 1990s period, they do little to explore Douglas himself in relation to these moments.

Often described as 'talkies' or 'social-problem movies', Douglas's films have sparked debate concerning their often-controversial content and message.[6] A considerable number of critics have made parallels between Douglas and notions of the 'zeitgeist', an inference that continues in academic studies of Douglas's films. For *The Daily Variety*, *Basic Instinct* 'marked Douglas as consistently savvy reader of the zeitgeist'. In its review of *Falling Down*, *The Washington Post* asserted Douglas 'again takes on the symbolic mantle of the zeitgeist'. Similarly, Philip Green asserts Douglas did not 'invent' his crisis-ridden character 'out of thin air, he clearly tapped into the zeitgeist, or part of the zeitgeist, as well'.[7] In each case, Douglas is seen to represent a specific cultural and historical moment, iconic of prevailing issues and concerns around feminism (*Fatal Attraction*, *Basic Instinct* and *Disclosure*), homosexuality (*Basic Instinct*), ethnic minorities and racial discrimination (*Falling Down*). Not only are Douglas and his films perceived as paralleling trends in American society, but his characterisations themselves are discussed as a recognisable social type: the 'persecuted figure'.[8] The typing of Douglas reaches its zenith in discussions that position him as the exemplary Everyman, 'an example of a specific type, the Average White Male, facing a crisis of power at a particular moment in US history,' and who is 'acutely symptomatic of masculinities of his moment'.[9] These statements are significant for the credit they allow Douglas in constructing his contemporary characters; it is Douglas who has 'tapped into', 'takes on' and 'reads' the zeitgeist. Rather than writers or filmmakers, it is Douglas who is afforded a sense of authorship concerning the roles he plays. How precisely did Douglas 'tap' into the zeitgeist? If Douglas is '*the* representation of flawed, crisis-ridden masculinity', what does the actor *do* to represent it? In exploring Douglas's role in constructing character, this section problematises the typing of the actor as 'Average White Male' by exploring the nuances and departures in his screen performances, considering his screen persona as comprised of several themes that are 'differentially activated' from role to role.[10] In order to assess the actor's agency, this section focuses in particular on Douglas's performances in *Falling Down* and *Wonder Boys* (2000).

Falling Down and *Wonder Boys* differ from the majority of Douglas's 1990s films in their emphasis on Douglas's characters 'as' crisis-ridden, while his other roles foreground the male protagonist's grad-ual downfall. In this respect, *Fatal Attraction*, *Basic Instinct*, *Disclosure*, and *The Game* (1997) can be considered 'fall from grace' narratives; Dan Gallagher in *Fatal Attraction*, Nick Curran in *Basic Instinct*, Tom Sanders in *Disclosure*, and Nicholas Van Orton in *The Game* are, at the start of each film, self-confident and dominant men. It is during the course of each narrative that their self-confidence is pulled apart by a duplicitous female (Alex Forrest/Glenn Close, Catherine Tramell/ Sharon Stone, Meredith Johnson/Demi Moore and Christine/Deborah Unger), to be replaced by paranoia, apprehension and insecurity. The initial security of the male protagonist's identity is increasingly threatened to the point where he is forced to retaliate or be destroyed fully.[11]

In *Falling Down* and *Wonder Boys*, however, the Douglas character's fall from grace occurs prior to the start of each film and he is a fallen man from the outset. In *Falling Down*, D-Fens (alluding to his car registration plate) has recently been fired from his job, a restraining order prevents him from seeing his young daughter and ex-wife Beth (Barbara Hershey), and he lives with his mother, factors suggesting a more apt title for the film would be 'Fallen Down' or 'Fell Down Further'. In *Wonder Boys*, Grady Tripp is a dishevelled, divorced and aging college professor who has failed to live up to the reputation he gained following the publication of his critically successful first novel seven years previously. Rather than focusing on the *process* of destabilising and restabilising male identity as is the case in *The Game* and the three 'erotic thrillers', *Falling Down* and *Wonder Boys* are fundamentally concerned with Douglas 'as' crisis-ridden; the presentation of pathetic, unstable masculinity is the prevailing image.

A recurring theme in Douglas's 'Average White Male' roles is his presentation of ordinariness. Whether playing an unemployed defence worker or billionaire investment banker, Douglas's performances are bound to notions of the ordinary. In the first instance, many of his characters are professional men: he is a legal attorney Dan Gallagher in *Fatal Attraction*, police detective Nick 'Shooter' Curran in *Basic Instinct*, computer company executive Tom Sanders in *Disclosure*, defence worker (albeit unemployed) Bill Foster/D-Fens in *Falling Down*, investment banker Nicholas Van Orton in *The Game*, and college professor Grady Tripp in *Wonder Boys*. Work for each character is much more than a plot point; their male status is not only defined in relation to their work but success in the workplace is presented as inseparable from male identity. D-Fens, or Bill Foster, experiences a crisis of identity when he is made redundant from his job as a defence worker and is no longer able to support his child as a result. Tom Sanders is twice passed over for a promotion in favour of a woman, causing him to question his masculine privilege. Grady Tripp has writer's block; his black-outs and general incompetence are attributed to his inability to finish his second novel. The inseparability of maleness and a professional work ethic present Douglas's characters as Middle Americans, in search of the American Dream that rewards hard work and ambition.

In the erotic thrillers, the gradual unravelling of the male characters' appearance assists in the construction of Douglas as experiencing a crisis of male identity. Each film starts by establishing Douglas's ordinariness via a 'front' of masculine heteronormativity, or what Jude Davies terms 'hypernormality'; clean-shaven, suit-wearing, middle-class professionals who are well educated and married with children (in the case of *Fatal Attraction* and *Disclosure*).[12] Not surprisingly, the suit serves as an immediate indicator of Douglas's professional status and white male professionalism; his masculinity is coded through his business attire. External threats to male normality are conspicuously revealed in the disintegration of visual appearance: an unshaven face, unkempt hair, a dishevelled or damaged suit. In *Falling Down*, D-Fens/Douglas's appearance immediately calls attention to an unstable sense of maleness. The absence of a suit jacket suggests D-Fens/Bill Foster's loss of identity, indicating the status of worker that has been stripped from him. The actor's atypical hairstyle in *Falling Down* was also acknowledged by more than one reviewer; his 1950s buzz-cut suggests nostalgia for an earlier time when male social roles were seemingly more traditional and straightforward (see Chapter 4).[13]

Wonder Boys is even more acute in its visual presentation of male angst. Reviewers stressed the visually different Douglas: 'in a *calculated* reversal of his standard lethal-lothario persona, Grady is overweight and unshaven, with a bad haircut, glasses, and a stocking cap'. For Andrew O'Hehir, 'unshaven, unkempt and frequently clad in a fuzzy pink woman's bathrobe, Douglas actually resembles a middle-aged human being for the first time'.[14] The publicity poster that accompanied *Wonder Boys'* initial release featured a close-up head shot of Douglas. Peering over his large-frame tortoiseshell glasses, his face unshaven and hair unkempt, the image was a clear departure from the slick-backed coiffure and professional clean shave that were signature trademarks of Douglas's earlier roles. The flash of grey hair suggests an aging Douglas, not the timeless and unchanging Douglas from *Fatal Attraction*, *Basic Instinct* and *Disclosure*; a red scarf and tweed jacket replace the sharp suit and designer shirt he so often wore in his other roles. As Tripp's problems increase during the course of the film, his appearance further deteriorates: his clothes get shabbier, his hair is messier and his facial hair becomes more and more unkempt; the limp that he gains after being attacked by a dog accentuates his vulnerability and incompetence. His physical appearance at the end of the film reinforces Tripp's emotional journey: in a smart polo-neck shirt, clean-shaven with his hair combed (and less grey); his 'crisis' is seemingly resolved.

However, very little of what I have described here can be solely attributed to Douglas's *performance* in either film. D-Fens and Tripp may offer a visual image of crisis and instability, but this is largely achieved via the script, costume, hair and props, and these are the province of the screenwriter, wardrobe department and stylists rather than the actor. In fact, the only examples of Douglas's actorly contribution to the image of instability mentioned here are his limp and weight gain for *Wonder Boys*, the latter being an example of what James Naremore refers to as 'biological performance'.[15] Where is

Douglas's agency in performing angst then? How does he perform ordinariness? Rather than presenting male instability through something he *does*, that is, something he exhibits or displays, it appears that the key to Douglas's performances in *Falling Down* and *Wonder Boys* is in what he apparently does *not* do. The portrayal of ordinariness so central to Douglas's image of Everyman seemingly hinges on the actor's ability to restrain his actions and 'do' very little. However, as John Ellis rightly notes, 'Under performance is not a question of restraint or lack of histrionics. It is a question of *producing the effect of behaving* rather than performing'.[16] Douglas's minimal acting in *Falling Down* and *Wonder Boys* is still acting, even if the technique is not immediately apparent.

The opening sequence of *Falling Down* is indicative in this regard. The four-minute scene juxtaposes images of Douglas sitting in unmoving traffic with the triggers of his escalating agitation: road signs flashing incessantly, school children screaming, a man shouting into his mobile phone, car radios blaring, broken air-conditioning, dirty exhaust fumes and beeping car horns, garish bumper stickers, and a fly buzzing round his hot car. Each time the camera returns to Douglas, it offers the actor in fragments: extreme close-ups of his mouth, nose and eyes; a medium close-up of the back of his neck; a medium shot of his hands. A number of critics have singled out this sequence in their discussion of the film, focusing on the framing of Douglas in relation to these external irritations. Fred Pfeil, for example, sees the combination of close-ups of Douglas's face and body, with the swivelling and panning camera, and build-up of diegetic and non-diegetic sounds, as creating an unsettling position for the viewer that problematises the actor's earlier hero status.[17] Similarly, Paul Gormley singles out the long takes, fast edits and close-ups, along with the 'overbearing soundtrack' as contributing to Douglas's 'strangeness' in the film: 'The discomfort caused by the fast-editing and the rising soundtrack', he notes, 'places the audience in a mimetic relationship with the figure trapped in the car, and it comes as a huge relief when D-Fens ends both his, and the audience's discomfort, by getting out of the car, and telling other drivers he is "going home"'.[18] Douglas's part in creating this discomfort is barely acknowledged in either reading, implying that it is technology, not actor, which creates meaning.

While the camera and soundtrack certainly feature heavily in the construction of agitation in the opening sequence, Douglas's actions frame the scene and contribute to the overall meaning in significant ways. His mouth trembles slightly, with droplets of perspiration across his upper lip. He slowly closes his eyes with heavy, weary eyelids. His breathing is shallow and laboured. He forces a swallow, a weak gulp, in an attempt to moisten his mouth. The trembling, sweating, closed eyes, stilted breathing and gulping all take place before the first pan away to the blaring radio, a demonic-looking Garfield toy, screaming children. Panning back to D-Fens/Douglas, the actor swats the back of his neck, followed by a medium shot of Douglas as his hands tightly grip the steering wheel. His pupils dart frantically from side to side. He slowly closes his eyes again. He clenches his jaw and purses his lips. His brow creases slightly. He vigorously rattles the car window handle. He furiously swats the fly with a rolled up newspaper.

The pans and close-ups may indicate what is causing the character's stress, but they do not present that stress; they point to the source not the display of angst. The close-up draws attention to this performance, fragmenting it and accentuating it. In her essay 'The Close-Up: Scale and Detail in the Cinema', Mary Ann Doane describes the power of the close-up to draw attention to an object and highlight its significance. More than any other type of shot, Doane argues that the close-up 'demonstrates the deictic nature of the cinematic image, its inevitable indexicality. Mimicking the pointing finger, it requires no language and is not comparable to it'.[19] The close-up singles out an object, or part of an object, and, in doing so, asks the spectator to give special attention to that which is framed and isolated. It is perhaps not surprising that Pfeil, Gormley and others focused their reading of the traffic jam scene on the movement of the camera yet, in doing so, they bypass the originator of the discomfort and 'strangeness': D-Fens/Douglas. The relationship between actor and camera is, to borrow from Cynthia Baron, 'mutually interactive', but this mutual interactivity starts and ends with the actor.[20] Removing the pans and cuts, the combination and arrangement of Douglas's actions – the trembling lip, the laboured breathing, the moistening of his mouth, the prolonged blink, the rigid grasp of his hands on the wheel, swatting the fly, rattling the crank handle – work together to portray anxiety, discomfort, increasing agitation and aggravation.

Douglas's shift in this scene from subtle, slight gestures and expressions to excessive, hysterical outbursts is repeated throughout the film; moments of interiority are punctuated by violent outbursts. D-Fens uses violence (verbal and physical) as a cathartic release for his anger and frustration; his 'flooding out', as Erving Goffman terms those moments of extreme emotion that burst out, is projected onto a rolled up newspaper and, later, a baseball bat (to destroy the shop of a Korean American as punishment for what D-Fens perceives as exorbitant prices) and a rocket launcher (when he obliterates some road works with a weapon acquired earlier from the homophobic white supremacist owner of a military surplus store).[21] Conversely, his face and gestures remain calm and almost motionless. Similarly, in *The Game*, Nicholas Van Orton/Douglas struggles to keep a straight face when his briefcase fails to open, forcing him to delay firing an employee. Moments later, when Van Orton is alone, we see him thrashing the briefcase against a bench, unable to contain his anger and frustration any longer. Emotion and the performance of emotions are seemingly restrained and internalised to the point of becoming damaging to the male characters. Douglas presents the illusion of containing his emotion until his characters explode into verbal and physical aggression.

While D-Fens and Nicholas Van Orton move between relative inaction and overblown action, Grady Tripp is more firmly associated with inaction, waiting for events to take place around him in moments of what Andrew Higson has termed 'doing nothing':

> Whether in a stylized acting practice, or in a naturalist acting practice ... there are moments when one or more actors are required to '*do nothing*,' thus calling for a minimalist style of acting (although still calling for work and concentration): shots involving characters waiting or watching, or thinking, or day-dreaming, where the key to the success of the scene is the absence of movement or expression (which is expressive in itself, of course).[22]

Rather than the *absence* of movement being the key to the success of the scene, however, doing nothing still requires the actor to do or not do *something* as part of the process of 'externalising emotion'.[23] 'Doing nothing' in film performance is an oxymoron that involves a level of skill and engagement on the part of the actor in order to convey the effect of not-acting or *being* rather than *doing*. Waiting, watching, thinking and daydreaming all involve some movement, action, gesture, expression, even if that movement is slight and apparently insignificant. In *Wonder Boys*, for example, numerous scenes see Tripp/Douglas sat in front of his typewriter or on his doorstep 'doing nothing' (see Figure 2.1). With a voice-over narrating Tripp's motivations (or lack thereof), his thoughts and feelings are projected more through his low and gravelly monotone than as gestures, expressions or corporeal movements. Props continue to be significant in determining emotion but instead of anger and frustration projected onto a briefcase or baseball bat, smoking marijuana during moments of introspection provides Douglas with an 'expressive object' onto which he can project Tripp's melancholy via deep inhalations and extended exhalations.[24]

Noting a difference from earlier roles, Douglas has said that 'compared with the characters in *A Perfect Murder* or *Wall Street*, [Tripp] is much more uncertain about himself, more like the guy in *Falling Down* ... *Wonder Boys* allowed me to play a man of inaction as opposed to a man of action'.[25] Reviewers also acknowledged the narratively different Douglas: '*Wonder Boys* found [Douglas] acting against himself', commented one reviewer, while *The San Francisco Examiner* noted: 'He has put his seething away; his paradigmatic, oppressed

Figure 2.1   Grady Tripp/Michael Douglas 'doing nothing' in *Wonder Boys* (Paramount, 2000)

white male has found a character in which to lose himself'.[26] Indeed, the audience is denied the opportunity to witness Tripp's most excessive moments of emotion; he experiences anxiety attacks causing him, and the screen, to black out. Whereas D-Fens erupts into physical aggression, Tripp passes out from his restraint, imploding rather than exploding with emotion.

It is in those moments of 'doing nothing' and relative inaction that Douglas's performance of angst and his presentation of ordinariness come together. Ordinariness in *Wonder Boys*, but particularly in *Falling Down*, is revealed as a *front*, an image that is put on and enacted. The scenes of Tripp privately 'doing nothing' demonstrate the artificiality of his public actions. When Tripp stands outside at a party to escape the networking and small talk, his pronounced intake of a cigarette and deep exhalations of smoke suggest his relief at exiting the room, as well as his boredom; an acknowledgement that his awkwardly jovial attempts to converse with guests a few moments earlier were forced and superficial. Tripp/Douglas may present an *image* of ordinariness – a successful writer and college professor – but it is in performance, especially in his social performance, that he fails. His presentation of angst is particularly evident in moments of private introspection, the quiet moments of thinking, typing, smoking, and passing out that are confirmed by his voice-over narration.

In *Falling Down*, D-Fens's ordinariness is also revealed as a façade and masquerade. As with Tripp, ordinariness is evident only as far as the surface, which is presented in particular by his costume: the stiff white shirt with pens clipped in the top pocket, the smart tie, and leather briefcase. However, in his response to everyday irritations (a traffic jam, overpriced Cola, not serving breakfast after 11.30 a.m.), the construction of his ordinariness is immediately evident. D-Fens's ordinary image breaks down in bursts of irrational violence and hostile action. D-Fens is also unable to meet the norms of his male social roles. At the start of the film, D-Fens is presented as a white-collar worker, a husband and a father. His inability to maintain these 'ordinary' male roles is gradually revealed as the source of his angst: D-Fens is divorced, and his ex-wife Beth (Barbara Hershey) has a restraining order against him, so he is not allowed access to his young daughter; he was fired or made redundant from his job and is not able to pay child support; he lives with his mother as a result of his unemployed, divorced status. In each case, D-Fens fails to perform the ordinary or achieve male social norms. It is only in coaxing police detective Prendergast (Robert Duvall) to shoot him at the film's finale that D-Fens is able to regain some sense of 'ordinary' fatherhood; in being killed, he can finally provide financial support for his daughter with his life insurance.

D-Fens/Douglas's presentation of ordinariness is particularly evident in a sequence in which he watches an old home video of himself as 'Bill Foster' in Beth's house (Figure 2.2). Filmed before his divorce and while he was still employed, the video shows a relaxed, caring, friendly and happy man; his 'natural' hairstyle and blue and white chequered shirt, unbuttoned slightly, gives Bill a homely look comparable with Douglas's fatherly image in *Fatal Attraction* and *Disclosure*. The scenes are intercut with images of D-Fens watching the video, wearing a dark buttoned-up shirt and a severe militaristic buzz-cut. His face is stiffer, older, unhappy. He wears the same glasses in both scenes and yet, as D-Fens, the glasses look larger, swamping his face and creating a more sinister feel as the light from the television reflects onto the lenses.

Not only does this conspicuous transformation highlight D-Fens's increasing anxiety and paranoia regarding his separation from his family, it also foregrounds Douglas's changing screen image. The images of Bill Foster deliberately play on Douglas's earlier version of

Figure 2.2 D-Fens/Bill Foster reads his performance of fatherhood in *Falling Down* (Warner Bros, 1993)

the crisis-ridden male, visually aligning Bill with Dan Gallagher, Tom Sanders and Nick Curran.

In watching the video, D-Fens self-reflexively reads his own performance of fatherhood. At first, Bill Foster is presented as 'ordinary' father. D-Fens/Douglas wistfully watches the scene. His fingers gently rub the knuckles on his left hand in anticipation of what the video will show. He smiles openly, mouthing along to Bill singing 'Happy birthday to you' to his daughter. The smile quickly fades as his daughter begins to cry and refuses to sit on the horse he purchased as a birthday gift. As Bill's voice gets angrier and more frustrated, swearing and demanding his wife to put their daughter on the horse, D-Fens realises the ordinary father is a false act, his nostalgic anticipation quickly gives way to melancholy and regret; he looks away from the screen and lowers his head in shame. Bill Foster is only seen briefly in the home video, trying to feed his daughter cake. He is present in voice rather than image, underscoring his disembodied and estranged fatherhood. At first, Bill/Douglas's voice is soft, encouraging, nurturing. With his daughter's refusal to eat the cake and sit on the horse, his voice becomes harsher, demanding. At the end of the film, a police officer returns to Beth's home and the camera focuses on the still-playing home video. Bill Foster holds his smiling daughter on one arm and a Labrador puppy on the other. Bill talks softly and lovingly, kissing his daughter's head and hugging her closely. Beth is heard laughing in the background and then joins father and daughter in front of the camera. This final scene underscores the performance D-Fens has struggled to maintain throughout; his status as 'ordinary man' is a complete fabrication.

Reflecting on his performance in *Fatal Attraction*, Douglas has talked about the act of 'wiping yourself off' in order to become an everyday character:

> I think what was a big breakthrough for me as an actor was when you start preparing for a part you start thinking about your character: what are you going to do, what mannerisms, who's the character? And I remember having a moment where I said: wait a minute, what character? This is not about putting on the makeup, or putting *on* the character, this is about wiping yourself clean; wiping yourself *off*. Because I *could* be a lawyer in New York City,

I *could* possibly have had an affair, this nightmare *could* have happened to me.[27]

Rather than putting *on* a performance, Douglas considers his performance as taking *off*, removing a mask in order to present that
which is underneath. The mask in this case is the Douglas star
persona that must be wiped off or contained in order to portray an
Everyman, highlighting a disparity between star and screen persona.
Douglas's performance of ordinary Everyman is problematised by
his star status. The portrayal of ordinariness so central to Douglas's
image of the 'Average White Male' seemingly hinges on the actor's
ability to restrain his actions, that is, by emphasising 'impersonation' over 'personification' to borrow from Barry King. In King's
definition, personification refers to 'the range of the actor [being]
consonant with his or her personality' while impersonation requires
skill whereby 'the "real" personality of the actor should disappear
into the part'.[28] However, the foregrounding of Douglas's ordinariness, while central to his screen characterisations, both opposes and
complements the extraordinariness of his star persona. As John Ellis
notes, 'The star is at once ordinary and extraordinary', presenting a
paradox that is 'repeated and intensified in cinema by the regime of
presence-yet-absence that is the filmic image'.[29] His extraordinary
identity clashes with his ordinary characterisation so that the very
act of taking off the mask – 'wiping yourself off' – is also revealed as
a performance since it involves an identity that must be hidden or
suppressed. The clash suggests that impersonation and personification are not as easily to distinguish as it would first seem.

Douglas's extraordinariness is revealed by his star status – as an a
Academy Award-winning actor and producer and son of Classical
Hollywood star Kirk Douglas – and amplified by his celebrity status
via frequent appearances on chat shows and in gossip magazines.
In these respects, his star identity starkly opposes his 'Average
White Male' screen performance persona and yet, at the same time,
it supplements it. In 1992, for example, rumours circulated that
Douglas had admitted himself into a rehabilitation clinic after then-
wife Diandra Luker accused the actor of having a sex addiction.
Ordinarily, such an accusation would have a damaging effect on the
star image, yet the news followed the release of *Basic Instinct*, blurring
the boundary between person and persona, actor and character, with

'confirmation' of the actor's hypersexuality.[30] In this case, Douglas's performance in *Basic Instinct* was less about 'wiping off' his star identity than extending his star persona onto the screen and bringing his celebrity associations to the fore. While his alleged sex addiction in the early 1990s complemented his characterisations in *Basic Instinct* and *Disclosure*, his performance in *Wonder Boys* generated discussion around his off-screen relationship with Catherine Zeta-Jones, 25 years his junior and becoming a father again in his fifties. 'In this case, it's life imitating art', Douglas quipped, but the comparison once again highlights the inseparability of star and screen persona, person and persona.[31]

Douglas's 25lb weight gain for *Wonder Boys* also blurs the line between persona and performance. On the one hand, his gain can be considered as what James Naremore refers to as 'pure biological performance ... an involuntary biological process' (see Chapter 5).[32] Douglas's weight gain for *Wonder Boys* can be considered as a voluntary biological process of sorts with the actor speeding up the aging process. The performance of ordinariness requires Douglas to adapt his extraordinary star body (made extraordinary via Hollywood fitness regimes and alleged plastic surgery, along with the extraordinariness of the star persona) yet, in the case of *Wonder Boys*, his body becomes hyper-ordinary when Douglas literally 'put on' for the role. Putting on weight in order to maximise authenticity in the role of aging college professor necessitates a departure from the extraordinary star persona of 'Michael Douglas'.

Douglas's performance of angst discussed here not only refers to what is done in a measurable sense but also an impression of what is not done: taking *off* the mask rather than putting the mask on. In Douglas's case, angst is presented as something to be exposed, an identity laid bare to reveal vulnerability and weakness. While the characters of D-Fens and Tripp internalise their respective crises, Douglas also exhibits angst via limited movements and gestures that are amplified by technological factors such as close-ups and lighting. The sequences explored thus highlight the impossibility of considering an actor's performance independently of technological factors affecting it but demonstrate that such factors assist or enhance performances rather than create them. In capturing and framing male angst, cinema technology repeatedly singles out one part of the body in particular as principal point of performance: the face. Focusing on

Bill Murray, the following section considers the role and function of the face in performing angst.

About face: Bill Murray's midlife crisis

Bill Murray embodied the male 'midlife crisis' in the late-1990s and 2000s. He is a disillusioned millionaire school benefactor in *Rushmore* (1998); a past-his-prime actor advertising whisky in Tokyo in *Lost in Translation* (2003); a depressed and cuckolded husband in *The Royal Tenenbaums* (2001); an oceanographer with fatherhood issues in *The Life Aquatic with Steve Zissou* (2004); and an 'over-the-hill Don Juan' on a road trip to find the mother of a son he has never met in *Broken Flowers* (2005). Murray has been considered to be a 'master of minimalist angst', and a 'poster boy for America's cynical, depressed midlife males', in short, an actor 'unrivalled at portraying middle-aged regret'.[33] While Murray's association with 'midlife crisis' is nothing new, of particular significance is the suggestion that midlife crisis can be performed in a specific way, portrayed by an actor so that he becomes synonymous with the angst besetting middle-aged men at the start of the twenty-first century. It would seem that Murray has so successfully embodied male angst that he has *become* the man-in-crisis; the line between man and performer has become increasingly blurred as if Murray himself is experiencing a midlife crisis. Jennifer Senior for the *New York Times*, for example, posed the question: 'Does a culture even need a definition of burnout when it has Bill Murray?' in her article on the midlife crisis. One critic even went so far as to suggest Murray had opened the eyes of the American public to 'male menopause' – a more 'serious side' to the male midlife crisis.[34] Why is it that Murray has been read as the epitome of midlife crisis? How, precisely, does Murray *perform* angst and how much, to borrow from Barry King, depends upon the 'given-ness' of Murray's physical and behavioural attributes?[35] Through a discussion of Bill Murray's performances, critical reception of his acting style and physical appearance, and the use of his image in promotional publicity, I explore the specifics of the actor's alignment with crisis-ridden masculinity, examining how angst is enacted on the screen and what methods are employed to create 'minimalist angst' or portray 'middle-aged regret', particularly focusing on the actor's face.

Extratextual images play a key role in the imaging of male angst.[36] According to Steven Cohan, the poster for *North by Northwest* (1959, Figure 2.3) 'offers an arresting image of male vulnerability: Cary Grant suspended helplessly in space':

> Although he stretches out his arms as if ready to break the fall with his hands, Grant's bent legs and flung feet indicate an utter inability to support himself were he to reach the ground. What's more, the expression on his face – his mouth agape, his eyes closed – testifies to, if not fear, then horror at his plight.[37]

The result is 'a rather haunting image of masculinity in crisis,' with Grant's masculinity presumably threatened by the woman who brandishes a gun behind him. For Cohan, the film's adventure and comedy were the reason for its popularity in 1959 and yet, he argues, Cary Grant's performance of Roger O. Thornhill a.k.a. George Kaplan was a 'commercially shrewd intuition of what fifties America wanted to believe, for better *and* worse, about masculinity in its contemporary setting'.[38]

It is revealing to compare the *North By Northwest* poster to the image of Bill Murray slumped on the end of a hotel bed on the poster for *Lost in Translation* (Figure 2.3). With his sagging shoulders and heavy limbs, Murray projects an air of melancholy and lethargy. Sadness is written all over his face; he stares vacantly at the camera with eyes hollow and lifeless. His mouth is turned down and eyebrows raised slightly suggesting perplexity or concern. With the short kimono-style dressing gown exposing most of his legs, forearms and neck, and white fluffy slippers, Murray is an image of disoriented masculinity. His loosely clasped hands resting between his thighs offer a modest sense of protection for the loss of dignity that the short and skimpy kimono threatens. At the same time, the unfamiliar sight of a white American male in a Japanese kimono heightens the impression of alienation and isolation. His drooping body, framed against a backdrop of Tokyo city, seems even smaller and less significant in comparison to the vibrant luminosity of the cityscape. The poster tagline – 'Everyone wants to be found' – only emphasises what has been so unequivocally and successfully created by a single image: loss, alienation and loneliness.

Figure 2.3 Advertising 'masculinity in crisis' 50 years apart (*North by Northwest* (MGM/The Kobal Collection, 1959) and *Lost in Translation* (Focus Features/The Kobal Collection, 2003))

Displayed on billboards and in movie theatres 44 years apart, the posters and the films they advertise share a number of similarities. Both posters feature comedy actors in their fifties. Both films are about a man's struggle to mature and take on responsibility. Both characters experience an identity crisis regarding their male identity and are disoriented by their position in the culture. The image of male angst that is presented by each poster, however, is entirely different. In 1959, Grant's depiction of masculine instability – consisting of

Figure 2.3 Continued

extended limbs and wide facial expression – is animated, exaggerated and dramatic. Murray, by contrast, appears languid and passive. Even though they are both static images, demonstrating outcome rather than process, male angst is revealed to be performative – something projected, depicted, put on. The two posters suggest there is a historical difference in the performance, or at least the presentation, of male angst. They highlight how performance styles have been used in different historical periods to connote masculinity and to demonstrate how male angst can be performed and projected as images in entirely different ways. While Grant's male vulnerability causes him to throw open his arms, legs and mouth in horror, Murray's midlife crisis is evident in what Andrew Sarris has described as Murray's 'seemingly effortless projection of inner turmoil'.[39] While it would be impossible to draw conclusions from the two posters alone about distinct modes of performance in the 1950s and 2000s, the similarities between the films regarding other significant aspects (age of actor, genre, narrative) suggest there are crucial differences at play in the presentation of angst.

Lost in Translation was not the first film to see Murray play a character experiencing a so-called midlife crisis or to see him placed in a situation causing him to question his male identity. While a number of critics asserted that *Groundhog Day* (1993) marked Murray's transition from 'wiseacre to wounded wise man', from 'live wire to lost soul',[40] Murray had already established his ability to combine comedy and melancholy in roles such as the miserly and lonely TV producer in *Scrooged* (1988), the clown 'crying on the inside' in *Quick Change* (1990), and the disenchanted gangster in *Mad Dog and Glory* (1993). Such roles illustrated Murray's ability to 'act against type' rather than being indicative of a changing image. More direct endeavours to challenge his screen persona, such as his 'straight' role in *The Razor's Edge* (1984), were commercially unsuccessful, reinforcing Richard Dyer's acknowledgement that 'attempts by a star to change may meet with box-office failure'.[41] Such roles were ultimately ineffective in changing public and critical conceptions of Murray's comedic persona and *Groundhog Day* was still largely perceived by the media as a typical Bill Murray vehicle in which he once again demonstrates a 'masterfully loony performance'.[42]

With the release of *Rushmore* (1998), the specificity of Murray's acting style began to generate a substantial amount of discussion in both popular and critical forums. Critics highlighted Murray's departure from previous overstated performances towards a more minimalist, 'exquisitely spare' style that quickly became fundamental to the construction of his revised persona.[43] Lynn Hirschberg of the *New York Times* magazine, for example, recognised that Murray's 'layered, complicated performance' was a long way from the 'goofy, funny guys who have made him famous'.[44]

The word 'crisis' usually implies something that is visibly chaotic or frenzied, active rather than passive, yet reviewers highlighted Murray's 'sense of stillness' as a distinguishing trait of his post-*Rushmore* angst-ridden characters.[45] Roger Ebert even goes so far as to suggest that 'No actor is better than Bill Murray at doing nothing at all, and being fascinating while doing it'. He writes:

> Murray has the uncanny ability to invite us into his performance, into his stillness and sadness. I don't know how he does it. A Bill Murray imitation would be a pitiful sight: passive immobility, small gestures of the eyes, enigmatic comments, yes, those would be easy, but how does he suggest the low tones of crashing chaotic uncertainty?[46]

The implication is that when Murray does 'nothing at all' (here referring to *Broken Flowers*), he is not acting; he is simply 'being'. To act, on the other hand, implies something that is measurable, obvious, stated. Of course, this defies the very logic of performance and this once again raises the issue of 'doing nothing' in performance that was discussed earlier in the chapter. Murray may well be doing nothing but he is 'doing' it nonetheless. Or, as Michael Kirby has pointed out: 'The motionless performer may convey certain attitudes and emotions that are acting even though no physical acting is involved.'[47] Murray is doing something to 'invite us into his performance,' even if he is merely sitting and thinking. Ebert himself is aware of the performance paradox of 'doing nothing' when he asks: how does Murray *suggest* the low tones of chaotic uncertainty?

Geoff King's reading of *Lost in Translation* similarly reinforces the difficulties in defining and describing minimalist acting. According to King, Murray's performance as Bob Harris moves between 'playing straight' and 'performative modes' of more comic expression. Those so-called performative modes are fairly easy to locate and describe – comedic and dramatic moments that call attention to performance as performance, such as filming a whisky commercial or fighting off the advances of an overzealous Japanese woman in his hotel room. Aside from describing moments where Murray plays straight as 'sincere', there is little indication of what the actor *does* to play straight or act sincere. Rather, for King, 'playing straight' is about the containment of Murray's trademark comic persona: 'no quirks, no wry deadpan glances'.[48] The implication is that 'performative modes' are defined, explicit and therefore measurable, while 'playing straight' is implicit, assumed and non-performative; what is done and what is not done.

Yet a minimalist acting style still requires work and concentration, as Andrew Higson notes, despite involving limited or no gestures. The most subtle of gestures – a flicker of the eyes, a slight facial tick, an intake of breath – can have a powerful impact and are central to the process of 'externalising emotion'.[49] The pool scene in *Rushmore* is a clear example of Murray's minimalism at play. Murray plays Herman Blume, a wealthy industrialist and school benefactor, in a role written specifically for him by Wes Anderson and Owen Wilson. Bored with life, hated by his wife and sons, Ronny and Donny, Blume befriends Max Fischer (Jason Schwartzman), a precocious 15-year-old schoolboy with a penchant for extra-curricular activities. Blume falls in love with Rosemary Cross (Olivia Williams), a young teacher at Rushmore Academy who has also become the object of Max's affections.

By the pool, defiantly throwing golf balls into the water, Blume/Murray sits at the edge of the frame, ignoring (and being ignored by) his sons opening presents on the other side of the pool. With his eyes near-closed, his eyebrows drawn together producing deep frown lines across his forehead, and a cigarette hanging limply from his pursed lips, Murray's face registers boredom, apathy and hopelessness. Looking over at his wife flirting with a party guest, his expression remains the same, aside from his eyes, which blink rapidly. Murray walks over to the diving board with an air of juvenility, his stomach and back hanging over the waistband of his Budweiser swimming trunks, visually contradicting his debonair Clark Gable moustache. Knocking back his glass of whisky, he climbs the stairs to the board. His isolation and detachment from the people around him is amplified as he scans the crowd of guests below. With the cigarette still in his mouth, he dive-bombs into the water. In a scene reminiscent of

The Graduate (1967) that underscored Benjamin Braddock's (Dustin Hoffman) cross-generational crisis, he closes his eyes and hugs his knees into his stomach, as if pondering the possibility of never re-surfacing. The intertextual reference to Mike Nichols' film intensifies Blume's unhappiness; both *The Graduate* and *Rushmore* are coming-of-age narratives but where Braddock's trajectory concerns his transition from college youth to career man, the *Rushmore* sequence emphasises Blume's inability, refusal or rejection to 'grow up' and 'be a man'.

In a later scene, after Blume and Rosemary have split up and Max has told Mrs Blume her husband is having an affair, Blume and Max encounter each other at the hospital. Standing in the elevator, Blume has visibly deteriorated. His hair is dishevelled, his face unshaven and moustache is overgrown. One eye is swollen and bruised from 'either Ronny or Donny. I can't tell the difference anymore'. Aside from these physical markers of disorder, Murray's face is relatively motionless. In response to Max asking if he is 'ok', with two cigarettes hanging from his mouth, Blume replies monotonously, 'Mmmmmm. I'm a little bit lonely these days.' The very subtle movements his face does exhibit – a slight twitch in the corner of his mouth, sporadic blinking of his eyes, the faint wincing of his cheeks – portray an anxiety deeply rooted in loneliness and melancholy.

Lost in Translation and *Broken Flowers* also feature a number of scenes of Murray sitting, waiting, watching, yet each is expressively potent. In *Broken Flowers*, these moments are integral to Murray's portrayal of midlife depression and a number of key scenes feature Murray's Don Johnston 'doing nothing', mostly while sitting on his sofa. As with the *Rushmore* pool scene, these moments of introspection and externalising emotion operate without dialogue, forcing the audience to sit and wait with him. The absence of dialogue amplifies the actor's subtle facial expressions and bodily gestures. His vacant stare bores through the television screen, eyes half-closed through boredom and lethargy, and an occasional glance around the room signals he may be waiting for something to happen.

Scene and shot duration increases the sense of awkwardness created by the moments of 'doing nothing', with some shots lasting longer than a minute at a time. However, the awkwardness of stillness and 'doing nothing' is also created in briefer, transitory moments that arguably have as much expressive potency. Visiting the grave of an ex-girlfriend, Michelle Pepe, Don becomes overwhelmed. Up until this point, Don/Murray's expression, gesture and voice have remained relatively 'blank'; the cemetery scene marks the peak of Don's emotional journey and offers his most emotive performance of angst. With a plaster on his head, a bloody cut across his cheek and bruised eye – resulting from a clash with another ex-girlfriend – Don displays his wounds both physically and emotionally. Murray's eyes and head move slowly and slightly to one side, hesitantly glancing at the floor and then away as if not knowing where to look. He gulps, his eyes well up, his lips tremble, and his shoulders rise and fall to correspond with his shallow and laboured breathing. The result is an emotion held back: a conscious attempt not to cry. The context of the wider film assists in the recognition that Don's sadness results not from the death of the ex-girlfriend but the realisation that he is a lonely bachelor in his fifties with no established relationships. It is Murray's performance in this scene, however, that demonstrates the depth of that sadness and the uncertainty and conflict Don faces in his process of 'growing up' and 'being a man'.

Commenting on these extended scenes of doing nothing, Murray said he spent most of the time *reacting* rather than acting: 'It's hard to shut up, to not speak all the time. ... You're really taking all the emotional hits and you have to respond just with your face and your body'.[50] The distinction between reacting and acting is an important one in locating the difference between the image of masculinity-in-crisis exhibited in the posters for *North by Northwest* and *Lost in Translation*. For Murray, *acting* refers to dialogue or obvious movement; *reacting*, on the other hand, is limited to the subtle and slight gestures of the face and body. The actor also admitted that Jim Jarmusch, director of *Broken Flowers*, gave him a 'very interesting but narrow range of takes' in order to contain Murray's 'goofball stuff'.[51] By this reasoning, 'doing nothing' involves the restraint and containment of action but is an action nonetheless; in fact Murray's comment suggests that reacting requires *more* work and concentration.

Fundamental to each of the examples explored here is Murray's face. Although he is described as 'doing nothing' and characterised by stillness and 'passive immobility', his face is often the locus of emotion. However, is the idea of 'doing nothing' at the heart of what Barry King refers to as an actor's 'given-ness'? That is, how much of

Murray's embodiment of 'midlife crisis' is to do with how he looks rather than what he does with those looks? In a review of *Broken Flowers* for the London *Sunday Times*, Edward Porter commented, 'The thinning hair, the bags under his eyes, the drooping cheeks, not since Walther Matthau has an American star been as well equipped to suggest a weary, battered soul, without moving a facial muscle'. For Jessica Winter of *The Village Voice*, Murray and his characters' emotions are 'written in the doughy contours of his goofy-handsome face and reflected in his doleful basset-hound eyes'. A *Philadelphia Enquirer* critic suggests that 'he seems perfectly capable of painting "The Last Supper" with a single eyelash'. For A. O. Scott of *The New York Times*, it is his 'pockmarked, pancake of a face' that intrigues.[52] While each reviewer may have a different approach or understanding of the film under review, at some point Murray's visage is scrutinised, commented on, drawn attention to and dissected in a way that suggests there is something remarkable, or even unique, about his face and facial performance.

It is not surprising that Murray's face has generated more media attention than any other part of his body. As Mary Ann Doane has pointed out, the face has been over-represented as '*the* instance of subjectivity' or what she refers to as the 'intensification of a locus of signification'.[53] Commenting on the changing performance style of the 1910s but arguably applicable today, Janet Staiger notes, 'Characters are developed when we know their thoughts and feelings. And we know their thoughts and feelings primarily through their facial motions.'[54] The face is a 'reflecting surface', wrote Lawrence Shaffer in 1977, 'never just a thing-in-itself but always a reflective metaphor'. For Roland Barthes, the face is much more than the features it contains: 'A mask is but a sum of lines; a face, on the contrary, is above all their thematic harmony.'[55] What is particularly interesting about the abundance of comments regarding Murray's face is the contrast between those that emphasise his subtle yet powerful use of facial gestures in the construction of his midlife-crisis male, and those where critics believe Murray achieves this effect *without* moving his face. In other words, a significant number of contemporary reviewers hint at the possibility that Murray's specific physiognomy signifies midlife crisis and infer that there is something particular about his face that marks him as crisis-ridden *prior* to his enactment of a character.[56] How much, then, is Murray's association with the male midlife crisis his own doing and how much is out of his control? Is his performance of male angst dependent upon what he looks like rather than what he does?

The practice of reading facial characteristics and their movement as indicative of specific emotions has a long history. As far back as 1927, Charles Aubert argued in *The Art of Pantomime*, his structuralist approach to facial expressions, that the face was made up of 'expressive components' with a vast number of combinations and permutations either 'stamped by will and intelligence' or without will and intelligence.[57] In other words, the face is intentionally expressive (a performance) or the expressiveness is already and unintentionally evident in the subject's face. In the 1960s, personality theorist Silvan Tomkins produced a list of eight 'affects' which he believed could be expressed facially: interest-excitement, enjoyment-joy, surprise-startle, distress-anguish, fear-terror, shame-humiliation, contempt-disgust and anger-rage. Categorising each expression according to the level of affectation – positive, negative or neutral – Tomkins' list highlights the associated facial characteristics of these specified emotions:

Positive:
1. Interest-Excitement: eyebrows down, eyes track, look, listen
2. Excitement-Joy: smile, lips widened up and out, smiling eyes (circular wrinkles)

Neutral:
3. Surprise-Startled: eyebrows up, eyes blink

Negative:
4. Distress-Anguish: cry, arched eyebrows, mouth down, tears, rhythmic sobbing
5. Fear-Terror: eyes frozen open, pale, cold, sweaty, facial trembling, with hair erect
6. Shame-Humiliation: eyes down, head down
7. Contempt-Disgust: sneer, upper lip up
8. Anger-Rage: frown, clenched jaw, eyes narrowed, red face.[58]

Such methods are as problematic as they are useful. Not only does reading the face in this way rely on a degree of subjectivity (there is a vast difference between 'grumpy' and 'sad,' although a concave face could imply both), but facial expressions and their interpretation are also culturally and historically specific. What one culture may interpret as a smiling, joyful face could signify madness for another. According to Tomkins' list, the most important facial markers of emotion are the eyebrows, mouth and eyes. The 'distress-anguish' affect described here corresponds to Murray's concave face – arched eyebrows, mouth down. The mouth, eyes, cheek structure, and brow turn down to form an arch '∩' shape (as opposed to a convex 'U' shape or neutral '−'). The negative concave face implies sadness, worry or grumpiness while the positive convex face appears smiling or surprised.

Comments about Murray's distinctive physiognomy certainly highlight the possibility that the performance of male angst and midlife crisis may be suited to some actors rather than others. According to Barry King, an actor can suggest a particular emotion or state 'merely because he or she has automatic or physiologically given qualities, e.g. lip shape and movement, facial mass and habitual expressions'. Moreover, King argues, actors are limited by their given-ness to perform particular characterisations.[59] *Groundhog Day* aside, Murray was looked on by critics less favourably before his performance in *Rushmore* when his facial expressions were more stated and dramatic. However, this could also explain why his post-*Rushmore* performances of male angst have been popular with critics – his physiognomy is deemed to be a better 'fit' with the angst-ridden roles. Indeed, while critics have readily aligned Murray with midlife crisis and male angst since his appearance in *Rushmore*, a number of other actors with similar facial features have found critical recognition in angst-ridden roles, such as William H. Macy in *Fargo* (1996), *The Cooler* (2003) and *Edmond* (2005) or Steve Buscemi in *The Big Lebowski* (1998) and *Ghost World* (2001). Murray, Macy, Buscemi, and indeed Walter Matthau, all have what could be described as naturally concave facial features.

The older Murray has become, the more he has been associated with 'midlife crisis'. Instead of an emphasis on the body as marker of crisis (the 'middle aged spread'), reviewers have again concentrated on Murray's face. Certainly, Murray does not have the chiselled Hollywood looks of Cary Grant or Tom Cruise, although this has not stopped him from becoming an American sex symbol. As Courtney Fitzgerald of

The Austin Chronicle has asked: 'Why settle for Johnny Depp when there's Bill Murray? Bill makes acne scars sexy. Tragicomedy lives on his face. His sagging jowls make you swoon.... Let's face it, Bill Murray is a luminary of American sex, his light glowing brighter with the broken capillaries'. Similarly, Shane Watson of the *Sunday Times* asserts: 'pockmarked, balding and in mid-midlife crisis (hence the Helmut Lang T-shirt), yet somehow irresistible. There isn't a woman who has seen [*Lost in Translation*] who hasn't fantasized about Murray.'[60] Many of these facial attributes were evident many years prior to *Rushmore* (particularly his hair, which has been receding since the 1980s). It is telling, then, that Murray epitomises midlife crisis not in his forties (the decade traditionally associated with midlife crisis) but in his fifties.

The association of 50-something Murray and 'midlife' crisis alludes to the cultural climate of the late 1990s and early 2000s whereby images of aging baby boomers and subsequent speculations surrounding the transformation of what it means to grow old abounded. Sociologists and gerontologists came out in droves to state that the boundaries of old age are shifting, both demographically, as a result of increasing life expectancy rates, and culturally, with the aging baby boomers refusing to grow old and 'act their age' (see Chapter 5). Murray's alignment with midlife crisis in his fifties can be read as testament to shifting age boundaries and it has also been suggested that his aging has added a new dimension to the midlife male. Kenneth Turan, reviewing *Lost in Translation* for *The Los Angeles Times* commented that not only has Murray's comic timing 'gotten sharper' with age but his aging has 'added to the gravitas and sense of wistful dignity' that has accompanied his performance of male angst.[61] 'Something miraculous has happened to him as he's aged,' declared Peter Travers for *Rolling Stone*, 'his blobby, pockmarked face has somehow become unexpectedly handsome, and he's grown as an actor to the point that he can communicate his inner state while being nearly comatose'.[62]

While Murray's physiognomy is fundamental to how he has been read as the epitome of male angst and midlife crisis, it is clear that this signification is inseparable from his facial performances. It would be more accurate to suggest a face like Murray's assists or amplifies the performance of male angst than it would to suggest his physiognomy is a prerequisite for the construction of the man-in-crisis.

Murray's physiognomy is just one factor, albeit a major factor, in the construction of midlife crisis for the screen and his presentation of angst relies on the belief that Murray is *doing* nothing. His facial performances of immobility have attracted comparisons with Buster Keaton – the 'great stone face' of silent cinema – an actor also famous for his melancholy and angst yet with an entirely different physiognomy. Like Murray, Keaton's 'stone face' was not quite set in stone. Writing in 1958, Christopher Bishop noted that 'when he wished, Keaton could create utter and hilarious disorder by the subtlest change of expression, the flicker of an eye-lid, the beginnings of a frown'.[63] Similarly, as Roger Ebert argues, it is in Murray's 'small gestures of the eyes', or what A.O. Scott has called his 'slightest ticks and flickers', that angst is created.[64] Even when Murray's face remains 'frozen' in his films, reviewers have observed how his eyes take on a life of their own, externalising emotion more effectively than any other face or body part. In his review for *Lost in Translation* for *Time*, Richard Corliss states:

> Watch Murray's eyes in the climactic scene in the hotel lobby: while hardly moving, they express the collapsing of all hopes, the return to a sleepwalking status quo. You won't find a subtler, funnier or more poignant performance this year than this quietly astonishing turn.[65]

Furthermore, director Wes Anderson's comment that Murray 'has his own way of moving. His eyes do things no one else's do', suggests this fascination also extends to filmmakers.[66]

Part of the fascination in watching Murray *do* nothing relies on the audience's understanding of Murray's star image – the roles he plays now but also the comedic persona he crafted prior to the emergence of his angst-ridden stone face. To believe he is 'doing nothing' implies Murray is 'being himself' and this requires understanding of who 'Bill Murray' is. It is here that Murray's earlier goofball persona and his later crisis-ridden persona converge; Murray 'doing nothing' may be fascinating because we are waiting for 'something' to happen: for the goofball to burst out. In the films considered here there are only momentary glimpses of slapstick and the 'old' Murray; the actor has become so quickly and firmly aligned with melancholy and stillness that even these glimpses appear out of place. The gym scene in *Lost in Translation* where Murray/Bob loses control of his elliptical trainer is a case in point. With his limbs flailing madly and shouting for help, he eventually falls off. Significantly, however, while his arms and legs are moving rapidly from the force of the machine, Murray's facial expression remains still while his eyes dart back and forth in panic and bewilderment.

It is the performance-within-a-performance set up by the film – Murray, an actor, plays Bob, an actor – that most clearly plays on the relationship between person and persona. At a photo shoot for Suntory, the whisky he has been commissioned to advertise, Murray (the actor) not only performs Bob (the character), but Murray also performs Bob performing. Notions of performance are further confused when the photographer asks Bob/Murray to incorporate the performances of other actors into his repertoire. Requests to 'do' John Wayne, the Rat Pack and '007' result in Bob/Murray adapting his facial gestures and mannerisms in order to imitate each particular actor or acting style. This sequence of conspicuous enactment provides a literal and explicit example of the constructedness of both masculinity and performance. It is telling that the actors Bob is asked to perform – Frank Sinatra, Sean Connery, Roger Moore – are aligned with particular versions of masculinity that are the antithesis of Murray's angst-ridden male: the tough, rugged Rat Packer and the suave, sophisticated James Bond hero. Murray's performances of these other men amplify Bob's crisis of identity; it is his performance of the expressions of others that is preferred over his own face (and, in fact, persona) since they do not want 'Bob', or an impression of one of his own characters. At the same time, the performances-within-a-performance calls attention to the performance process; even in moments of 'doing nothing,' Murray is doing something to present his character.

It is important to recognise the role of the filmmaker in assisting the restyling of Murray's star persona and Murray's choice of films certainly play a crucial part in determining how he has been read in popular culture and film criticism. Jeffrey Sconce has classified a new generation of filmmakers, including Sofia Coppola, Wes Anderson and Jim Jarmusch, as exhibiting a 'smart sensibility' defined in opposition to the mainstream while, at the same time, being dependent on it.[67] Characterised by irony, nihilism, disaffection and 'blankness', films by these directors undoubtedly provide Murray with an arena for 'externalising emotion' and utilising minimalist modes of acting. According to *The Times*, Murray has become 'a touchstone for the younger generation of Hollywood directors', suggesting that 'they saw in him something Hollywood had never seen before — something hidden in that pudgy, malleable, acne-scarred face, in the deep bags under his eyes, in the irredeemable melancholy that oozes from every aging pore'.[68]

Not only does the director provide the opportunity for Murray to refine his minimalist acting style, but this is amplified though specific techniques – the longer than average shot length or 'low-budget long-take' that David Bordwell suggests is 'the major distinguishing mark of off-Hollywood directors'.[69] Sconce describes what he sees as a number of new ways of framing employed by many 'smart' films: 'the "awkward couple" shot (a strained couple shot in tableau form separated by blank space); the "awkward coupling" shot (a camera placed directly over the bed recording passionless sex); and in "family" films, the "awkward dining" shot (long-shots of maladjusted families trapped in their dining rooms)'.[70] *Rushmore*, *Lost in Translation* and *Broken Flowers* employ all three 'stock' shots to underscore and accentuate feelings of alienation, apathy and angst. *Broken Flowers* in particular repeatedly employs the 'awkward dining' shot in each scene that Johnston meets with an ex-girlfriend; with each drawn-out silence, the camera lingers on Murray's face, closely observing his awkwardness and discomfort and waiting for him to act or react. It is through the drawn-out silences, close-ups and long-takes that Murray's presentation of male angst is more acutely observed, capturing those extended scenes of sitting, waiting and watching. However, it is what Murray *does* during these scenes that takes precedence; the 'smart sensibility' or directorial techniques do not create male instability, they accentuate and draw attention to the actor's performance. This is evident in the final scene of *Broken Flowers*, which uses a 20-second arc shot, circling around Murray's face and head (see Figure 2.4). Only his eyes move; they blink, his pupils move rapidly from side to side as if thinking, processing the encounter with the teenager who is perhaps his son, pondering his next steps. The circling camera, pulling in from long-shot to close-up, creates a sense of disorientation, confusion and vulnerability, but it is finally his eyes, darting back and forth while his expression remains frozen, that underscores his loneliness.

Figure 2.4 Cinematography calling attention to facial expression in *Broken Flowers* (Focus Features, 2005)

Murray's performance of angst, while composed of minimal and slight movements, demonstrates the significance of the face in creating meaning. The case study of Murray reveals that the 'facial performance' involves the actor's 'given' physiognomy as well as what is done with it. Once again, cinema technology plays a key role in the construction of angst but the actor is always the originator of meaning. Does Murray's performance of angst tell us anything about the contemporary period? As Roberta Pearson points out in *Eloquent Gestures*, any analysis of performance needs to be constantly aware of the 'cultural and historical specificity of performance codes and of the implicit judgements inherent in familiar descriptive terms such as melodramatic and naturalistic'.[71] Critics in the late 1990s and early 2000s may consider Murray's performances minimalist, subtle and 'not acting', yet this is not to say that his performances in the films released during this period will always be deemed to work in this way. Many film critics in the 1950s viewed Marlon Brando's use of The Method in *A Streetcar Named Desire* (1951) and *On the Waterfront* (1955) as naturalistic and subtle – a form of acting offering a very different approach to 'externalising emotion' than the one displayed by Murray in *Broken Flowers* or *Rushmore* but one that has also drawn associations with 'masculinity in crisis'.[72] Although Murray is firmly aligned with male angst in the contemporary period, it does not necessarily mean angst will always be central to his persona; he has, after all, already managed to redefine his screen persona once in moving from goofball in the 1980s to melancholic male in the late 1990s and 2000s. The historical and cultural specificity of performance codes thus underscores the usefulness of film reviews, helping to locate performers and performances in their particular contexts.

Not only does a case study of Murray reveal ways male angst can be performed and read in popular culture but it also adds a historical dimension to the feminist claim that men are *always* in crisis. Murray played angst-ridden characters in his earlier film career but was not firmly associated with 'crisis' until his performance in *Rushmore*. Thus, it was a particular performance style that assisted this alignment. The angst is specific to Murray, that is, it is Murray's 'given-ness', particularly as he has aged, that has aligned him with crisis. Furthermore, this performance style and 'given-ness' has been appropriated by a group of directors, characterised by a particular tone or sensibility that enhances the alignment with male instability through the use of specific techniques and storylines. In order to further explore the relationship between director and actor in creating male angst, I turn to a case study of the voice as performance tool in David Mamet's *Oleanna* in the final section of this chapter.

Tongue-tied: Mamet and Macy's verbal and vocal angst

The voice as an acting tool has received little sustained attention in critical studies of film and performance. While a small number of key studies were published in the early 1980s, including Mary Ann Doane's 'The Voice in the Cinema: The Articulation of Body and Space' (1980) and Michel Chion's *The Voice in Cinema* (1982), only recently has there been some resurgence in studies of the voice and these are still limited in number.[73] The dearth of scholarly material has been explained by the tendency in film studies to concentrate on 'the image', viewing film as primarily a visual medium with sound as a subsidiary component.

The work of David Mamet presents an opportunity to explore this critical insufficiency. The dialogue that characterises his plays and screenplays has become widely known as 'Mametspeak': a rhythmic and manifestly dramatic style consisting of broken sentences, interruptions, long pauses, overlap, and repetition. It is this distinctive relationship with language and the voice that apparently distinguishes him from other playwrights. As Anne Dean notes:

> Perhaps more than those of any other American playwright, David Mamet's works constitute a *theatre of language*: the lines spoken by his characters do not merely contain words that express a particular idea or emotion; they are the idea or emotion itself.[74]

The idea that meaning in Mamet plays is not just represented in the words that are spoken but in *how* they are spoken is the focus of this chapter's final case study. While dialogue is central to Mamet's work, *Oleanna* (1994) explicitly foregrounds the power of language in its three-act, two-character story about political correctness and sexual harassment in the education system. The use of language in *Oleanna*, particularly the relationship between words and power, has already been the subject of a number of studies.[75] However, as Martin Shingler has noted, 'there is much more to the voice than dialogue', and it is the centrality of the voice in *Oleanna* that I wish to address in more detail here.[76] This section will consider the voice as a performance tool, exploring the verbal (what is spoken) and vocal (how it is spoken) mechanics of performance employed in the construction of male angst on the screen. After addressing some difficulties raised when studying the voice, I examine how words are used in *Oleanna* to create male instability before going on to consider the relationship between director and actor in constructing vocal performance.

Unlike the film still, photographic image, script or screenplay, the voice cannot be 'captured'. An image can be paused, enhanced or magnified; a passage from a play or screenplay can be read, re-read and deconstructed. 'Capturing' a voice, however, proves much more problematic. Certainly, the voice can be recorded and repeatedly played back, to allow the listener multiple opportunities to hear the sounds of the voice, to analyse the pauses, inflections, accents, tone and textures. However, the very act of recording distorts or affects how the voice is heard. As Gianluca Sergi argues in his essay 'Actors and the Sound Gang', this is the main characteristic of the film voice: 'the film actor does not simply speak ... like any aspect of filmic performance, the voice is mediated'.[77] On the one hand, the presentation of the film voice is influenced by the need to create optimum sound quality – using the correct number of microphones and the best type of microphone for the scene or film, for example. On the other hand, choices regarding sound technology can be more to do with practicalities than aesthetics, that is, factors such as the cost-effectiveness of the technology used can be more influential than achieving optimum sound. The cinematic voice, therefore, is a constructed voice, the product of external influences outside the actors' control.

The process of recording and editing dialogue has been seen as a sanitising process, cleansing the voice of blemishes and imperfections. James Naremore, for example, has posited that:

> The microphone is capable of bringing us the 'grain' of an actor's voice, but in usual practice it tames and naturalizes the vocal instrument, detheatricalizing language in much the same way as close-ups detheatricalize gesture.[78]

Sergi expands on the impact of technology in his assertion that the film voice 'is not a given, fixed value, but a variable'.[79] By this reasoning, the film voice is the product of any number of technological influences, from microphone choice to post-production sound editing. While it is true that the film voice is a mediated voice, it is also a documented and documentable voice. Once the film reaches cinemas it becomes fixed; the cinema patron will hear the same voices whether they watch the Sunday matinee or a Wednesday evening performance (there is always the possibility, of course, that the sound equipment in the cinema is not up to standard, thus affecting the quality of the sound). In the cinema auditorium, the sound absorption that poses a problem in the theatre is reduced with surround sound technology; speakers are placed around the room for optimum sound reflection and refraction.

In the age of DVD, it can be played back and looped with a remote control, made louder or quieter using the volume dial, and altered by turning on (or off) numerous sound technology devices (Dolby Digital, DTS, THX), each time transforming the acoustic properties of the sound. Technology thus has the potential to radically alter our perceptions of the voice. As Michel Chion notes in relation to Dolby:

> Dolby helps to give a direct, close, and palpably physical presence to the voice, entirely changing the way we perceive it. More generally,

it focuses finer attention on vocal texture, subtle variations of timbre, vibration of vocal cords, resonances.[80]

With this sound technology, the voice can be presented to the listener as clearly as possible. Filmmakers are also able to choose between sound technologies depending upon the effect they wish to achieve – to 'define cinematic space' – and can influence what the audience actually hear.[81]

Added to the difficulties in studying and 'capturing' the voice, selecting one of Mamet's films as a case study inevitably runs up against particular problems of how to approach the voice as an acting tool since the playwright and director is renowned for his control over the acting process. It is clear from Mamet's own writings that he does not believe in deviating from or elaborating on what exists in the play or screenplay. In *On Directing Film*, his most sustained study of film acting, Mamet asserts that the actor's job is to 'accomplish, *beat by beat*, as simply as possible, the specific action set out for them by the script and the director'.[82] For Mamet, it is the script that becomes the most important tool for the actor – the words written on the page – and it is the director, *not the actor*, who controls the performance. This polemic is central to his beliefs about the processes involved in stage and screen acting on which he has written extensively.[83] However, as I will go on to demonstrate, such an approach ignores the fact that an actor will always bring *something* to their role and this is particularly the case with the voice with its specific idiosyncrasies and characteristics.

The importance Mamet places on the words in the script recalls his own training as an actor under Sanford Meisner, an acting coach who closely followed the Stanislavsky System. Mamet frequently refers to Stanislavsky in his essays; the stress he places on the dialogue for the 'aesthetic integrity of the play' is reminiscent of Stanislavsky's emphasis on 'verbal action'. Stanislavsky maintained that the script should be closely analysed by the actor whose task it is to decide the vocal intonation required to convey meaning, which words to emphasise, and where the pauses should appear. However, with his scripts written so precisely, with emphasis on certain words, pauses and interruptions written in, Mamet sets out to minimise the actor's contribution to the creative process. Critical of those actors who 'try to use their intellectuality to portray the idea of the movie ... performing mundane and predictable actions in an overblown way', Mamet suggests that the director (both stage and screen) prefers to work with what Stanislavsky called the 'organic' actor who acts according to the words in the script, adding nothing nor taking anything away.[84]

Mamet's work is almost exclusively concerned with masculinity and its discontents; from his award-winning screenplay and play *Glengarry Glen Ross* (1992) to his critically successful plays *Sexual Perversity in Chicago* and *Speed-the-Plow*, to his films *Homicide* (1991) and *Heist* (2001), men and male issues are at the centre of the narrative, and this focus on the masculine extends to the dialogue. Expletives punctuate the male characters' speech, asserting power through coarse language. Carla McDonough has argued that male power and loss of power are indicated by the sound and delivery of words:

> [Male characters] attempt to use language to establish a place for themselves that does not exist in the reality of their play worlds. But, if their language is the last masculine space that they can find for themselves, it, too, is ineffective as it breaks down, repeats itself, pauses. Because they have no adequate vocabulary to fully express their fears and desires, Mamet's men end up speaking their confusion in broken syntax and hysterical invective.[85]

While this is true, as well as asserting power through the very words that are spoken (in the case of the habitual use of expletives), Mamet's male characters also assert power and demonstrate loss of control through *how* the words are spoken: in broken, incomplete sentences with recurrent pauses and repetitions.

As a text that began on the stage and has been revised for the screen, *Oleanna* is a revealing case study for the use of the voice in both theatre and film.[86] A student failing her course (Carol/Debra Eisenstadt) approaches her professor (John/William H. Macy) to ask for help. What John believes are innocuous, accommodating suggestions to help Carol understand, are interpreted by Carol as sexual harassment and 'rape', resulting in John losing his university tenure, his wife and his new house. Words take centre stage: the breakdown of power is demonstrated by the breakdown of language as John's grasp of the powerful properties of language are gradually stripped away as a result of Carol's manipulation of his words. Initially, John demonstrates power through his knowledge and understanding; he uses words or concepts such as 'term of art', 'paradigm', and 'index' that Carol does not understand and asks John to define. In Act II, Carol demonstrates her ability to manipulate John's words, to change their meaning, and the power over words begins to be transferred to Carol. By Act III, the transference of power is complete; her ability to know which words to use has increased and she has also gained access to the space in which to say them. It is Carol who dominates the verbal space at this juncture, delivering long speeches while John is relegated to the position of listener, sporadically interjecting in the same manner that Carol was fighting to be heard in Act I.

However, it is not necessarily *what* is said but *how* it is said that governs the transference of power. By comparing John and Carol's dialogue, it becomes evident not only how a masculine dialogue is constructed, but also sets this apart from 'female' dialogue, demonstrating how language serves to deconstruct male identity through emasculatory vernacular. This is first made clear in the language tussle at the beginning of Act I:

JOHN: I know how ... *believe* me. I know how ... potentially *humiliating* these ... I have no desire to ... I have no desire other than to help you. But. I won't even say 'but.' I'll say that as I go back over the ...

CAROL: I'm just, I'm just trying to ...

JOHN: ...no, it will not do.

CAROL: ...what? What will...?

JOHN: No. I see, I see what you, it ... but your work ...

CAROL: I'm just: I sit in class I ... I take notes ...

JOHN: Yes. I understand. What I am trying to *tell* you is that some, some basic ...

CAROL: ...I...

JOHN: ...one moment: some basic missed communi...

CAROL: I'm doing what I'm told. I bought your book, I read your ...

JOHN: No, I'm sure you ...

CAROL: No, no, no. I'm doing what I'm told. It's *difficult* for me. It's *difficult* ...

JOHN: ...but...

CAROL: I don't ... lots of the *language* ...

JOHN: ...please...
CAROL: The *language*, the 'things' that you say ...
JOHN: I'm sorry. No. I don't think that that's true.
CAROL: It *is* true. I...

The pace of the exchange is determined by the words. Sentences are left in mid-air, overlapped. Words are left incomplete creating a sense of urgency but also frustration as each character tries to gain verbal authority over the other, creating the impression of incoherence and inarticulateness as the words are stumbled over in an attempt to verbalise thoughts as quickly as possible. When a character finally manages to complete a sentence, the effect is final and infers a confidence and authority that is missing from the broken sentence. Rather than presenting dialogue in a straightforward manner, allowing the actor room for interpretation, Mamet directs the actor in the script to those important words that should be emphasised. Certain words are italicised in order to reinforce a point, to stress a particular idea and to demonstrate how the meaning of a word is affected by how it is spoken. John's emphasis on *believe* and *tell*, for example, underscores his intention to help Carol understand the information he is imparting. Carol's double emphasis on *difficult* and *language*, however, reinforces her frustration, making her speech more urgent and frenzied.

In *Oleanna*, shouting operates in a similar way. In *The Voice in Cinema*, Michel Chion distinguishes between male and female exclamation. He notes, 'The man's shout delimits a territory, the woman's scream has to do with limitlessness. ... The scream gobbles up everything into itself – it is centripetal and fascinating – while the man's cry is centrifugal and structuring.'[87] The male shout can be seen as a marker of power, indicating the boundary or territory and implying a degree of control. The scream on the other hand, is a feminine action, implying a loss of control or powerlessness, inferring a degree of hysteria and disorder. Similarly, Eisenstadt's shouting in *Oleanna* takes on a number of different forms, emphasising her frustration ('I DON'T UNDERSTAND. DON'T YOU SEE???'), her anger ('NO! YOU FOOL!'), to make demands ('I WANT UNDERSTANDING!!') and to gain control of the conversation ('I BELIEVE THAT I'M SPEAKING!').

By contrast, Macy's voice is balanced, his pitch constant and his volume remains steady. According to Sergi, vocal authority can be gained through difference, 'by adopting a different pitch'; independence, 'through adopting a different metre, syncopating the lines where he extends his and vice-versa'; and authority, 'by setting the tempo of the exchange'.[88] In Act I, John has complete control over the exchange. He refuses to raise his voice in response to Carol's shouting, keeping his voice at the same pitch and level which forces Carol to lower hers. John talks over Carol, breaking up her sentences so he retains control over the pace of the dialogue; he employs repetition and emphasis to make his points stronger. Carol continues to resort to shouting, even when she has gained power over John, positioning her character as overly emotional and irrational against John's rationality.

By Act II, John's waning power over words is evident when he begins to raise his voice in an attempt to retain control. In a similar way to how John asserts authority by changing his tempo and style in Act I, by Act III Carol talks over John, interrupts him and cuts him short. John loses authority as Carol gains confidence in her ability to use language, making it increasingly difficult for John to remain rational. That Carol continues to raise her voice in the final act only reinforces the emasculatory effects of shouting since she is portrayed in a hysterical light. When John resorts to shouting in an attempt to regain verbal authority, it is all the more clear that he has lost control over the verbal arena and thus his power over Carol. His masculinity is called into question precisely because he resorts to using the tactic that Carol has so unsuccessfully employed, a tactic which portrayed her as irrational, hysterical and emotional. John is thus feminised through his loss of vocal power.

By the film's finale, John has lost all command of the dialogue, reinforced first by his use of expletives and then by violent action against Carol. In the first act, John is constructed as an educated, intelligent, knowledgeable man on account of the abundance of words he effectively employs. By the third Act, he can only react to Carol's comments with 'Get the fuck out of my office ... you vicious little bitch' and 'I wouldn't touch you with a ten-foot pole. ... You little *cunt.*' Rather than reasserting John's masculinity, as McDonough has argued is the case with the majority of Mamet's other plays, these limited instances are even more powerful in emphasising John's fall from grace and go to demonstrate just how far he has moved from the articulate, rational professor of the first act. That John has to resort to expletives (and arguably two of the most sexually offensive and derogatory of words) in an attempt to usurp power, underlines John's emasculation.

The ending of *Oleanna* has often been discussed in terms of its verbal ambiguity. At the end of Act III, John has found out that Carol is accusing him of rape. Realising he has lost the battle of words and nothing he can say will better the situation, John attacks Carol violently and forces her to the ground. After a pause, John says:

JOHN: ...well...
        (Pause. She looks at him)
CAROL: Yes. That's right.
        (She looks away from him, and lowers her head. To herself:)
        ...yes. That's right.

The ending has been interpreted by Kellie Bean as evidence of the misogyny and patriarchal dominance which underlines the whole story. She states:

> No matter what Carol has visited upon John, he finally dominates her unequivocally, and in a paradigmatically masculine style – through violence against her. He forces her to the ground, where she acknowledges her final defeat, head bowed and *'To herself: ...yes. That's right.'*[89]

From the written words alone, it is certainly possible to come to this conclusion. There is no indication in the stage directions of precisely which emotion each character should reveal in their voice. While Mamet limits the possibility of interpretation for much of the play, the ending is left open, leaving the elucidation of the lines completely to the actor or director (or reader). However, a line is added to the film that challenges this reading. After John has beaten Carol, he looks around the room as if collecting his thoughts and addressing his actions, and says, 'Oh, my God.' He sits down on a chair and slowly puts his hands through his hair. Looking at Carol, who has lifted herself off the floor and is sitting on the sofa, John looks away from her and repeats 'Oh, my God', this time in an almost inaudible whisper. 'Yes. That's right', Carol replies, her voice shaky but definite. According to Bean, 'Although the plot punishes John for his treatment of Carol, the visual argument of the play celebrates John's power over Carol. *Oleanna* ends with a stark image of female submission to masculine dominance.'[90] The addition and repetition of the line 'Oh, my God', challenges Bean's contention and removes the ambiguity apparent in the script by shifting the power from John to Carol with his verbal and vocal surrender. Confirming this, Carol's 'Yes, that's right' is spoken quickly, strained yet factual, acknowledging John's validation of the charges against him. In the film, therefore, the voice is contained, removing the ambiguity that was present in the script.

As a writer and director for both the stage and screen, Mamet is consciously aware of what he perceives to be the differences between the two performance forms:

> in a play ... the only way you have to convey the action of the plot is through the action of the characters, what they say to each other. With a movie, the action has to be advanced narratively. To advance it through the dialogue is just boring; it is not the proper exploitation of the form.[91]

However, in the film version of *Oleanna*, dialogue continues to be the most important aspect of the performance; for the majority of the film the only noises we hear are the voices of the two characters and the incessantly ringing telephone which figures as a third 'voice' in the film, interrupting the narrative and signalling key moments in the story. The achievement of simplicity supports Mamet's assertion that 'The acting, the design, the direction should all consist only of that bare minimum necessary to put forward the action. Anything else is embellishment.'[92] By keeping the sound as simple as possible, the importance of the dialogue over all other elements of the play is retained. Mamet's emphasis on remaining faithful to the script and to the precise way in which dialogue is written, directing the actor towards how the lines should be spoken, suggests that the published stage play is a consistent documentation of dialogue, at least for those performances directed by Mamet himself. Although there is no aural record of the theatre voice, we have an indication of which words should be emphasised, when the silences should occur, and when voices should overlap. However, there will always be ambiguity, particularly as there is no indication of the 'qualities' of the voice in the stage play, that is, how should the words *sound*, what emotions should be conveyed by the voice.

The highly structured and precisely written dialogue goes some way towards removing this ambiguity by constraining the actor to the words in the script. As Macy has commented, dialogue in Mamet's plays 'is so finely tuned that improvising is nearly impossible. If you paraphrase it, it suddenly becomes very clunky in your mouth as if you stumbled over it'.[93] The key word here is *nearly*; while Mamet writes in a way that minimises or limits the actor's contribution to a role, the opportunity to improvise (even if it is slight) still exists. This also raises a possibility that Mamet refuses to acknowledge in his writings – that the actor invariably brings an element to the role that does not nor cannot exist in the written words.

According to Sarah Kozloff, the actor's 'natural vocal qualities, combined with his or her vocal skills, greatly influence the viewer's perception of the character's personality'.[94] In the role of John, William H. Macy reprised the character he had played in the theatre but was yet to establish his iconic role as the 'loser' or 'wimp' that he would later present in *Fargo*, *Magnolia* (1999) and *The Cooler*. However, Kozloff's statement suggests that a character can be created through the actor's particular vocal inflections. While Macy's voice in *Oleanna* may not have had any cultural currency in aligning him with a particular kind of character, the vocal dynamics he employs in the film effectively construct him as angst-ridden. As John's verbal authority is threatened, for example, Macy's voice becomes increasingly shrill and whiny; his matter-of-fact tone is replaced with exasperation and his vocal range widens. The shrillness and whining emphasised by drawn out, nasal vowels add to the sense of John's waning power. The sounds of Macy's voice become feminised to the point of sounding childlike, undermining the maturity and control the character exhibited at the beginning of the film.

In her essay 'Screen Performance and Directors' Visions,' Sharon Marie Carnicke argues that 'while performances in individual films emerge from the complex connections among directorial vision, narrative demands, camera work, mise-en-scène, sound and design, the actors still embody characters by means of physical and vocal gestures'.[95] The response of actors to working with David Mamet suggests that actors are willing to surrender their control over verbal performance in order to work with the writer-director. Commenting on the dialogue in *Glengarry Glen Ross*, Jack Lemmon noted: 'You learn quickly to leave Mamet's dialogue alone. It's like playing the piano. You have to learn the notes. ... There's no ad-libbing. Every syllable has meaning.' Similarly, Al Pacino has referred to Mamet's dialogue as 'actor-proof', stating 'You just have to hit the notes.'[96] Mamet may control what is written by giving a complex and poetic structure to dialogue that makes it difficult to change or to improvise, but he can only control the sounds of the voice to an extent and has limited control over what Roland Barthes has referred to as the 'grain' of the actor's voice.[97] In the case of *Oleanna*, Macy's grain – the vocal essence that he takes from role to role – complements the written dialogue; the 'jittery' and 'pleading whine' so central to the 'sad-sack, milquetoast persona' the actor would revise in *Fargo*, *The Cooler* and *Edmond*.[98] There is, then, no such thing as 'actor-proof' dialogue since the actor always brings an element to a role, even if that element is heavily restricted.

Conclusions

In examining Douglas's performances in *Falling Down* and *Wonder Boys,* and Murray's performances in *Rushmore, Lost in Translation* and *Broken Flowers*, angst is characterised by stillness and immobility with minimal movements and gestures, acting 'ordinary' in the case of Douglas or 'playing straight' in the case of Murray. Angst is expressed via a concave expression, a down-turned mouth and drooping eyes, a look of dismay and bewilderment. For Macy in *Oleanna*, angst is revealed through a changing vocal pitch and tone – shrillness and whining – that undermine his male authority. Angst for all three actors is presented as vulnerability and exposure: for Douglas, this involves 'wiping off' the star persona and externalising inner emotion; for Murray, emotion is externalised through numerous scenes of 'doing nothing', and close-ups of the actor's expressive physiognomy; for Macy, angst is portrayed in a stutter, a hesitation, a whine.[99] The performers not only expose themselves as angst-ridden but, in doing so, expose the performative nature of 'normative' masculinity in their failure to achieve the male ideal. In *Falling Down* and *Wonder Boys*, Michael Douglas/D-Fens/Tripp masquerades in all his male social roles: father, white collar worker, husband, son, college professor, and writer. In *Lost in Translation* and *Broken Flowers*,

Bill Murray/Bob Harris/Don Johnston struggles with his role as father, husband, and adult male. In *Oleanna*, Macy/John's male status hinges on his identity as husband, father, and university professor, his angst escalates as each role and identity is threatened. In each case, male-ness is foregrounded as an act, an identity to be staged. With each actor, the failure to live up to the perceived expectations of male social roles is key to their downfall and angst.

This focus on Murray's face and Macy's voice, makes it clear that certain parts of the body have more cultural impact than others in the creation of angst. Yet this is not to say that it is solely Murray's face or only Macy's voice that are responsible for creating an image of angst, for these bodily fragments, no matter how powerful, work alongside numerous other elements affecting performance. Macy's whiny, jittery voice may well assist his performance of angst but the power of the voice as performance tool is also complemented and amplified by his face: the actor's 'given' characteristics such as the concave mouth as well as his facial gestures (frowning, drooping eyelids, wrinkling the brow, pouting) that play on his 'given-ness'. The analysis of Douglas's performances may highlight the part played by the body in constructing anxiety and instability, but his face is often presented as the focal point of performance, further accentuated by the use of cinematographic techniques such as the close-up.

As the case studies indicate, the performance of angst is indebted to such film techniques yet the performer is always the instigator of emotion and expression. The final case study also foregrounds the pivotal role played by the writer-director in performance construc-tion. The case studies highlight the necessity to consider actors' performances within a continuum comprised of directors, edi-tors, cinematographers, sound technicians, reviewers (who inscribe meaning onto a performance), marketers, promoters, agents, and screenwriters. The case studies may reveal the collaborative nature of performance, yet actors are the crux – they are the ones credited with the creation of character and the intricate mechanics of performance are projected onto them, despite not being wholly responsible. It may be possible to determine a repertoire of performance signs in the enactment of angst, yet the case studies also reveal the difficulties in determining such a repertoire and, certainly, the impossibility of determining a *fixed* repertoire of performance signs.

While the performances examined in this chapter associate angst with vulnerability, it would be misleading to suggest that the performance of vulnerability is unique to this group of actors or this historical moment. Indeed, the vulnerability of male angst is central to the performance of masculinity in film noirs such as those found in *Double Indemnity* (1944), *Laura* (1944) or *Gilda* (1946).[100] On the one hand, the performances examined in this chapter depart from these earlier manifestations in foregrounding the performance of angst and angst as a performance; *Falling Down*, *Lost in Translation* and *Broken Flowers* centre on the presentation of male *as* angst-ridden while the film noirs are more concerned with gradually revealing male instability and anxiety. On the other hand, the moment in which the performances are produced and consumed also differentiates them. Although the chapter's main objective was to focus on the ways angst is performed, the case studies also reveal the cultural specificity of performing angst: Douglas's performance in *Falling Down* and Macy's in *Oleanna* can be read in terms of the racial and gendered discourse around political correctness at the start of the 1990s; the alignment of Murray with 'midlife crisis' at the start of the 2000s taps into debates around the shifting parameters of life stages in response to the aging of the baby boom (examined in detail in Chapter 5); Douglas and Murray's inability to be 'good' fathers in *Falling Down* and *Lost in Translation*, and their difficulties in coming to terms with the possibility of being a father in *Wonder Boys* and *Broken Flowers*, can be read in relation to changing perceptions of fatherhood in the contemporary period (examined in Chapter 4). Establishing the performance of angst as vulnerability in two different historical moments (1940s film noir and 1990s/2000s) thus highlights the importance of situating performances in their social and cultural context.

In 'The Voice in the Cinema', Mary Ann Doane concludes that 'film is not a simple juxtaposition of sensory elements but a discourse, an enunciation'.[101] This chapter has focused on the 'sensory elements' comprising performances of angst but a number of restrictions are imposed due to the complex and contradictory nature of reading performance, the impact of cinematographic and editing techniques on constructing performance and, in Goffman's terms, the 'mobile and transitory' nature of performance signs.[102] Seeing film as 'a discourse, an enunciation' is particularly important when studying the performance of masculinity which, as Judith Butler tells us, is always socially constructed. Since male social roles are also socially, politically and culturally constructed and performed, performance analysis must account for this by locating performances historically; we cannot consider performances in isolation but must locate them and relate them to the context in which they are performed and consumed. It is therefore vital that performances are considered in relation to the discursive moments that inform and are informed by performances of male instability and angst. Such moments shape both the images and performances of angst and our interpretation of them.

The discussions of films and actors in Part II examine the relationship between image and socio-cultural discourse in more detail and locate performances of male angst in relation to the social and historical context of the 1990s and 2000s. The circulation of extratextual material is crucial in locating performances contextually. The following chapters draw from material directly related to performances and performers (marketing and promotional publicity, interviews, television appearances, online discussion forums). The blurring of boundaries between or 'convergence' of entertainment, politics, and popular culture in the contemporary period has made it impossible to divorce film performance from the wider culture.[103] As the previous chapter discussed, 'performance' can be seen as an interdisciplinary term that has been appropriated in numerous fields of research. The following case studies acknowledge this interdisciplinarity by considering the impact of popular cultural forms in shaping and determining male identities: the 'genres of cultural performance' that Victor Turner has suggested affect performances and actions.[104]

In this way, the following chapters draw from film reviews, the popular press, news items and stories, marketing literature, self-help books and popular fiction and non-fiction. Such methods should not be seen as representing the views of the general population; as Richard Dyer has noted, 'the relationship of what the media call "public opinion" to the opinion of the public must always remain problematic'.[105] However, reviews and news stories do assist in the construction of images and identities. Covers from magazines such as *Time* and *Esquire*, for example, are used to illustrate popular perceptions of male identity, which, in turn, contribute to the discursive construction of masculinity and shape how performances are read in the period under examination. On-screen performances of male angst are thus located at the point of convergence – between film, television and other media platforms, politics, journalism and popular culture – for it is the combination of such elements that determines how they are produced and understood.

Part II
Roles and Representations

3
From Wimps to Wild Men: Bipolar Masculinity and the Paradoxical Performances of Tom Cruise

The Wild Man was a prevalent popular cultural figure that raised questions about the state of masculinity at the start of the 1990s, frequently appearing in self-help books, on magazine covers, in politics, and on the screen. At first a mythical figure, popularised in the writings of American poet Robert Bly and his bestselling self-help book for men, *Iron John* (1990), the Wild Man was personified by Jeff Bridges on the cover of an *Esquire* special issue titled 'Wild Men and Wimps' in October 1991 (Figure 3.1). Scowling into the camera, Bridges looked animalistic with his lion-like mane growing past his shoulders and a week's growth of hair on his face. In contrast to his facial appearance, Bridges wore a black bowtie, jacket and white shirt; a contradictory mix of 'civilisation' and 'nature', both cultivated and feral. With the 'Wild Men' cover line stamped in bold font across the actor's forehead, the words resting atop his slanting bushy eyebrows and piercing grey-blue eyes, Bridges became in a single image a figurehead for the men's movement championed by Bly at the start of the decade.[1] In smaller font and pushed to the edge of the *Esquire* cover, the Wimp was almost absent. Yet the presence of the Wimp, as the title of the special issue implies, was central to the construction of the Wild Man in the 1990s: the antithesis of Bridges' wild, hyper-male. It is the performative relationship between masculine opposites – in this case, between the Wild Man and the Wimp, between hyper-masculinity and hypo-masculinity – that is the focus of this chapter.

Part I of this book assessed the usefulness of 'performance' to the study of masculinity, understanding performance in terms of gendered and cinematic enactments. I have been thus far interested in

95

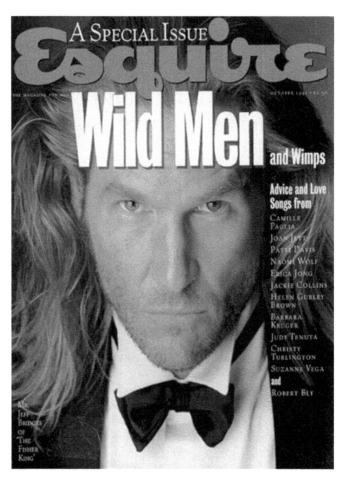

Figure 3.1   Embodying the Wild Man (Esquire/The National Magazine Company/
Matthew Rolston, 1991)

the role that performance plays in the creation of character and persona, examining in detail a number of performers who, through their
screen performances and physical characteristics, have been aligned
with male angst and dramatised 'the male condition' in the 1990s
and 2000s. Part II builds on the theories and issues addressed in Part I
but examines in more detail particular extratextual moments in which

masculinity has been contested – that is, moments in which the idea of male instability is made particularly prominent or visible. The following chapters explore a number of tropes of unstable masculinity in circulation during the 1990s and 2000s and their representation in contemporary film and popular culture.

The previous chapter examined William H. Macy's vocal performance of angst but also considered his alignment with angst-ridden masculinity as a result of his 'given' facial characteristics; the whining voice, hangdog cheeks and sagging eyes all contribute to his persona. These facial and vocal performances are evident in the later ineffectual male characters the actor plays: the pathetic, emasculated wimps of *Fargo* (1996), *Boogie Nights* (1997), *Magnolia* (1999), *State and Main* (2000) and *The Cooler* (2003). It is not just the actor's physical appearance and screen character that construct the image of masculine instability in these examples, however. The performance of the Wimp is also reinforced by its opposite: Dirk Diggler/Mark Wahlberg's hyper-male with his corresponding hyper-penis in *Boogie Nights*; Frank T. J. Mackey/Tom Cruise's chest-beating men's seminar leader in *Magnolia*; or Shelly Kaplow/Alec Baldwin's knee-capping bully in *The Cooler*. Together, the Wimp and the Wild Man exhibit a dichotomous relationship. Yet their relationship is also one of interdependence with each masculine trope reliant on the other for validation and definition. This idea offers a stark contrast to earlier studies of masculine tropes by Susan Jeffords and Fred Pfeil, for example, which argue representations of masculinity historically shift from decade to decade, such as the 'hard body' in the 1980s and the 'Year of Living Sensitively' in 1991.[2]

Following a discussion of the relationship between hard and soft masculinity, the second half of the chapter considers the centrality of performance to constructions of 'bipolar masculinity' through a case study of Tom Cruise in *Magnolia*. While not an actor aligned with 'male crisis' as in the case of Michael Douglas in the early 1990s or Bill Murray a decade later (see Chapter 2), Cruise's performance of hyper-masculinity via Frank T. J. Mackey – Bly's *Iron John* taken to the extreme – reveals the interdependence of the Wimp and Wild Man. Moreover, Cruise's paradoxical performances not only problematise the relationship between the on-screen and off-screen performance of masculinity but they also raise questions about the nature of contemporary stardom.

Hard and soft: Wild men and wimps in popular culture

Constructions and perceptions of male identity have strong links with the wilderness versus civilisation debate or what Karen Lee Ashcraft and Lisa A. Flores term 'civilized-primitive dualism'.[3] In her true story of Wild Man Eustace Conway who moved out of his parental home and into the wilderness when he was seventeen, Elizabeth Gilbert describes the history of America as follows:

> There was a frontier, and then there was no longer a frontier. It all happened rather quickly. There were Indians, then explorers, then settlers, then towns, then cities. Nobody was really paying attention until the moment the wilderness was officially tamed, at which point everybody wanted it back. Within the general spasm of nostalgia that ensued ... there came a very specific cultural panic, rooted in the question *What will become of our boys?*[4]

Gilbert's book highlights the alignment of masculinity with nation; Conway is presented as the 'last American man', his wild masculine image representing the wildness of America: strong, natural and untainted by the feminising effects of mass culture. As Richard Slotkin's historical studies of the mythology of the American frontier attest, the 'frontier' is a complicated concept with shifting definitions, from Frederick Jackson Turner's 'frontier thesis' in 1893, to the supposed collapse of the frontier myth in the wake of Vietnam and John F. Kennedy's promise of a 'new frontier' in 1960.[5] Fears over the loss of masculinity with the loss of the American frontier are thus by no means new. The masculine frontier has come to stand for nature over culture, implying nostalgia for any moment where traditional definitions of masculinity have been threatened or usurped by the capitalist forces of modern society.

At the start of the 1990s, fears over a lost frontier for men were brought to the fore once again in the writings of 'mythopoetic' author Robert Bly. Bly, a prize-winning poet and anti-war activist in the 1960s, had been organising male gatherings since the 1980s for men to go back to nature by 'drumming, reciting poetry, learning aikido, playing volleyball, telling stories, making masks, listening to presentations ... and dancing a wild samba late into the night'.[6] These rural gatherings were staged as a response to consumer culture, the perceived 'feminisation' of society, and feminism. With the publication of Bly's *Iron John: A Book About Men*, a Brothers Grimm fairytale refashioned as a commentary on the deteriorating state of masculinity in the late 1980s and early 1990s, the mythopoetic men's movement was officially launched into the public spotlight, spawning similarly masculinist manifestos and anti-feminist diatribes from Warren Farrell to Sam Keen.[7] According to Michael Kimmel, Bly, Keen and others tapped into 'a deep current of malaise among American men' compounded by 'fears of feminization – that we have lost our ability to claim our manhood in a world without fathers, without frontiers'.[8] The mythic and nostalgic frontier was being re-imagined by hoards of men across America who left their corporate lives behind for a weekend to go deep into the forest, beat drums and dance around campfires.

The cultural significance of *Iron John* is undeniable, especially considering the upsurge of debates concerning masculinity during this period, and how its themes have consistently been recycled in American film. On the one hand, the Wild Man in *Iron John* is displayed as a performer and a performance, a male identity to be acted out, sometimes literally with the use of masks and costumes. On the other hand, the book not only borrows from culture but also feeds back into the culture, assisting in the circulation of images and in the formation of the Wild Man trope. *Iron John* remained on bestsellers' lists for much of 1990 and 1991; it paved the way for spin-off books (itself contributing to the *Esquire* special issue); it was the subject of numerous talk shows and current affairs programmes; it was cited in both men's and women's magazines across America and in Britain; and it was analysed and scrutinised by media commentators and newspaper columnists, and in gender studies scholarship.[9]

In Bly's formation, maleness for the Wild Man is an essence, something that exists from birth rather than something learned or bought. Bly writes, 'every modern male has, lying at the bottom of his psyche, a large, primitive being covered with hair down to his feet'.[10] The Wild Man must be uncovered through a 'bucketing-out process' in order to re-establish the male ideal in the contemporary period, an idea that has been explored by films as different as *Dances with Wolves* (1990), *Tarzan* (1999), *Human Nature* (2001) and *Grizzly Man* (2005). A recurring storyline revolves around the idea that attempts to tame or domesticate the Wild Man have destructive social and historical implications. Key to this bucketing-out process is initiation. Much of the problem with men in contemporary America, Bly argues, is a result of the father or, rather, absence of fathers in modern families, an idea that frequently featured in political, popular and academic discourse during the 1990s (see Chapter 4). Bly maintains that the failure of men to initiate boys in contemporary culture is the reason men lack access to the Wild Man and this failure to initiate is largely due to the increasing absence of a father figure in the household. Not only is the absence of a father figure at the root of men's inability to enter into manhood but also, according to Bly, their inability is fuelled by the increasing dominance and influence of the female in men's lives: 'When we walk into a contemporary house', he writes, 'it is often the mother who comes forward confidently. The father is somewhere else in the back, being inarticulate'.[11] For Bly, fatherhood is a central masculine signifier that has been usurped by the mother figure in the contemporary period. Bly repeatedly returns to this idea of father lack or loss as a significant explanation for the softening of men. The father or father figure, as Bly's pseudo-Freudian reading suggests, is central to the process of initiating boys into manhood thus the rejection of the mother is a necessary step in reclaiming masculinity.

However, for feminists and other critics of the mythopoetic men's movement, the Wild Man signifies the destructive nature of masculinity; he is a symbol of misogyny, indicative of the damaging effect of patriarchal masculinity and is ultimately 'nativist, separatist, homophobic, and expressed through concocted myths of ancient men's rituals'.[12] Despite Bly's claims in *Iron John* and his seminars that he 'does not seek to turn men against women nor to return men to the domineering mode that has lead to repression of women and their values for centuries', his polemic could certainly be construed as anti-feminist and indeed anti-female.[13] Susan Faludi worryingly recalls a 1987 seminar:

[A] man in the audience told Bly, 'Robert, when we tell women our desires, they tell us we're wrong'. Bly instructed, 'So, then you bust them in the mouth'. After someone pointed out that this statement seemed to advocate violence against women, Bly amended it, 'Yes. I meant, hit those women verbally'.[14]

The recuperation of masculinity for the contemporary man ultimately depends on the extrication of the boy from the mother, the husband from the wife, the man from the woman, and it is only in the company of other men that man's 'inner warrior' can be revealed.

Bly perceives male instability as existing apart from dominant or normative constructions of masculinity, foregrounding a desire or need to 'return' to an earlier, more secure cultural moment for men. He admires the stoicism of the 'fifties male', bemoans the feminine 'soft male' of the 1970s and calls for men to uncover the 'deep' masculinity inherent in all men than has been hidden as a result of social and cultural changes of the past few decades, particularly feminism. In this way, Bly's work appears to conform to a wider pattern in film and masculinity studies in seeing masculinity as either 'hard' or 'soft'.

A number of film scholars have discussed masculinity in popular American film according to a number of types or tropes, exhibiting certain characteristics at particular moments in history that can be said to reflect or embody a specific cultural moment or decade.[15] Surveying this scholarship, one would assume that masculinity operates in phases or cycles. Susan Jeffords, for example, describes the dominant masculine form in the 1980s as the muscular 'hard body' embodied by actors such as Arnold Schwarzenegger and Sylvester Stallone and reflected in the image and presidency of Ronald Reagan. Jeffords' narrative of the Reagan years is ultimately one of contrasts: from the sensitivity of the seventies, to the macho eighties and a return to sensitivity and soft men at the start of the nineties; from the 'hardened, muscle-bound, domineering man of the eighties [to] the considerate, loving, and self-sacrificing man of the nineties'.[16]

Similarly, Fred Pfeil suggests the 1990s signalled a shift in masculine subjectivity towards a more sensitive, domesticated male, as performed by Harrison Ford in *Regarding Henry* (1991) or Schwarzenegger in *Kindergarten Cop* (1990). Accordingly, Pfeil terms 1991 'The Year of Living Sensitively' and suggests such representations offer a direct contrast to the 'rampagers' of the *Lethal Weapon* (1987 and 1989) and *Die Hard* (1988) films from the previous decade.[17] Jonathan Rutherford has even gone so far as to categorise supposedly conflicting masculine identities as the 'New Man' and 'Retributive Man'. The Retributive Man, epitomised by Sylvester Stallone's Rambo, 'represents the struggle to reassert a traditional masculinity, a tough independent authority'. The New Man, on the other hand, is 'an expression of the repressed body of masculinity.... It is a response to the structural changes of the past decade and specifically to the assertiveness and feminism of women'.[18]

Ultimately, these position pieces argue that the masculine tropes described emerge from a critical convergence of events shaping masculine identities during specified periods. Masculinity is inscribed antithetically as 'hard' or its antonym 'soft'. The collapsing of distinctions regarding masculine identity is particularly evident in the field of politics where campaigning strategies often resort to essential notions of masculinity to emphasise the perceived maleness of the candidate in relation to the weakness of the opposition. As the first president in a dual-income marriage, Bill Clinton was a prime target for 'wimp-baiting' during his election campaign and presidency; his transition between soft and hard masculinity is underscored by Kenneth Walsh's reference to Clinton as an 'Iron John in the Oval Office ... the first New Age president, in touch with his emotions, sure of his masculinity'.[19] Seeing divergent examples of masculinity dominating at different historical moments, however, ignores the part each male trope plays in the identity formation of the other. In fact, by separating them in this way, Jeffords, Pfeil and Rutherford do not address the possibility that male identity exhibits both hard and soft masculinity *at the same time.*

Rather than existing in stark contradiction, hard and soft masculinities depend on the existence of the other for definition. Representations of masculinity are inherently bipolar, moving between hard and soft modes. The term bipolar is predominantly used in psychiatry to refer to a mood disorder whereby a person experiences mixed emotional states that are characterised by episodes of mania (high) and depression (low). A modern term dating back to the 1970s, bipolar was distinguished in early studies from 'unipolar', which referred to a person only experiencing episodes of depression. Significantly, bipolarity is characterised by *episodes* of high and low, not discrete shifts between the two, and it is those extreme episodes which are remembered above all else. Masculinity, as scholars such as R. W. Connell have pointed out, is a fluid identity and constantly in flux.[20] Since what constitutes 'being a man' continually changes according to the particular social or cultural moment, it is necessary for men to also adapt, change and, in effect, recycle their male identities. Yet movement too far in either direction is considered to undermine masculinity. Rather than using 'bipolar' to refer to an unstable personality disorder, I employ it here as a way of usefully describing the fluidity of both normative and non-normative constructions of masculine identity as they are enacted on the screen.

The most noticeable examples of such movement is in the extreme altering or recycling of male identities, as in the case of Arnold Schwarzenegger's seemingly dramatic shift from hard body in *The Terminator* (1984) to sensitive and soft Detective John Kimble in *Kindergarten Cop* and Dr Alex Hesse in *Junior* (1994). Both hard and soft are equated with excess; from excessive 'masculinity', as Yvonne Tasker terms it, to the excessive softness of Schwarzenegger's pregnant body in *Junior*.[21] However, rather than a direct transition from hard to soft as Jeffords and Pfeil suggest, male identity demonstrates both; although one is usually dominant at any particular moment, each is simultaneously defined in relation to the other. In *Kindergarten Cop*, Kimble's job as policeman initially conflicts with the more maternal role of kindergarten teacher yet he finds he must move between hard and soft modes of masculinity, taking on the role of both physical and emotional protector. Furthermore, Schwarzenegger's film roles from the 1980s onwards undermine the reductive tendency to collapse ideas of masculine identity onto decades or cultural moments; the actor resumed hard body roles in the 1990s and 2000s (*Terminator 2: Judgment Day*, 1991; *Terminator 3: Rise of the Machines*, 2003) not to mention moving away from the hard body in the late 1980s (*Twins*, 1988) thus problematising the easy alliance of the hard body with the 1980s or sensitivity with the 1990s. Hard and soft masculinity should instead be seen as a sliding scale; a hierarchy of masculine tropes demonstrated both across roles and within them.

The idea of bipolar masculinity as the convergence of hard and soft masculinity is crucial to an understanding of the Wild Man in popular culture. As the *Esquire* cover suggests, it is impossible to consider the Wild Man in isolation for the soft Wimp is central to his identity: one cannot exist without the other. Rather than achieving a natural state or normative masculinity, the Wild Man is constructed as *hyper*-masculine, characterised by excess and echoed in Bly's sensationalist and often contradictory writings. The performance of masculinity reveals the constructed nature of male (and, indeed, female) identity;

masculinity is something to be demonstrated, staged, put on. In this respect, the Wild Man has a somewhat paradoxical relationship with performance. He is, according to Bly, inherent in all men, the result of nature not nurture. Yet he is firmly aligned with ideas of ritual, masks and ceremony – all forms of performance and enactment. Bly's *Iron John* sets out to reject the idea of masculinity as performance by viewing maleness as an essence yet, at the same time, the performative *nature* of the Wild Man proves this impossible. The Wild Man, as he has been popularised by Robert Bly and the mythopoetic men's movement, is framed as spectacular and excessive rather than natural or normal, a spectacle that was subsequently amplified by the mass media. The 1991 *Esquire* special issue, for example, featured images of men covered in swamp algae, hugging trees and thrusting spears into the air while dressed in Tarzan-like loin cloths, and described the initiation ceremonies and group rituals taking place across America in sweat lodges, with poetry recitals round the camp fire, and beating drums. The 'therapeutic circus', as *Esquire* journalist Doug Stanton called it, involved 1990s men growling and yodelling, weeping and moaning, with animal names like Fox, Zebra and Wolf.[22]

The excessive, performative nature of the Wild Man has been explored in numerous literary and cinematic examples but arguably most prominently in Chuck Palahniuk's 1996 novel, *Fight Club*, and via the 'excess and absurdity' of the 1999 film version starring Brad Pitt as Wild Man Tyler Durden.[23] The novel and film have received an extraordinary amount of critical and academic attention, mostly focusing on the portrayal of destructive, misogynist masculinity. Although Palahniuk said in interviews that he had not read *Iron John*, Tyler and Jack (played by Edward Norton in the film) could have been lifted from its pages, resonating themes of father loss and overdependence on the mother, initiation ceremonies (the 'chemical kiss', homework assignments, head shaving), and the supposedly feminising effects of consumer culture.

Jack (or 'the narrator' as he is listed in the film credits) is a self-labelled 'thirty-year-old boy' and the epitome of the commodified male, obsessed with consumer goods, catalogue shopping and condiments. By day, Jack is a claims investigator for a major car manufacturer; at night he is a chronic insomniac, a condition he attempts to alleviate by visiting support groups for victims of testicular cancer, brain parasites, and tuberculosis. On a business trip, Jack meets Tyler who opens his eyes to the shallowness of consumer society, delivering tirades about how men need to regain their masculinity by returning to the hunter-gatherer era that they are denied in their culture of consumption and celebrity obsession, albeit in a postmodern and urban context:

> In the world I see – you are stalking elk through the damp canyon forests around the ruins of the Rockefeller Center. You'll wear leather clothes that will last you the rest of your life. You'll climb the wrist-thick kudzu vines that wrap the Sears Tower. And when you look down, you'll see tiny figures pounding corn, laying strips of venison on the empty car pool lane of some abandoned superhighway.[24]

After his apartment is mysteriously blown up, Jack moves into Tyler's dilapidated house and they start an underground boxing club to give men the opportunity to release their primal aggression and reclaim their sense of masculinity. When the fight clubs become a national success, Tyler decides to 'take it up a notch' and Project Mayhem is born: a full-scale anti-capitalist terrorist organisation with the ultimate aim of overthrowing corporate America and eradicating consumer debt. However, women are ultimately more threatening to men than consumerism and Tyler's misogyny culminates in his verbal and emotional response to Marla (Helena Bonham Carter); women are 'tumours', 'scratches on the roof of your mouth', and 'predators posing as house pets'. At the same time, in labelling herself as 'infectious waste', Marla corroborates the image of women as dirty and contaminated, further reinforced by Tyler's donning of rubber gloves during a sexual encounter.

Representations of the Wild Man in *Fight Club* explicitly model themselves in opposition to the figure of the Wimp. Tyler Durden's Wild Man is repeatedly set against Jack, whose softness is amplified when framed in conjunction with Tyler's excessive or hypermasculinity. *Fight Club* demonstrates a self-conscious awareness of this opposition by playing with the conventions of masculinity and femininity. In one scene, while discussing recipes for making bombs, Tyler parades around the kitchen in a pink dressing-gown. In another scene, Jack is caught listening in on Tyler and Marla's sexual antics by Tyler, who is wearing a pair of yellow rubber gloves. Rather than feminising Tyler, these props – the dressing-gown and the 'Marigolds' – are such palpable symbols of femininity that their comedic value counteracts any feminising effects they may have. Additionally, the excessiveness of his masculinity in the rest of the film – from a macho physique to patriarchal diatribes – means his masculinity not only remains intact but is in fact amplified. While Tyler's Wild Man and Jack's Wimp are continually depicted as opposites, their interdependence is fundamental to the storyline. In a narrative 'twist' near the end of the film, it is revealed that Tyler is Jack's alter-Ego, a projection of the man he really wants to be. Jack and Tyler literally depict bipolar masculinity; they are hard and soft, Wimp and Wild Man within the same body.

The centrality of 'other' masculinities in the definition of male identity is a long way from R. W. Connell's observation that: 'Our conventional meaning for the word "masculinity" is a quality of an *individual*, a personal attribute that exists in a greater or lesser degree ... an analogue of physical traits like hairiness of chest or bulk of biceps'.[25] Indeed, masculinity depends on the existence of a multitude of male identities to define it – the definition of masculinity is essentially a collective process whereby men compete with other men for validation and confirmation. Masculinity is collectively enforced, protected, and threatened. While it may at first appear to follow in the footsteps of Jeffords, Pfeil and Rutherford in its categorisation of men as soft and deep, Robert Bly's *Iron John* is noteworthy for its engagement with the idea of masculinity as a collective and communal practice.

The mythopoetic men's movement (and the same could be said of the Million Man March a few years later) demonstrates the idea of masculinity as collective experience whereby groups of men come together to 'reclaim' and 'reassert' their manhood, which involves the containment of the Wimp and what the Wimp represents: the feminine (women are excluded from these gatherings). In this way, the mythopoetic men's movement can be seen as a form of 'protest masculinity' which, according to Gwen Broude, 'represents an unconscious defensive manoeuvre on the part of males who are in conflict about or who are insecure about their identities as males'.[26] While most frequently applied to the behaviour of boys in the playground, the idea of protest masculinity shares similarities with the 1990s men's movement and pursuit of deep masculinity. It is, for Connell, a 'collective practice and not something inside the person', and is mostly characterised by 'an ambience of violence'.[27] While the Wild Man depends on his opposite for identity confirmation, it also requires confirmation from a collective group of men who are similarly looking to authenticate their male identities. The all-male 'fight clubs' organised by Jack and Tyler are evidence of the collectivity behind protest masculinity; they provide men with a space in which to vent their frustrations against society, functioning in a similar way to Bly's woodland retreats.

The collective masculinity on display in a number of 1990s ensemble films provides fertile ground for the exploration of male tropes and competing identities. Films including *Reservoir Dogs* (1991), *Glengarry Glen Ross* (1992), *Short Cuts* (1993) and *Magnolia* illustrate competing and antithetical masculinities at play. With the hard/soft masculinity spectrum dramatised in various ways – the brass balls and 'cunts' of *Glengarry Glen Ross*, the colour-coded masculine monikers in *Reservoir Dogs* – the performative nature of masculinity is markedly evident in the ensemble film. *Magnolia*, directed by Paul Thomas Anderson and with Tom Cruise, William H. Macy, Jason Robards, Philip Seymour Hoffman, John C. Reilly, Philip Baker Hall, Alfred Molina and Jeremy Blackman comprising the polymorphous male ensemble, not only highlights the centrality of the Wimp to the construction of the Wild Man, foregrounding the Wild Man as performance, but also locates the Wimp and Wild Man within a matrix of male identities, each searching for validation and definition.

As a prominent figure in the ensemble, Tom Cruise's performance of men's seminar leader, Frank T. J. Mackey, is striking for how his character moves unsteadily between wildness and softness. Numerous reviewers read Cruise's performance as a clear departure from his established persona and it is in this movement away from the security of his conventional all-American leading man roles that Cruise's performance of angst should be understood. As an actor who, according to Gaylyn Studlar, straddles hard and soft modes of masculinity, Cruise is a particularly interesting example for the way his performance of hyper- and hypo-masculinity in *Magnolia* anticipates his off-screen performances on television talk shows only a few years later.[28] Tom Cruise's relationship to constructions of male identity – on screen and off – provides a pertinent case for exploring the performance of masculinity in the 1990s and 2000s whereby his unstable star persona resonates in his on-screen enactments of unstable masculinity. Not only is a movement between hard and soft evident in his on-screen performances, a case study of Tom Cruise also reveals the bipolar nature of the contemporary film persona in its necessary move between stardom and celebrity. Bipolar masculinity is thus evident in Cruise's movement between film and television, dramatisation and self-presentation, actor and persona, star and celebrity.

From *Magnolia* to Oprah: Performing instability

Although released eight years after *Iron John*, Magnolia's treatment of masculinity is uncannily similar to the one offered in Bly's publication. The film foregrounds Bly's major themes: a concern with uncovering 'deep' or true masculinity; the precarious relationship between men and women in contemporary America; the centrality of fatherhood to male identity formation; and the distinction between hard and soft modes of masculinity. *Magnolia* focuses on nine major characters whose individual storylines are juxtaposed via a game show, *What Do Kids Know?*: Earl Partridge (Robards), the show's producer, who is dying of cancer; Phil (Hoffman), Earl's nurse; Linda (Julianne Moore), Earl's suicidal wife; Frank T. J. Mackey (Cruise), Earl's estranged son; the show's host, Jimmy Gator (Hall), in the early stages of cancer; Jimmy's daughter, Claudia (Melinda Dillon), a cocaine addict; Jim (Reilly), a policeman who falls for Claudia; Donnie Smith (Macy), the winner of *What Do Kids Know* in the 1970s; and Stanley (Blackman), a child genius and current champion of the show.

The distinction between hard and soft masculinity is reinforced through the juxtaposition of storylines with hyper-masculine men's seminar leader, Frank, positioned at one end of the scale, and pathetic 'quiz kid' Donnie at the other. The other men are situated in between: Jim, the incompetent cop who advertises for love in the small ads and loses his gun; Phil, the sensitive and compassionate nurse who goes out of his way to find Earl's son; Stanley, the solemn boy who wants his father to be less overbearing; Earl, the philandering millionaire; and Jimmy who, it is implied, sexually abused his daughter. Out of all the characters, Jim and Phil are constructed as the closest to acceptable masculinity. Jim, in rescuing Donnie during the climactic frog storm, is given the chance to prove himself and restore the masculine image that was threatened when he lost his gun. Phil, the emotional nurse, succeeds in reuniting father and son, Frank and Earl. He has, in Bly's terms, assisted in the initiation process that restored the father–son bond and supported Frank's development from boy to man. Such instances present masculinity as a collective and communal experience, confirmed but also threatened by the existence of other masculinities.

The softness of male characters in *Magnolia* is amplified in their contrast to men's seminar leader, Frank T. J. Mackey, Bly's Wild Man taken to the extreme. In his 'Seduce and Destroy' seminars, he vents his anger against women and tells his audience members that in order to authenticate their male identity they need to put women back in their place. Mackey's mission is to re-educate men, to guide them into fulfilling their potential as men, to teach them how to become 'masters of the muff', and to bed the women that would ordinarily turn them down. Like the spiritual leaders of the mytho-poetic movement, Frank adopts the role of initiator, leading men through the 'bucketing-out process' where they must reject their softer, more feminine side, towards a manhood defined by virility, potency, heterosexuality, power, and domination over women. Like Bly, Frank blames an increase in female power for the softness of men, but Frank takes it one step further, treating women as objects to be toyed with for men's enjoyment and thereby demeaned.

From the moment Frank is introduced, the wildness in men is revealed as utter performance. Frank ostentatiously spreads his arms in the sky, adopting a messiah-like stance as the dramatic accompanying music builds and his silhouetted figure is gradually revealed by spotlight. As he lowers his arms and slowly brings his palms together, cupping the space around his groin, the 'Seduce and Destroy' banner behind him is revealed, with an image of a ferocious dog chasing a petrified kitten. 'Respect ... the cock!' Frank loudly proclaims, 'and tame ... the cunt!' he bellows to the delight of the diegetic audience. From the extravagant gestures and dramatic music to the scripted speeches and excessive language, masculinity is something to be 'put on', performed through games ('How to fake like you're nice and caring') and recited through mantras. Even Frank's 'costume' – a figure-hugging leather waistcoat – gives the impression of a suit of armour or the gothic attire of a comic book caricature. Rather than the actor's trademark boyish crop, Frank/Cruise's hair is chin length, half tied up, less unruly than Jeff Bridges' hair on the *Esquire* cover but a clear departure from the interminable boyishness on display in his earlier roles. At no point is this performance constructed as a normative display of masculinity. Frank's is a performance of excess; it is staged, theatrical, consisting of grinding hips, gyrating groins, pumping arms, wild movements and chest beating.

Frank's performance climaxes during his scenes with Gwenovier (April Grace), an African American interviewer, presumably for a television exposé. As Gwenovier sits and waits for Frank to ready himself for the interview, he strips down to his underpants and, with his trousers still round his ankles, performs a variety of 'Iron Man' poses, flexing his muscles, puffing out his naked chest, rotating his arms as if slapping someone's rear and performing handstands and somersaults across the room, all the while proclaiming 'I'm Batman! I'm Superman! I'm a fucking action hero!' (Figure 3.2). Frank's referencing of Batman and Superman as a declaration of male potency to a female interviewer is a fitting analogy. The comic book icons epitomise the idea of bipolar masculinity: two hyper-masculine superheroes, characterised by their excessive strength and ingenuity but whose alter-Egos (Bruce Wayne and Clark Kent) are softer and more vulnerable in comparison. However, in evoking action heroes, Frank calls attention to his own masculine excess as well as highlighting the difference between their 'hard bodies' and his own sculpted, but hardly disproportionate, physique.

A far cry from the dance Cruise performs in his underwear and socks in *Risky Business* (1983), his display undermines rather than

Figure 3.2   Tom Cruise as Frank T. J. Mackey in *Magnolia* (New Line, 2000)

amplifies Frank's masculinity. His muscles, while honed and chiselled, appear puny; his posing highlights the vast difference between his body and the superheroes and action men he evokes. His musculature may not be as excessive as Schwarzenegger in *The Terminator* or George Clooney's moulded body armour in *Batman & Robin* (1997) but his posturing and prancing push his performance to the verge of the ridiculous; his angst is revealed in his performative display of 'hard' masculinity. The image of his trousers round his ankles, for example, while intended to depict the urgency of his sexual power – simulating sex with an invisible partner as he thrusts his groin into the air – also evokes a vulnerability, or even sexual deviance, as in the cliché 'caught with his pants down'. Frank's immaturity and lack of control is confirmed by an uncomfortable-looking Gwenovier, who adopts a motherly role, lowering her voice and requesting that Frank calm down and button his shirt properly. With his tongue hanging out of his mouth and panting like a dog, Frank obediently settles.

While Frank's excessive, highly stylised display is already visibly a performance enacted for the benefit of, first, his male diegetic audience and, second, Gwenovier and the camera crew, it is the interview that fully reveals the extent of the masquerade. Frank tells Gwenovier that his mother is alive but his father is dead. Yet, probing Mackey about his family, Gwenovier admits that she knows this is a lie constructed for publicity purposes; she reveals Frank's real identity as Jack, the son of game show producer, Earl Partridge. Significantly, in a departure from *Iron John*, it is a woman, not a man, who adopts the role of initiator, forcing Frank to commence the 'bucketing-out process' that will uncover his deep masculinity. In a reversal of the *Iron John* narrative, Frank's deep masculinity is revealed to be a softer, gentler identity hidden beneath his wild exterior. Although Gwenovier begins this process, Frank refuses to cooperate with her investigation, silently glaring at her for the remainder of the interview like a petulant child. In keeping with *Iron John*, Frank's 'bucketing-out' becomes a collective male experience in which Phil and Earl feature. Phil is instrumental in this process, tracking down Frank in order to reunite him with his 'remote father'.[29] When Frank breaks down by his father's bedside, his tears and declaration 'I fucking hate you, you fucking asshole. Don't go away', underscore the importance of the father in defining maleness and socialising boys. Forced to care for his sick mother when Earl deserted his family, Frank has followed in his father's footsteps by treating women as objects to use and abuse. His misogynistic seminar performance is explained as resulting from his father 'lack'; his attempt to define himself as a man without paternal guidance and his infantile regressions point to the conclusion that he has been unable to 'grow up'.

While the distinction between hard and soft masculinity is achieved in *Magnolia* through the juxtaposition of diverse male performances, it is through Cruise's character that the most significant contrast of hard and soft masculinity takes place to reveal a bipolar masculinity. Frank's 'bucketing-out process' demonstrates how individual characters also exhibit this distinction within themselves. 'Frank' the hyper-masculine seminar leader is revealed to be a mask, hiding the softer, more sensitive 'Jack' who can cry and make peace with his estranged father. The last step in uncovering the deep male is Frank's visit to the hospital to meet Linda, Earl's young widow and the stepmother he has never met. In this development from arrogant playboy to mature sensitive man, Frank T. J. Mackey seemingly follows the same trajectory as many of Cruise's earlier characters, from *Cocktail* (1988) to *Jerry Maguire* (1996). As Gaylyn Studlar notes, 'his films consistently move his characters from a performance of manliness into "authentic" manliness'. Yet this authentic manliness, she argues, is also a performance, 'held up for scrutiny as a construction, a masquerade'.[30] While Jack could be considered as the authentic male to Frank's excessive hyper-masculinity, Jack's masculinity is also revealed as a performance. On the one hand, Jack is revealed as authentic, reinforced by his unrestrained emotional episode at his father's bedside. Yet his emotional outburst is also depicted as excessive and over-the-top, so that rather than moving from a performance of manliness into 'authentic' manliness, Jack's childlike weeping implies a shift from excessive hyper-masculinity to excessive softness. His angst is performed differently at either end of the hard/soft spectrum but, in both cases, it is characterised as excess, revealing the impossibility of achieving a normative state of manliness. The implication is that before he can reject the destructive nature of the Wild Man, Jack must embrace his softness, evident in his crying for the father who abandoned him.

Following *Magnolia*'s release, a number of reviewers suggested Cruise's role was a complete departure from his established screen persona, an idea that was also apparently maintained by the actor.

In an interview with director Paul Thomas Anderson, for example, Lynn Hirschberg suggested Cruise did not actively promote the film because he felt his role was 'so inconsistent with the Tom Cruise Trademark that, contractually, he insisted on distance'.[31] Another source, however, suggests it was Anderson who tried to play down Cruise's appearance in the film to avoid 'overhyping Cruise at the expense of the rest of the cast'.[32] Cruise's absence from promotional publicity offers another reason that Cruise's performance of hard and soft overpowers the presentation of bipolar masculinity offered by the ensemble cast: the weight of Cruise's persona inevitably removes the possibility of an *ensemble* film. The dominance of the Cruise image is reflected in film reviews that repeatedly called attention to his 'transformation' from earlier roles.

Commenting on the all-American boy-next-door persona established in *Risky Business, Top Gun* (1986), *The Color of Money* (1986) and *Cocktail*, Dennis Bingham has argued that Cruise's performances were more *re*action than action:

> Cruise gives the kinds of performances conventionally expected of a male lead, emoting much less than the other actors around him. He tends to react, to be the still center around whom things happen, the initiator of action, about whom the audience does not give much thought because none is necessary. This kind of film actor traditionally performs 'naturally'; that is, his acting is disciplined and minimal in its movement. Thus it does not call attention to itself.[33]

Cruise's performance in *Magnolia* is certainly a departure from this established persona. It is a performance that explicitly calls attention to itself. There seems to be nothing natural about the performance, it is stagy, theatrical, wild and excessive; a performance consolidated by the raucous whoops and cheers of the male diegetic audience and reaffirmed in his histrionic cries for his dying father. Conversely, others have viewed his performance of Frank T. J. Mackey as a parody or culmination of all his previous roles and characters: the performative, 'exhibitionist masculinity' described by Studlar; the gleaming toothy smile; the cocky, self-assured, over-confidence; the transition from boy to man. Critics saw his performance as 'an outrageous parody of the pumped-up roles he played in *Cocktail* and *Top Gun*' and 'a scorching critique of his other performances'.[34] Their comments imply the actor's role in the construction of his screen persona, demonstrating a self-conscious awareness of who or what 'Tom Cruise' is and playing with that construction and image.

Cruise's performance in *Magnolia* has also been discussed as somehow more 'real', less performative than earlier roles. On *The Charlie Rose Show*, Alec Baldwin commented, 'if I had seen Tom Cruise only play the range that he is typically asked to play, in big-budget studio films, I might not have the same opinion I have of him as when I saw Tom Cruise *take off* that mask and do *Magnolia'*.[35] Cruise's performance in *Magnolia* can thus be considered alongside Michael Douglas's 'wiping off' of his star persona (see Chapter 2) and yet while Douglas's 'wiping off' was an attempt to display his ordinariness, it is Cruise's mask here that is perceived as ordinary, suppressing an extraordinary and uncharacteristic personality. The notion of masks not only play a part in the construction of Frank as a mask hiding Jack, the 'real' man underneath, but are key to understanding Cruise's star persona and, as Bingham notes, masks were a recurring feature of Cruise's film repertoire in the late 1990s and early 2000s. 'It is as if Cruise were dramatizing a desire to obscure his famous face', he argues, 'to cover it, and to acknowledge it as a meaningless façade, a hindrance to expression'.[36] This idea is taken literally in *Vanilla Sky* (2001) with Cruise's character, David Aames, wearing a prosthetic face plate to cover his supposedly disfigured face and the actor is virtually unrecognisable as a bald, overweight studio executive in *Tropic Thunder* (2008). While the masks in *Vanilla Sky* and *Tropic Thunder* are literal, *Magnolia* utilises masks figuratively, hiding the 'real' man behind the mask but also non-diegetically with Cruise 'taking off the mask', revealing the 'real' Tom Cruise in a departure from his earlier, 'false' roles. Nonetheless, the 'real' Tom Cruise is also a projection and performance, created and sustained by his film and media appearances.

The perceived exposure of the 'real' Cruise in his turn in *Magnolia* uncannily foreshadows the later exposure and break down of Cruise's off-screen persona. Cruise's excessive performance of Frank and his 'taking off the mask' to reveal a softer, more sensitive male underneath was reversed by a series of events taking place in 2005 and 2006 that suggested the actor had reached some sort of crisis point in both his personal and professional lives. In the same way that Cruise's performance in *Magnolia* revealed normative masculinity to be a performance, this series of events exposed his established, 'normative' persona as artifice and construction. Despite persistent speculation about his sexuality circulating for some time, Cruise had remained one of the most popular contemporary Hollywood stars, managing to stay relatively clear from paparazzi attacks. In the 2000s, however, Cruise's popularity and star power was threatened; a USA Today/Gallop poll in 2006 found 51 per cent of respondents registered an unfavourable opinion of the actor and his 'Q scores' (a marketing strategy to measure the reputation of an actor or brand) apparently dropped 40 percent in 18 months. Cruise's vociferous endorsements of Scientology were cited as a major contributory factor. On television show *Access Hollywood* in May 2005, he criticised Brooke Shields' use of medication for postpartum depression, a criticism that was ill-received by the media and general public; a month later, when the subject of anti-depressants and Scientology was brought up, he challenged *Today* show presenter Matt Lauer, calling him 'glib' and proclaiming psychology a 'pseudo-science'. Cruise's alignment with Scientology contributed to the actor becoming 'a punch line in Hollywood', and was amplified by his whirlwind relationship and marriage to *Dawson's Creek* actress, Katie Holmes, sixteen years his junior, adding to the rumours that the actor was experiencing a 'midlife crisis'.[37] A *South Park* episode titled 'Trapped in the Closet' (16 November 2005) took direct aim at Cruise's sexuality and religious beliefs: 'Come out of the closet, Tom. We know you're in there', Stan shouts at a cupboard, as Cruise's cartoon sheepishly emerges.

The moment which arguably had the biggest effect in foregrounding Cruise's increasingly unstable star image was his sofa-jumping exploits on *The Oprah Winfrey Show* in May 2005. Invited onto the show to discuss *War of the Worlds* (2005), Cruise proceeded to punch the air, jump on the sofa, and bounce around before a visibly shocked and bemused Oprah (Figure 3.3). The frenzy of actions were verbalised in Oprah's repeated cries of 'He's gone! He's really gone!' along with the raucous whoops and cheers of the studio audience. The reason for his display was revealed to be his newfound love for Holmes ('It's beyond cool', Cruise proclaimed). With the help of his host, he dragged Holmes from backstage to greet the audience. The event uncannily recalled Frank T. J. Mackey's somersaults in his underwear in front of a bewildered Gwenovier in *Magnolia*. Cruise and Mackey

Figure 3.3 Expressive incoherence on *The Oprah Winfrey Show* (Harpo Productions, 2005)

were both exposed and vulnerable, their male personas called into question by their hyperactive performances.

The televised event quickly went viral, becoming the most played video clip on YouTube. Streamed to computers around the globe, the scene was relayed to audiences who ordinarily would not have been privy to Cruise's exploits. Spoof videos appeared almost simultaneously; videos of the original broadcast were modified to make it look as though Cruise was murdering Oprah on her sofa. The inanely reflexive *Scary Movie* franchise parodied the Oprah sofa scene in their fourth instalment. Even Katie Holmes parodied Cruise at the MTV Movie Awards, madly propelling her arms around as the actor had done on *Oprah* and asking the audience, Should I bring him out? Whilst the stability of Cruise's star persona had been threatened before with intermittent rumours of his closeted homosexuality, the quick succession of publicly derided instances meant 'Cruise had, in just a few short months, morphed from public icon into a pop-culture joke'.[38]

Figure 3.4 Performance-of-a-performance on *The Tonight Show* (NBC, 2005)

The caricatures climaxed in Cruise's 'presentation of self' when he appeared on *The Tonight Show* in June 2005 (Figure 3.4).[39] This time jumping on Jay Leno's sofa, Cruise's performance-of-a-performance was a conspicuous attempt to regain some of the credibility he had arguably lost three weeks earlier. Yet his endeavour to poke fun at himself was acknowledged by only a handful of critics; it seemed his star persona had been irrevocably damaged.[40] Citing the actor's recent 'unacceptable conduct', Paramount ended their fourteen-year relationship with Cruise in August 2006. According to Sumner Redstone, chairman of parent company Viacom, 'As much as we like him personally, we thought it was wrong to renew the deal. ... He's a terrific actor. ... But we don't think that someone who effectuates creative suicide and costs the company revenue should be on the lot'. His relationship with Katie Holmes was also singled out as a per-formance; according to a *People* magazine poll, 62 percent of readers believed the Cruise–Holmes relationship to be a publicity stunt.[41] Cruise's once-secure persona had quickly become something to be questioned, a false act.

Like the breakdown of Frank T. J. Mackey's persona in *Magnolia*, the waning popularity and credibility of the 'Tom Cruise' persona and star image can be considered in terms of Erving Goffman's 'synecdochic responsibility' or 'expressive coherence' whereby an actor must strive to create an impression that is 'compatible and consistent with the overall definition of the situation that is being fostered'.[42] Cruise's unconventional behaviour on *The Oprah Winfrey Show* and his outspoken advocacy of Scientology challenge the coherence and 'front' of the Cruise persona – the brand constructed by his box office hits such as *Jerry Maguire*, *Mission: Impossible* (1996), and *Minority Report* (2002). In the same way that reviewers were quick to point out Cruise's departure from his established persona in films such as *Vanilla Sky*, *Collateral* (2004), and *Magnolia*, his off-screen actions in 2005 contradicted the previously private and enigmatic Cruise. While the actor's changing film roles can be seen as an essential element of film stardom, what P. David Marshall has described as 'transgressions ... to break the conventional mold of the specific screen personality', Cruise's screen transgressions must be distinguished from his off-screen performances, which can be considered to be more severe and damaging than acting against type. His actions are closer to the Roscoe 'Fatty' Arbuckle scandal, whereby 'the transgression virtually destroyed his power as celebrity sign'.[43] Cruise has been forced to revise his persona or risk having the power of his celebrity sign destroyed completely. Considering Cruise's sofa-jumping episode as an 'unmeant gesture' which is markedly different from the officially projected image, Cruise's actions force a 'wedge between the official projection and reality'.[44] Whether the performance was meant or 'unmeant', Cruise's actions were perceived as so inconsistent with the established persona that it exposed the artifice of the 'Tom Cruise' image.[45]

Responses to Cruise's actions suggest the impossibility of locating what is performance, further confounded by the actor's expressive *in*coherence in television interviews.[46] The spectacle of Cruise's sofa-jumping and verbal attacks can thus be considered in terms of what Guillermo Gómez-Peña describes as the 'mainstream bizarre ... a perplexing oxymoron [which has] effectively blurred the borders between pop culture, performance and "reality"; between audience and performer'.[47] In his move from dramatisation to self-presentation, from credible to ridiculous, Cruise has arguably moved from star to celebrity; no longer mysterious or revered, Cruise's star 'status' has been modified by his off-screen performances and his 'private' life has overtaken interest in his films.

Cruise's public fall from grace raises questions about the gendered nature of celebrity, what Diane Negra and Su Holmes have referred to as 'gender-based representational incongruities'. In their introduction to a journal special issue on female celebrity, Negra and Holmes refer to a *New York Times* article that notes: 'Men who fall from grace are treated with gravity and distance, while women in similar circumstances are objects of derision, titillation and black comedy'.[48] Citing Britney Spears' breakdown, celebrity crotch flashing, and Jade Goody's racist slurs on *Celebrity Big Brother*, which they say 'invite questions about the extent to which dignity and privacy are increasingly gendered in the context of celebrity representation', Negra and Holmes suggest such moments of female humiliation and excessive exposure offer a stark contrast to the mystery around Heath Ledger's death by accidental overdose in 2008 (widely rumoured to be suicide) and reinforce their claim that the behaviour of male celebrities is 'largely immune from public referendum'.[49] Cruise is clearly an exception to such gender-based representational incongruities, suggesting his fall from grace is akin to female shame, his masculinity usurped by his excessive public exposure. The difference between Cruise and Ledger lies in the distinction between public and private, hyper-visibility and mystery. While Ledger's death called attention to itself as public event, it was unseen and retained a sense of 'dignity and privacy'; the death was the event not the actor. With his sofa-jumping and controversial public criticism of psychiatry and psychology, both the actor and his actions overtly call attention to Cruise as public event.

The impact of Cruise's 'bizarre' televisual performances has superseded the established 'Tom Cruise' brand to the extent that his persona is now considered in terms of its inconsistencies and excess. Cruise was well received for his brief role in *Tropic Thunder*, for example, a Hollywood parody that saw the actor don a fat suit and bald cap in a performance that largely consisted of Cruise shouting a stream of profanities and dancing histrionically to rapper Ludicris, complete with groin thrusts and rear-slapping. *Tropic Thunder* unequivocally and self-consciously calls attention to Cruise's hyper-masculinity as performance. Cruise's performances, both on screen and off, foreground a concern with distinguishing the real from the unreal, or acting from not-acting. In *Magnolia*, Cruise displayed a bipolar masculinity in his movement from Frank T. J. Mackey's manic misogyny to Jack's emotional hysteria at his father's bedside. Cruise's bipolar masculinity extends past the cinematic stage to his televisual performances to Oprah, Jay Leno and Matt Lauer, moving from manic declarations of love for Katie Holmes to angry attacks on chat show hosts and interviewers.

In shifting between masculine extremes – *Magnolia*'s Wild Man and soft son, his public displays of elation and fury – Cruise's performances have exposed his normative masculine persona as performance and act so that his bipolar masculinity (no matter how excessive and 'bizarre') has been replaced as the norm. Just as masculinity can be undermined by movements too far away from the perceived norm, Cruise's actions suggest that extreme shifts away from a star's established persona can undermine star power to the point that the actor no longer has the option or ability to return to his earlier normative position. Instead, the normative identity must be reworked. In this case, the unstable Cruise persona becomes the norm, presenting the performative and paradoxical nature of masculinity and uniting the two extremes of hyper- and hypo-masculinity, Wild Man and Wimp.

4
Performing Paternity: Clinton, Nostalgia and the Racial Politics of Fatherhood

A discussion of 'The American Family' in 2001 in US Department of State Journal, *US Society and Values*, underpins the complex and contradictory discourse around family and fatherhood during the 1990s and early 2000s. The journal special issue acknowledged that American society increasingly encompasses a variety of family units including single-parent households, adoptive households, stay-at-home dads, and step-parenting. Yet the overwhelming message of the journal issue, reinforced by the large accompanying image, was that the model, ideal, best family structure remained that of the 'traditional' family comprised of 'mother, father and children'.[1] Starkly opposing the notion of the father as head of the family, the personification of the crisis of father absence was encapsulated by a 1992 *Newsweek* cover. The cover featured the image of a white, villainous-looking moustached man on a 'wanted' poster with the caption: 'Deadbeat Dads: Wanted for Failure to Pay Child Support'.[2] Two years later, fatherlessness was highlighted by President Bill Clinton as the 'single biggest social problem in our society'. David Blankenhorn – founder of the Institute for American Values and the National Fatherhood Initiative – called the deadbeat dad the 'reigning villain of our contemporary fatherhood script', claiming that 'no other family behaviour, and no other family policy issue has generated such an urgent consensus on what is to be done'.[3]

The two examples problematise the naturalness of fatherhood, suggesting that 'traditional' notions of fatherhood have less relevance in the contemporary period. The problem of the 'deadbeat' dad and of fatherlessness reached a new level in the 1990s as what constituted a

Figure 4.1   'The American Family', *US Society and Values* (IIP eJournals 2001)

'good' father increasingly became the subject of interrogation. What is a good father? What does or should a father do? Do we even *need* fathers? With the endemic image of the deadbeat dad voluntarily shirking his 'responsibilities' as a father and parent, along with the apparent erosion of the marriage institution and the decline of the male breadwinner role, the American father was running the risk of becoming an endangered species.[4] Fatherhood, the role often considered *the* defining characteristic of masculinity and taken for granted as fundamental to male identity construction, was undoubtedly now seen in political discourse and in the media as an identity to be proved and acted out.

Examining competing ideas around the figure of the father in the 1990s, this chapter considers fatherhood as a performance bound by definitions of 'normative' masculinity no more evident than in the image of 1950s traditional fatherhood, particularly as the image has been presented in Hollywood. The four films discussed in this chapter engage with the complex debate around family values in the 1990s. Foregrounding fatherhood as an image and performance, *Pleasantville* (1998), *Far from Heaven* (2002), *John Q.* (2002) and *The Pursuit of Happyness* (2006) each attempt to renegotiate the terms of 'traditional' fatherhood and problematise the relationship between fatherhood and male identity in contemporary American culture. The uneasy negotiation of the terms of fatherhood presented in the films is, I suggest, comparable to Bill Clinton's shifting discourse on fatherhood during his presidency, that ran the gamut of liberal and conservative responses to the American family and fatherhood in the 1990s. Clinton's emphasis on 'responsible', rather than 'traditional', fatherhood demonstrated an attempt to rework and renegotiate the image of fatherhood in the contemporary period and to reconsider the place of the father in the American family. This reworking and renegotiation is evident in the four films under consideration here with varying degree of success.

Managing contradictions: Clinton, family values and valuing families

On 16 October 1995, President Bill Clinton delivered a speech on race relations to a University of Texas audience. On that same day, over 80,000 African American men marched in Washington, DC, in support of 'unity, atonement and brotherhood'. The resounding message of both events was for men to 'take responsibility' for their families and lives, to improve race relations and perceptions of African Americans. Where they differed was in their consideration of race. Million Man March organiser, Nation of Islam leader Louis Farrakhan, highlighted the racial injustices preventing black men from adequately fulfilling their familial responsibilities and named 'white supremacy' as the main obstacle for the black community. Clinton spoke emphatically about the need for Americans to 'take responsibility' for their families and to 'clean the house of white America of racism' in order to fulfil his vision of 'One America'. At the end of his speech, Clinton identified fatherhood as a 'crucial area of responsibility' for American society, and vowed to catch fathers evading their child support payments. While race was repeatedly stressed as a 'problem' and a 'burden', issues of race were deflected when Clinton turned to the topic of fatherhood: 'This, of course, is not a black problem or a Latino problem. Or a white problem', Clinton asserted, 'It is an American problem'.[5] His consideration of fatherlessness as a cross-racial and national problem offered a stark contrast to Farrakhan's speech and also to former vice-president Dan Quayle's singling out of the 'particularly acute' problem of black families and fathers just three years earlier.[6] In their comparable requests for men to take responsibility and demonstrate their worth as fathers, Clinton's speech and the Million Man March reinforce the idea of fatherhood as an act. 'Responsible fatherhood' implies a social role to be publicly enacted rather than a natural or inherent process that men automatically enter into on becoming a biological father. In employing the phrase 'responsible fatherhood', Clinton offered an alternative to traditional fatherhood, suggesting earlier images of fathering were less applicable or valid in the contemporary period.

The American family has been a frequent contender for the political spotlight and vociferously adopted by both media and cultural critics, instigating debates over 'hot button' issues such as abortion, homosexuality, divorce, and the welfare of children. In James Davison Hunter's assessment in the early 1990s, the family was 'the most conspicuous field of conflict in the culture war', and along with other 'instruments of warfare' such as education, the media, law, and politics, became a contested and highly politicised site of conflict for academics, politicians and pundits.[7] In the 1990s and 2000s, a rhetoric of 'family values' permeated political commentary and domestic policy issues, featuring heavily in both conservative and liberal presidential campaigns at the beginning of the decade, and was subsequently taken up in various and conflicting ways by social and cultural critics.

On the one hand, conservatives such as Blankenhorn and Wade F. Horn vigorously attacked the increasing diversity of American families and strenuously promoted the traditional two-parent, heterosexual marriage as the normative model. For such conservatives, the apparent crisis of fatherlessness could be solved, or at least reduced, by strengthening the family unit. The nuclear family – the most 'stable' of family units – was therefore considered the ideal environment for the welfare of America's children. In a *Washington Times* op-ed, for example, Horn bemoaned the demise of 'The American Father' and speculated that if Americans did not act soon 'future generations will go to the Museum of Natural History to view "The American Father" right next to a display of the woolly mammoth'.[8] On the other hand, liberal family commentators, such as Judith Stacey and Stephanie Coontz, have been highly critical of the traditionalist and nostalgic family values rhetoric, arguing that the 'collective nostalgia' purposefully ignores the growing diversity of family units in America.[9]

However, despite conducting themselves as battling in contradistinction, conservative and liberal critics were a lot closer on family issues than they appeared, particularly over the problematic figure of the father. The urgency and sensationalism of Horn and Blankenhorn's tone is evident in Cornel West and Sylvia Ann Hewlett's summary of the contemporary discourse around fatherhood in *The War Against Parents*:

> The bottom line seems to be that fatherhood and fathering are enormously important, and when fathers are crippled and cast aside, serious repercussions are felt throughout the nation. A withering of the father-child bond devastates children, stunts men, and seriously erodes our social capital. For make no mistake about it: fatherlessness is much more than a private agony. It creates an open, festering wound that saps the strength of the entire nation.[10]

Fatherhood is equated with nationhood and considered to be an inherent part of masculinity; if the central position of the father to the family is threatened, the threat constitutes a direct attack on the US, and its absence critically damages men and male identity. In stressing the importance of elevating 'the cultural status and responsibilities of fatherhood' in her call to 'rethink' family values, Judith Stacey proceeded to 'agree with Blankenhorn that the sort of family values campaign *we most urgently need* is one to revise popular masculinities'.[11] While the array of family forms was the subject of many books by social scientists and cultural observers such as Coontz and Stacey, in what seemed a unanimous decision, politicians, media pundits, academics, and even celebrities, turned to the father as the figure most critical to the future of the American family.[12]

The problematic figure of the father illustrated by the competing constructions of American fatherhood that opened this chapter and the seemingly contradictory family values debate is reflected in

Clinton's public commentary on fatherhood in the 1990s. As the first baby boomer president, Clinton's victory at the 1992 elections marked the passing of the American presidency from one iconic generation to the next: the 'Greatest Generation' was being replaced by the 'pig in the python'.[13] Indeed, Clinton's term in office promised to be a direct contrast to former 'GI Generation' president, George Bush.[14] Almost immediately after entering the White House, pro-family, pro-choice and pro-change Clinton campaigned for massive health care reform, signed the Family and Medical Leave Act of 1993, which provided job security for Americans needing to take unpaid leave from work, and moved to revoke the ban on homosexuals in the military. However, after his ill-regarded 'Don't ask, don't tell' compromise on gays in the military and as his promises for health care reform failed to materialise, Clinton shifted to the right in his approach to the family, ardently adopting a pro-marriage position.

Contradiction was a central tenet of Clinton's presidential performance during the 1990s; his presidency and persona were widely noted for their seeming inconsistencies. 'Have you ever noticed how a child walking along after a rain can manage to get at least one foot in every puddle?' asked a *Washington Times* reporter in 1993; 'President Clinton has the same knack for contradictions. None escape him'. Five years later, Walter Shapiro for *USA Today* called Clinton the 'epitome of paradox' and suggested the president would make a befitting 'mature icon' for Calvin Klein's new fragrance: Contradiction. Cultural critic Greil Marcus has even compared the former President's political performances to Elvis Presley, noting how the two icons 'are alive in the common imagination as blessed, tawdry actors in a pretentious musical comedy cum dinner-theater Greek tragedy about their country's most unresolved notions of what it means to be good, true, and beautiful – and evil, false and ugly'.[15] The notion of Clinton as a performer was encapsulated by two news magazine covers from 1996 and 2001: the 21 October 1996 cover of *The New Yorker* pictured a cartoon Clinton dancing with Bob Dole in front of stage curtains and the February 2001 cover of *The Atlantic* shows Clinton wearing a tuxedo and white box tie and tipping his top hat with the cover line: 'Thanks for the memories'.

Clinton not only adapted and refocused his policies but also shifted and reworked his persona in order to boost his popularity with voters. The popular press often highlighted how Clinton would emphasise specific personality or identity traits over others at pertinent moments in his career. Critics suggested that he moved readily between a working- and middle-class identity, taking advantage of his roots in Hope, Arkansas and his education at Georgetown, Oxford and Yale Law School. He played on his 'unconventional' upbringing – the child of a low-income single mother with an abusive step-father – but also foregrounded his own 'conventional' family values in spite of alleged infidelities. 'He has created for himself an unprecedented persona', Andrew Ferguson commented in an article for *Time*, 'We have always known him by his contradictions – the raging moderate, the compassionate realist, the hardheaded dreamer. But now Clinton emerges as something new: a feminist Lothario, a New Age Don Juan, Alan Alda with a zipper problem'.[16]

News publications carried stories of 'The Protean President', commenting on Clinton's persistently shifting political agenda 'lurching left and right and back again in search of a winning message'. As journalists for *US News and World Report* observed: 'He is a deficit hawk one day, a tax cutter the next; a backer of gays in the military but an advocate of family values'.[17] In another association with an entertainment icon, Randy Roberts compared Clinton to Madonna's chameleon-like persona, going so far as to call Clinton the 'first postmodern president' who, Roberts said, regularly changed his political masks in order to generate wider support.[18] Clinton's contradictions and ambiguities may be recognised as a tactic to increase his supporters. They also underscore the complexity of discourses around fatherhood in the contemporary period as evidenced in the seemingly disparate, yet not dissimilar, debates about family values raging between liberals and conservatives.

The President acknowledged the growing diversity of families in America (he was, after all, raised by a single mother), but ultimately espoused traditionalist themes of 'family values' and individual responsibility, asserting the married, two-parent family with a strong father presence was best for American society. At the National Baptist Convention in 1994 Clinton remarked, 'I know not everybody is going to be in a stable, traditional family like you see in one of those 1950s sitcoms, but we'd be better off if more people were'. A year later in a speech on race relations, Clinton spoke of the 'old-fashioned American values' regarding work, family and the law that he believed were shared by all Americans, regardless of race or ethnicity.[19] Despite his endorsement of 'alternative' families during his presidential campaign, Clinton ultimately voiced the same rhetoric championed by Blankenhorn and Horn.

In Steven Cohan's analysis, the traditional 1950s family invoked by Clinton was characterised by the 'breadwinner ethic' and was central to the construction of normative masculinity during the period: 'the unquestioned norm of heterosexual masculinity'.[20] The stability of the breadwinner's family, and his place within it, became essential for boosting postwar morale, signifying the strength of the American economy and the moral fibre of the American people. As Barbara Ehrenreich has noted, breadwinning was so completely aligned with mature heterosexual masculinity in the 1950s and 1960s that men who failed to achieve the role were considered to be either 'not fully adult or not fully masculine'.[21]

Although fundamental to the construction of 1950s normative masculinity, the breadwinning father has continued to dominate popular ideas of masculinity, regardless of an apparent decline in number in actual terms. According to historian Robert Griswold, breadwinning has prevailed throughout history as a marker of men's masculinity:

> Despite men's differences, breadwinning has remained the great unifying element in father's lives. Its obligations bind men across the boundaries of color and class, and shape their sense of self, manhood, and gender. Supported by law, affirmed by history, sanctioned by every element in society, male breadwinning has been synonymous with maturity, respectability and masculinity.[22]

The idea that breadwinning is central to definitions of fatherhood and, in turn, is inseparable from definitions of masculinity is increasingly problematic in an era where dual-earning households outnumber households consisting of only male earners, where stay-at-home dads are rising in number and the 'deadbeat dad' has replaced the traditional patriarch as the dominant model of fatherhood. If fatherhood in the 1950s was, according to Cohan, performative, 'an ongoing process of acting out his masculine position as head of the family', 1990s fatherhood is arguably even more of a performance; without breadwinning to define his masculinity and identity as a father, he must confirm his fatherhood and masculinity in other ways. The implication is that with contemporary changes to the family structure, it has become increasingly necessary to devise new cultural scripts for fatherhood and to redefine the parameters of masculinity.

However, Clinton's commentary on fatherhood and the family also indicates an uneasy negotiation of nostalgia for 1950s traditionalism. It is not the 'stable, traditional' 1950s *family* that Clinton recalls but the 1950s *family sitcom*.[23] In other words, Clinton is all too aware that the family he and others nostalgically look to is an image fabricated for entertainment purposes but he is nostalgic for the image nonetheless. In fact, Clinton's repeated uses of the phrase 'responsible fatherhood' during his presidency suggests an attempt to move away from the restrictive and constricting model of traditional fatherhood offered by the 1950s sitcom and to accommodate the changing composition of the American family.

Imaging traditional fatherhood in *Far from Heaven* and *Pleasantville*

In both politics and popular culture, the 1950s have been persistently invoked as a time of conservativism and affluence. Despite being the decade that saw the Korean War, McCarthyism and the threat of Communism, the Beats, and the burgeoning Civil Rights Movement, the 1950s have been seen as a period dominated by cultural as well as political consensus that set it apart from neighbouring decades. This was the decade when the media were dominated by the image of the white nuclear family, consisting of the dutiful housewife, her fresh-faced children, and their breadwinning father – an image typified and reinforced by popular television sitcoms of the period, such as *Father Knows Best* (1954–60) and *The Adventures of Ozzie and Harriett* (1952–66). It is significant that Clinton hearkens back to the 1950s sitcom rather than romanticising the 1950s, recalling the popularised image of traditionalism rather than the historical decade. By invoking the sitcom family, Clinton reminisces about the idyllic image of the 'traditional' family and yet his comments also indicate a wariness of invoking the 1950s as an uncomplicated period of traditionalism.

Released in 1998 and 2002 respectively, *Pleasantville* and *Far from Heaven* turn to the 1950s as a supposed golden age of family values in contrast with the apparent demise of American society and the family in the 1990s. Both films engage with nostalgia as a mode of dealing with the past, but this is not to say the films themselves are nostalgic, as some indeed have argued.[24] By returning to the 1950s, both films highlight the problematic nature of nostalgia, depicting the image of the 1950s family as a misremembered past or what Paul Grainge refers to as a 'form of idealized remembrance' that employs an 'aesthetic of pastness'.[25] The past becomes a vehicle through which to comment on the present, depicting the 1950s as a repressive and constricting period via metaphor and irony.

The idea of the 1950s traditional family headed by the traditional father as constructed *image* is central to both films. In *Pleasantville*, the 1950s sitcom family is revealed as an image when two teenagers from the 1990s are literally transported into the world of the eponymous sitcom through their television screens. In *Far from Heaven*, the 1950s family as image is played with through the framing of Frank Whitaker (Dennis Quaid), an executive at television company Magnatech, and his homemaker wife, Cathy (Julianne Moore). As the columnist for the Hartford society paper informs Cathy, 'You *are* Mr and Mrs Magnatech' – the embodiment of 1950s consumerism and suburban affluence. Posing for a photograph in front of the fireplace, Cathy's performance of the perfect housewife is framed in the Magnatech advert featuring the Whitakers on the wall behind her.

Both films are set in the 1950s but they speak to concerns about the family and role of the father in the 1990s. A parallel between the 1950s and 1990s is unambiguously presented in *Pleasantville*'s opening sequence. The opening montage constructs the 1990s as a period of decline, disaster and danger as teachers warn their students of poor job prospects, global warming, famine and HIV. 'For those of you going on to college next year', the college counsellor informs a room of cheerless teenagers, 'the chance of finding a good job will actually *decrease* by the time you graduate'. The sequence cuts to a 1950s suburban street complete with white picket fences and perfectly manicured lawns, all shot in black and white. Off screen, a man's voice calls 'Honey! I'm home'. George Parker (William H. Macy) enters the front door to his suburban home and is greeted with a cocktail and a kiss on the cheek from his wife. The film cuts back to 1996 where 17-year-old David (Tobey Maguire) watches the television screen, transfixed by George and Betty's (Joan Allen) cheerful pleasantries, while his mother talks on the telephone, cursing David's father over custody issues. Scenes of George and Betty's friendly banter with their children are juxtaposed with the telephone conversation: 'Sure, they can stay by themselves.... But that's not the point. You're supposed to see them.... Well fine, you'll just see them some other time'. Idyllic domestic scenes offer a polar opposite to David's broken family, implying that his fascination with the television show is rooted in a longing for a simpler time when the nuclear family prevailed.

The breadwinning father is fundamental to the construction of family as image in *Pleasantville* and *Far from Heaven*, offering status and legitimacy to his homemaker wife. In *Far from Heaven*, Cathy is defined by Frank's breadwinning status – she is Mrs Magnatech, the wife of a television executive. The breadwinner ethic abounds in the Whitaker household; husbands are the sole financial providers while their wives literally wear their husbands' work successes with their opulent dresses and excessive 'party budgets'. All three of Cathy's identities – homemaker, wife and Mrs Magnatech – are dependent upon Frank's middle-class breadwinner identity; 'you are the proud wife of a successful sales executive', the society columnist tells Cathy, 'planning the parties and posing at her husband's side on the advertisements'. In *Pleasantville*, Betty's role as homemaker revolves around George's work hours; on his return from work (his work is never defined, only his status in the labour market), Betty greets George at the door with a cocktail and cooks his favourite meat-loaf. Just as Cathy busies herself at the Whitaker party, 'freshening' drinks for her husband and their guests, Betty is defined in relation to the food she cooks and the drinks she provides: as homemaker and hostess.

However, both *Far from Heaven* and *Pleasantville* problematise the 1950s family and, in particular, the 'traditional' father, most evident in Dennis Quaid/Frank's and William H. Macy/George's construction of the breadwinning father role. Both films question the nostalgic vision of the family by explicitly interrogating the image of the bread-winning patriarch as normative masculinity. The films reflect what Lynn Spigel refers to as a 'false utopia': the illusion or façade of nor-mality that hides the repression and austerity that really characterised the period.[26] In *Far from Heaven*, Quaid plays Frank Whittaker with a stiffness and severity that maintains his character's façade at the head of the family. Frank's formal and detached relationship with his wife, and especially his children, is embodied in the rigidity of his body movements, gestures and stern facial expressions. From the film's outset, Frank's actions and behaviour are revealed to be a front, the result of his suppression of homosexual urges; we first meet his character in the police station, having been mistaken, Frank asserts, for a 'loiterer'. Later, Frank follows two men out of the back of a movie theatre to a gentleman's only club where he exchanges knowing glances with another man. Frank's performance of 'normative' masculinity and fatherhood is powerfully exposed when Cathy 'surprises' her husband at the office only to find him kissing another man.

Frank fails as a husband to Cathy as a result of his masquerade as a 'normal' heterosexual father when he is in fact homosexual, yet it is not his 'unconventionality' that marks his failure as a father, as Stella Bruzzi has stated, but rather his *con*ventionality.[27] His stiffness underscores his disengagement from family life as a result of his closeted homosexuality, yet his angst is twofold as it also results from his marginalisation from the domestic space of the home. Reduced to the role of financial provider, Frank cannot live up to society's expectations of him. Family life revolves around the father yet Frank barely acknowledges his children, leaving their upbringing to their mother while he concentrates on paying for the suburban lifestyle to which they have all become accustomed. His disengagement conforms to contemporary psychiatric accounts that the breadwinning husband is 'deprived of any real goal except that of acquiring the skills needed to make money enough to "settle down" into an existence which he accepts rather than chooses'.[28] Frank provides the family with status, legitimacy and finances but is emotionally and physically absent and absented (by Cathy's dominant position in the home), turning to alcohol as a way of ignoring his discordant personal life. In this way, Frank/Quaid's performance of angst evokes the malaise and confusion experienced by the breadwinner that was portrayed in a number of popular films of the postwar period, such as *The Best Years of Our Lives* (1946), and *The Seven Year Itch* (1955), and critiqued by authors such as Sloan Wilson (*The Man in the Gray Flannel Suit*, 1955) and Richard Yates (*Revolutionary Road*, 1961; *Eleven Kinds of Loneliness*, 1962). The breadwinning fathers portrayed in these examples offer a stark contrast to the image of the contented hegemonic breadwinner that has come to represent the 1950s.[29]

Figure 4.2 Performing normalcy in *Far from Heaven* (Focus Features, 2002) and *Pleasantville* (New Line, 1998)

Far from Heaven and *Pleasantville* demonstrate how the breadwinning husband is a role played out by Frank and George, yet they also stress the importance of Cathy and Betty's performances of motherhood and homemaking in relation to the image of the traditional family and the 'normative' breadwinning husband. Their performances of motherhood and as wives accentuate George and Frank's performances of normative masculinity. The women play the dutiful housewife excessively, highlighting the artifice and construction of their husband's masculinity: busying around, refreshing drinks, preparing meals, humouring their husbands' jokes. Both films poke fun at the construction of normalcy in telling scenes of excessiveness and parody (see Figure 4.2). Dressed ostentatiously in a Mrs Claus outfit, Cathy asks Frank if they should go to Miami for a New Year's vacation: 'El says it's just darling. Everything is pink!' she proclaims. 'Oh, really?' Frank ponders, 'Maybe we ought to consider Bermuda?' The exaggerated and overzealous laughter highlights the artificiality of Frank and Cathy's relationship and the constructed image of normative family life. This is one of the few instances where Frank does not put on a mask of heterosexuality for the benefit of his wife.

The breadwinning husband and homemaker wife are mutually dependent on each other for the successful projection of normativity. As *Pleasantville* demonstrates, the husband is so reliant on the role of woman as homemaker and housewife that he is unable to carry out his patriarchal function in the absence of his wife. In one scene, 'Honey, I'm home!' – the call denoting the breadwinning father's entrance into the domestic sphere – signifies the threat to George's guise rather than confirming it, becoming an empty signifier that undermines his control when Betty is not there to greet him with a cocktail and his dinner. The future is left uncertain for George after his wife's affair with local diner owner, Bill Johnson (Jeff Daniels); divorce and separation are alien to the 1950s sitcom family in which George resides. He is no longer defined as head of the household since the performance of the breadwinning patriarch is only possible with a family to govern; the patriarchal breadwinner is nonexistent without the subordinate dependents. George's angst is displayed in his visual deterioration in the following scene where he turns up at the bowling alley wet and dishevelled from the rain. The previously animated and exaggerated smile is replaced with a hunched demeanour and morose expression; George/Macy's slouching body reflects the fading of dominant masculinity that has been instigated by his wife's departure.

Similarly, Frank relies on Cathy's performance to maintain his patriarchal identity and any deviation from the 'norm' taints the breadwinner image. When Frank discovers that Cathy has developed a close friendship with their African American gardener, Raymond Deagan (Dennis Haysbert), he accuses his wife of ruining the family image he has worked so assiduously to construct: 'Don't you realise the effect it's going to have on me and the reputation I have spent the last eight years trying to build for you and the children and for the company?' he shouts. Cathy's friendship with a black man of lower status is considered more detrimental to the acceptable image of the white American family than Frank's homosexuality.

Perhaps the most important prerequisite for the breadwinning father, however, and also the least discussed in critical accounts of the father, is his whiteness. The achievement of traditional father-hood was the model ascribed to American men, although it was not achievable to the vast majority of the male population. In fact, the 1950s breadwinning father was specific to a certain type of American male: 'the white, heterosexual, corporate, WASP, suburban breadwin-ner as personified by the ubiquitous figure of The Man in the Gray Flannel Suit'.[30] The suggestion that normative fatherhood is bound to notions of race and class raises a further contradiction evident in the family values discourse of the 1990s and Clinton's wary nos-talgia, which also has ironic implications for the man described as the 'first black President'.[31] With the president hearkening after the 1950s sitcom family, the stable, traditional family headed by the white breadwinning patriarch was considered the American model, exemplified by the blank, white faces of 'The American Family' that opened this chapter (Figure 4.1). By taking aim at the 'deadbeat dad', Clinton and others also firmly aligned 'responsible fatherhood' with the breadwinning ethic now associated with white 1950s fatherhood in popular memory.

Even more than the breadwinning ethic, the normativity of the tra-ditional 'American' father is rooted in the security of his whiteness; his whiteness is implicit to his performance since the given-ness of his role resides in his supposedly 'raceless' ordinariness. The 'father-hood crisis' as it was mapped in political and media discourse thus presents a racial paradox. Clinton and others perceived problems with fatherhood as an 'American problem' not defined by race or class. Nevertheless, the same commentators hearkened after a traditional model of fatherhood rooted in white, middle-class patriarchy. For Richard Dyer, the security of whiteness and its presentation as ordinary is achieved through the construction of 'whites as non-raced'. 'Whites are the one particular group that can take the non-particular position of ordinariness', he observes, 'the position that claims to speak for and embody the commonality of humanity'. Non-whiteness, by contrast, is 'already peculiar, marked, exceptional: it is always, in relation to notions of the human in Western culture ... particular and has no ordinariness'.[32] By this reasoning, the 'traditional' father can never be anything but white since he is dependent upon his normality in order to convey his normative cultural value. The non-white father can never become a 'traditional' father because he is marked; his race, unlike the white father, is made explicit to his identity in American society in whichever decade he is made representative. Blackness, as Manning Marable argues, is 'always simultaneously the negation of whiteness'.[33] The whiteness of the white father, on the other hand, is unmarked and rendered unremarkable.

In their white-centric narratives of family breakdown, *Far from Heaven* and *Pleasantville* play on the invisibility and ordinariness of the white breadwinning father yet also succeed in displacing issues of race through their privileging of whiteness. Both films treat whiteness as un-raced. The suburbs are depicted as a white space occupied solely by the white middle class. On the one hand, *Pleasantville* takes a liberal approach to issues of 'colour' and racial integration in its allegory of the Civil Rights Movement and critique of contemporary nostalgia for 1950s traditionalism. On the other hand, however, it could be argued that the film actually promotes racial uniformity and social conventionality over diversity and difference. The 'black and white' world of Pleasantville misleadingly suggests a place inhabited by white and non-white citizens. In actuality, whiteness not only prevails but also exists in isolation. When David and his sister Jennifer (Reese Witherspoon) educate the monochrome Pleasantville residents about sex, literature and geography, they begin to 'colourise', erecting racial divisions between 'true' citizens and 'coloureds'. Problematically, the solution to the ensuing chaos sees *all* residents turn from 'black and white' into colour, effectively un-racing the residents and reinstating them to the powerful position of invisible, supposedly unmarked and non-raced whiteness. In fact, the residents are now even *whiter*; their whiteness is amplified and presented in Technicolor.

Blackness is also seemingly relegated to the margins in *Far from Heaven*. Conforming to racial stereotype, African American characters exist as ancillary support to the white suburban family – as maid (Sybil) and gardener (Raymond). However, the relationship between Raymond and the traditional white family is not so easily dismissed.

Through the character of Raymond Deagan, director Todd Haynes critiques the racialised aspects of fatherhood, and the notion that whiteness is a prerequisite of the traditional father is challenged. Raymond, an educated man who takes over his father's gardening business after he dies, is a widower. We are told that his wife died when his daughter Sarah was five but that they 'do just fine' without

Figure 4.3   Two faces of fatherhood in *Far from Heaven* (Focus Features, 2002)

Mrs Deagan. Raymond's concern for his daughter is represented in stark contrast to the Whitaker father–child relationship. Frank has little time for David and Janice; Raymond is depicted as a devoted, caring father who takes his daughter to an art show and puts her interests and needs ahead of his own (see Figure 4.3). He even admits that he has left his 'own world' – that is, the black community in Hartford – in order that his daughter have more opportunities in life: 'I only want what every father wants for his child', he declares, 'the opportunities growing up I never had. Naturally'. When Sarah is taunted by white school boys about her father's friendship with Cathy, and has stones thrown at her, he decides to move his family to Baltimore and declines Cathy's offer to visit him there because, 'What happens now, what has to happen the most, is what's right for Sarah'. Raymond prioritises his daughter's well-being whereas both Frank and Cathy appear to be more involved in their personal quests for happiness than their children's welfare; the Whitakers can take their white children's opportunities for granted in ways that Raymond, as a black single father, cannot.

However, while Raymond is portrayed as a 'good' father despite being a black single father (it is important that he is single as a result of his wife dying not through choice), he struggles to comfortably occupy the position of traditional father in the narrative. Ejected from the normativity of the suburbs and by his 'own people' as a result of his attempted integration, Raymond is forced out to live with his brother in Baltimore. Raymond achieves what Clinton would call 'responsible fatherhood' but he continues to be marked by his race and excluded from the white space of the Hartford suburbs. In a film that is a pastiche of a movie made in a decade when racial segregation was enforced de jure in the South and often de facto in the North, Raymond is only allowed access to the white space of the suburbs because he abides by the rules of white suburbia – he is educated, cultured, has a strong work ethic – but he must remain an outsider. His attempts at integration alienate him from white acceptance and also invoke disdain from the black community. While *Far from Heaven* questions the naturalness of white patriarchal privilege and also implies that the white traditional father is not necessarily easily equated with 'good' fathering, Raymond's position remains solidly that of the racial intruder in the white suburbs even after he takes over the role of the father hero from Frank. Nevertheless, Raymond is still constructed as closer to the traditional image of fatherhood than Frank, despite being a black single father.

Both films confirm that whiteness is as much a given prerequisite of the traditional father as the fatherhood role is a prerequisite for normative masculinity; but they also question this image, revealing it as a construction and performance. The films demonstrate that whiteness does not equate with good fathering and, particularly in *Far from Heaven*, diversity and supposed 'unconventionality' can be closer to good fathering than the white father of 1950s popular consensus. *Far from Heaven* implies that Frank is a better father once he is removed from the nuclear family unit; after they have separated, Frank calls Cathy to arrange a divorce and for the first time in the film asks about the children. In *Pleasantville*, David realises that the traditionalism and conformity of the nuclear family do not necessarily equate with contentment and happiness; in fact, he plays a significant role in the disintegration of the nuclear unit, inadvertently bringing together Betty and Bill in helping them find expression for their sexuality. Paradoxically, David establishes a relationship with two father figures – Bill and George – in the world of the 1950s television show but his own father is absent from his contemporary reality. The implication that the traditional family is restrictive opposes the conservative nostalgia for the 1950s that featured in 1990s political discourse. It also suggests another side to the figure of the absent 'deadbeat' dad that politicians such as Clinton failed to acknowledge: in some cases, a father who does not live with his children can be a better father. Ultimately, *Pleasantville* and *Far from Heaven* attempt to dispel the mythical image of the 1950s sitcom family, problematising it as a model for the American family in the 1990s. Sceptical of the white breadwinning patriarch, both films offer an 'alternative' that underscores the performative nature of fatherhood and asserts that the 'traditional' father only exists as an outmoded image.

Responsible fatherhood in *John Q.* and *The Pursuit of Happyness*

The linking of father absence to the black family in Farrakhan's speech and Quayle's earlier pronouncements that opened this chapter was by no means a new occurrence; in 1965, Senator Patrick Moynihan's controversial report blamed father absence in the black community for the increase in welfare-dependent mothers, child delinquency, illegitimacy, crime and violence.[34] Escalating concern for African American men at the start of the 1990s led Louis Sullivan, US Health and Human Services Secretary to George Bush, to go so far as to state that 'not since slavery has so much calamity and ongoing catastrophe been visited on Black males'.[35] African American fathers were scrutinised and criticised for incompetence, absence and failure to nurture, fuelling the debate about a 'crisis of black masculinity'. bell hooks, for example, claimed that, 'From slavery on many black males have chosen to avoid parenting ... they believe that father-love is not essential to a child's well being'.[36] Responding to negative images of African American men that pervade contemporary media, social and cultural commentators have called for more images of 'strong black men' to counteract negative depictions of African American men as drug-dealers, rapists and murderers.[37] The Million Man March was one such attempt to rejuvenate the black male image. *John Q.* and *The Pursuit of Happyness* interrogate fatherhood as a key social role, engaging with issues that were at the forefront of media and political debates around fathers in the 1990s. Both films speak to concerns about the representation of African American men and fathers in focusing on two fathers' transition from 'Deadbeat Dad' to 'Responsible Father'. While the films are concerned with promoting black fatherhood and images of black masculinity, they also demonstrate attempts to displace racial anxieties in their narratives of individualism.

In *John Q.*, John Quincy Archibald (Denzel Washington) is a blue-collar steelworker who has recently had his hours at the plant cut and is unable to find a second job. John's eight-year-old son Mike (Daniel E. Smith) suddenly collapses and is rushed to hospital; he has a rare congenital heart defect and will die unless he has a transplant. John discovers his health insurance policy (HMO) has changed and will only pay out $20,000 – considerably short of the $250,000 needed for Mike's name to be added to the donor list. With his wife, Denise (Kimberly Elise), pleading for her husband to 'do something', John takes the hospital emergency room hostage, demanding that his son be added to the donor list or he will start shooting.

In *The Pursuit of Happyness*, which is based on a memoir, Chris Gardner (Will Smith) spends his life savings on bone density scanners to sell to hospitals, a venture that no longer provides enough income to support wife Linda (Thandie Newton) and five-year-old son Christopher (Jaden Smith). Linda walks out and Chris is evicted from his apartment, leaving him homeless and caring for his son on the streets. He and Christopher spend their nights in homeless shelters and subway restrooms while Chris takes an unpaid internship at prestigious brokerage firm Dean Witter, in the hope that he will achieve the 'American Dream' and be the one-in-twenty selected for a paid position after six months.

John and Chris's position as breadwinning patriarch are compromised by their inability to support their family financially, and they are constantly reminded about their failure to act as providers by their wives, who have been forced to work double shifts. Although neither father conforms to the prescriptions of traditional fatherhood defined by the breadwinning ethic, they do conform to Clinton's notion of 'responsible fatherhood' and the similar buzz phrase 'active fathering' circulating at the time, which promoted fatherhood as something to be dynamically acted out and confirmed. In both films, emotional support takes precedence over financial support; despite being financial 'deadbeats', John and Chris *prove* their ability to be responsible fathers who play and joke with their sons, hug and kiss them and offer physical protection. For those audience members who may consider their drastic attempts to protect their sons irresponsible, the fathers' actions are frequently validated; John is declared a hero for his persistence in saving his son and Christopher repeatedly tells his father, 'You're a good papa'. *John Q.* and *The Pursuit of Happyness* negotiate the terms of traditional fatherhood, questioning the dominant father role as economic provider. Fatherhood is considered less an essential male right than something to be proved, reinforced and maintained.

Although they struggle financially, John Archibald and Chris Gardner are depicted as strong black men who achieve success in the face of adversity and function as positive role models for their sons. Both films go to great lengths to portray their protagonists as American Everymen. From the promotional publicity (the poster describing him as an 'ordinary man') to his name, John Q. (Public) is depicted as a common man who finds himself in a situation that could happen to any American: he works hard and is considered 'overqualified' for the positions for which he applies and his HMO provider fails to tell him his insurance cover has changed as a result of his reduced working hours. According to director Nick Cassavetes, Washington was chosen for the role for representing 'a lot of things I like about America – hardworking but proud'.[38] This is consistent with Washington's appearance, from the visible paunch he displays, to the casual attire consisting of t-shirt with over-shirt, jeans, and a baseball cap worn back-to-front. Predictably, Washington empha- sised his ordinariness in press statements and promotional interviews on the film's release: 'This is me, man. I'm not big', he told one inter- viewer, 'I'm the guy who drives my kids around and helps coach some of their teams'. The actor also recalled his days as a sanitation worker and post-office employee before becoming a Hollywood star.[39]

In *The Pursuit of Happyness*, Chris's pursuit of the American Dream – 'Our right to life, liberty and the pursuit of happiness' as he quotes from the Declaration of Independence – is constantly reinforced as a goal all Americans aspire to; the film suggests that with enough moti- vation and dedication, anything is possible. As with Washington's physical alterations in *John Q.*, Will Smith wears a grey-flecked afro and moustache that place him in the 1980s and give him an older, more mature appearance. In interviews, Smith emphasised his own family values of 'communication, education and truth', and criti- cised the tendency for African American families to 'raise their chil- dren based on slavery concepts' instead of guiding them.[40] Smith's authenticity as a father was further played on via the pairing of the actor with his son, Jaden Smith, which was also emphasised in pro- motional publicity (see Figure 4.4).

The promotion of fatherhood and black masculinity comes at a price, however. Wives in both films are demonised or marginalised: Linda is depicted as a shrieking and emotionally unstable harridan who gives up her son with little resistance; Denise constantly berates her husband and is dispensed with when John demands his son is brought to the emergency room he is holding hostage. With the wives marginalised or depicted as deficient or unnecessary and then expelled from the narrative, it is no longer the father who is dispen- sable but the mother, effectively reversing the contemporary absent father discourse. John and Chris's quest for responsible fatherhood can be considered a 'male-centred strategy' whereby it becomes the responsibility of black men to save themselves while the mother is absented or helplessly weeping at the margins, unable to save her

Figure 4.4   Authenticity in *The Pursuit of Happyness* (Columbia, 2006)

son.[41] John and Chris challenge negative images of African American masculinity in their performances of responsible fatherhood yet there is, to borrow from Herman Gray, 'little disturbance to the "patriarchal order of things" where masculinity and manhood are concerned'.[42]

The films are also ambiguous in their treatment of the individual's relationship to wider political implications. On the one hand, the films attempt to reverse conservative family values rhetoric by blaming social structures, rather than the individual, for the protagonists' inability to be good fathers. Actual news footage is inserted in both films to emphasise the 'real' problems that are at stake in these fictionalised accounts. In *The Pursuit of Happyness*, Chris watches Ronald Reagan discuss the struggling economy on television. *John Q.* ends with a montage of images highlighting the injustices of the American health care system, with sound bites from Hillary Clinton, chat show host Jay Leno, feminist lawyer Gloria Allred and hip-hop artist Nas advocating free health care for all. Both films stress that the power of the individual is limited and that change is also necessary on a political level. Only when John Archibald threatens to take his own life in order to give his son a heart does the hospital capitulate and arrange for Mike's operation. Despite personal sacrifices, Chris ultimately relies on the brokerage firm to help him achieve the American Dream. Foregrounding individual responsibility can be seen as a political manoeuvre to take the emphasis away from government accountability. The tactic, Judith Stacey has argued, could be an attempt to 'displace anxieties over race, gender, sexual and class antagonisms that were unleashed as the modern family regime collapsed'.[43] In line with Clinton's 'responsible fatherhood' thesis, individual responsibility is emphasised over government accountability; the father is the site of action and must 'do something' in both films. More problematically, each film offers solutions to the problems it raises only on a personal level; neither John's nor Chris's actions offer a feasible solution to the larger problems with the American health care system and economy.[44]

In offering superficial solutions to their respective problems and projecting both issues onto the figure of the father, *John Q.* and *The Pursuit of Happyness* mirror Clinton's political positioning strategy during his presidency. Through their blend of liberalism and conservativism, the films echo Clinton's ambiguous politics, presenting liberal approaches to issues such as health care reform and single fatherhood, buffered against a more conservative reading of family values. In the same way that Clinton moved between liberal and conservative approaches to the family during his presidency, *John Q.* and *The Pursuit of Happyness* take a liberal approach to fatherhood by recognising family diversity with their solution to the problem of 'fatherhood' also informed by a conservativism that works to reinforce the breadwinning ethic.

Clinton's contradictions and ambiguities underscore his identity as a political performer, an identity that is essential in the contemporary political arena. As Daniel Marcus notes, 'Contemporary political candidates are the quintessential performative selves, seeking to be many things to many people, reconfiguring their identities according to specific social or political situations'.[45] Rather than the sign of a confused and hypocritical president as some contemporary news commentators would have it, Clinton's incorporation of liberal and conservative ideas was an incisive and largely successful ploy to appeal to a wider electorate. Jude Davies and Carol R. Smith argue a similar tactic is evident in Hollywood whereby films 'court ambiguous and incomplete audience identifications, so as to appeal to several audiences simultaneously and to engage with individual audience members in multiple ways'.[46] While the films were received by many critics on their release as offering a particularly liberal message, *John Q.* and *The Pursuit of Happyness* also adopt a conservative approach to the family and particularly to the father. In projecting social anxieties onto the figure of the father, and considering the father as the solution to political and social problems in the US, *John Q.*

and *The Pursuit of Happyness*, for all their overt foregrounding of family diversity and attempts to question the dominance of the traditional father, place the father at the centre of social anxieties and reinstate the father as dominant. Nonetheless, both films are also concerned with raising the profile of African American fatherhood, and fatherhood more broadly; fatherhood is not a given or essential right but something to be proved and acted out. The films reflect the complex, ambiguous and largely unresolved socio-political family values discourse in the 1990s, unresolved except in their emphasis on the figure of the father as central to the future of the American family.

While all four films considered in this chapter ultimately foreground the father as crucial to the future of the American family, key differences can be observed between the white-centred and black-centred narratives. In *Pleasantville* and *Far from Heaven*, the notion of the traditional father is explicitly presented as constructed image, perpetuated by the wider culture. In their self-conscious parodying of nostalgia for the 1950s, both films attempt to disrupt notions of the traditional family, and the traditional father as its natural head; Raymond Deagan and Bill Johnson offer more positive alternatives to the restrictive conventionality of the white traditional patriarch. Yet, no matter how scathing the critique of traditionalism, the power of the image prevails: Raymond leaves Hartford because his image does not conform to the ideological norm; David returns to the 1990s and must take on the role of responsible 'man of the house' to support his emotionally drained single mother. Significantly, however, the emphasis in both films is more on the father as supportive and responsible than on the father as breadwinning patriarch. The black-centred stories, on the other hand, endorse notions of responsible fatherhood as enunciated by Bill Clinton but are quick to promote the father as natural head of the family, and breadwinning prevails as the normative father function. The present-day realism of *John Q.* and *The Pursuit of Happyness* offers an aesthetic and ideological contrast to the highly stylised world depicted in *Pleasantville* and *Far from Heaven*, suggesting that contemporary Hollywood is only able to challenge the traditional fatherhood role by employing a nostalgic lens to look back at a time when image was apparently everything.

5
Aging Men: Viagra, Retiring Boomers and Jack Nicholson

A caricature of an elderly man, complete with white hair and exaggerated wrinkles, appeared on the 4 May 1998 cover of *Time* magazine. With one arm wrapped around a naked blonde woman, who clings to his neck in an intimate embrace, the man holds a small blue pill close to his pursed lips. His eyes peer anxiously in the direction of the woman to see if she had noticed his guilty secret. His angst realised in the mediated treatment of male impotence, the suspicious-looking character personified the 'dirty old man' stereotype of the aging male. Seven years later, in the wake of mounting fears that the imminent mass retirement of America's largest demographic would cause a 'retirement crisis', aging made the cover of *Time* once again. This time, a middle-aged man looks up in the air to see a flock of one-hundred dollar bills with wings fly off into the distance. 'The Great Retirement Ripoff', the headline proclaimed, 'Millions of Americans who think they will retire with benefits are in for a NASTY SURPRISE.'

The two covers are very different from the multitude of images of senescent baby boomers evident on newsmagazine covers around the same time. The 14 November 2005 cover of *Newsweek*, for example, featured a group of smiling celebrities and politicians, including Diane Keaton, Sylvester Stallone, Tommy Lee Jones, Bill Clinton, Donald Trump, George W. Bush, Dolly Parton and Cher. 'Ready or Not', the headline proclaimed, 'Boomers Turn 60.' Similarly, the 24 October 2005 cover of *Business Week* had an image of two smiling, waving boomers on a surfboard and announced that we should 'Love those Boomers!' because 'Their new attitudes and lifestyles are a marketer's

146

dream'. With the Viagra-popping Dirty Old Man approaching an unstable retirement at one end of the representational spectrum and the youthful boomers defying aging at the other, the covers reinforce the conflict between positive and negative images of aging that abound in studies of the aged and their representation.[1]

Two 'events' in the late 1990s and early 2000s amplified the public profile of the aging male, instigating a reassessment of the correlation between age and masculinity: the introduction of Viagra and the imminent mass retirement of the baby boom generation. Both events have received, and continue to receive, extensive media attention focussing not only on the event itself (Viagra as a cure for erectile dysfunction and the associated economic problems and possibilities for the retiring baby boom), but also on the widespread cultural and social implications affecting definitions of masculinity.

In 1998, the aging male was thrust into the public eye with the launch of Viagra onto the market place as a treatment for impotence (or the more clinical sounding 'erectile dysfunction' (ED), as the marketing department preferred), ushering in an 'era of widespread performance anxiety'.[2] Pfizer Pharmaceutical's campaign called ED a 'common problem' and claimed their new drug would allow men who had difficulties in achieving or maintaining an erection to once again function 'normally', that is, to regain control of their 'manhood'.[3] As a 'masculinity pill', Viagra encouraged a normative understanding of masculinity through the alignment of maleness with potency and virility.[4] An initial promotional advertisement featuring Senator Bob Dole presented ED as a potentially embarrassing 'condition' men would need 'courage' to talk to their doctor about. In what began as a strategy for normalising impotence in aging men, the marketing of Viagra essentially reinforced the positive/negative duality of aging, pathologising erectile dysfunction and presenting aging as decline so that aging masculinity became a 'problem' to be fixed through the consumption of a little blue pill.

The second significant 'event' foregrounding and questioning the construction of aging men is the mass retirement of the baby boom generation and the corresponding 'retirement crisis' it will apparently cause. Headlines proclaiming the 'graying of America' and coming 'age wave' have become commonplace with news stories earnestly addressing the potential fiscal implications of this demographic change.[5] With over 78 million boomers reaching the retirement age of 65 by

2030, the baby boom generation is the perceived instigator of the economic strain this mass retirement will ostensibly bring. At the same time, however, boomers are widely held to be the solution to negative images of retirement and aging in contemporary American society and are predicted to redefine and revitalise retirement and traditional notions of aging. This is, after all, the generation that swore it would never grow old nor trust anyone over 30. The image of affluent boomers clearly contradicts the *Time* cover that opened this chapter and the headlines proclaiming an impending 'retirement crisis' that suggest a significant proportion of Americans cannot *afford* to retire. The 'baby boom', as it is mapped in social discourse, thus distinctly refers to the aging middle classes with enough disposable income to challenge existing stereotypes of aging. Aging baby boomers have thus become both the economic symptom *and* the cultural cure of the American 'retirement crisis'.

Central to this discursive battle is the figure of the aging male. Writing in 1993, iconic feminist Betty Freidan feared, 'all our assumptions and definitions of masculinity are based on *young men*'.[6] However, in foregrounding the aging male, the collection of newsmagazine covers highlights the centrality of age to constructions of masculinity and what it means to 'be a man' in the late 1990s and early 2000s. On the one hand, the first of these images presents aging as decline, with maleness threatened as a result of this life change. The aging man is presented as a 'problem' that needs to be fixed, for example through the treatment of impotence offered by Viagra. On the other hand, the images of baby boomers present the possibility of revitalised notions of aging, calling, as they do, for a reassessment of what it means to grow older. Both events highlight the performative nature of age as it relates to masculinity, suggesting that 'aging' has its own prescriptions and proscriptions that are socially and culturally determined.

This chapter examines aging as performance, and considers the relationship between performances of aging and cultural conceptions of masculinity. Exploring cinematic treatments of aging men alongside social discourses of aging, the first half of the chapter outlines existing scholarship on aging and masculinity, examining key tropes of aging and old age. Aging as performance is then considered through a case of study of Jack Nicholson, examining how his performances interact with and challenge social discourses of aging and existing social stereotypes of old age. I argue that through his characterisations in *About Schmidt* (2002) and *Something's Gotta Give* (2003), Nicholson embodies cultural fears around aging, specifically addressing fears that centre on definitions of masculinity in the contemporary period.

Ripening, rotting and revitalising

In her chapter on 'The Aging Clint' in *Impossible Bodies*, Chris Holmlund provides one of the few substantial discussions of the aging male in cinema. Highlighting recent academic attention given to femininity and aging by Linda Dittmar, Vivian Sobchack, E. Anne Kaplan and Pat Mellencamp, Holmlund argues that masculinity and aging have been overlooked.[7] In an attempt to rectify this critical deficiency, Holmlund examines the longevity of Clint Eastwood's film career, from his early westerns to his more recent action and adventure films, considering the changes in Eastwood's performance and star persona that have been brought about by his aging. Focussing on Eastwood's aging body, Holmlund suggests the actor's (and his characters') attempts to mask age, or render it unimportant, fail to completely conceal the aging process. The failure to successfully deny aging takes place both physically and symbolically; the visibly declining male body is confirmed by Eastwood's 'slight gut and love handles ... spreading waistline ... and breasts [that] are slightly sagging', his waning manhood accentuated as his guns 'get ever bigger as he ages'. So while Eastwood continues to take on film roles that call the aging process into question, his aging body and ineffective 'props' nonetheless expose the masquerade. However, despite being unsuccessful in masking the aging process completely, Holmlund argues that, 'Clint's character and Clint himself, make aging look more like a good-natured, robust "ripening" than a despondent, rickety "rotting"'.[8] Given away only by his *slight* gut and *slightly* sagging breasts, Eastwood still manages to 'age well' and thus succeeds in escaping harsher effects of aging that might destabilise his masculine identity.

Holmlund's essay is an effective starting point in discussing the imaging of aging men on screen, since her reading of Eastwood establishes two major oppositions at play in constructions of aging: successful aging or aging well ('Good-natured, robust "ripening"') and unsuccessful aging or aging badly ('despondent, rickety "rotting"').

According to Mike Featherstone and Jeff Hearn, the image of defying or denying aging is dominant in contemporary society. These 'heroes of aging', Featherstone suggests, approach aging in a positive manner and remain youthful 'in their work habits, bodily posture, facial expressions and general demeanour'. Similarly, Jeff Hearn suggests this trope is most evident with 'formally successful men' such as politicians, businessmen, judges and broadcasters: those who defy aging through their continued demonstration of power and authority.[9]

Clint Eastwood and Robert Redford can be seen as emblematical 'heroes of aging'. Despite being in their seventies, both actors continue to play successful professionals (*Spy Game*, 2001; *Blood Work*, 2002; *Million Dollar Baby*, 2004) and take on challenging and active roles (*Absolute Power*, 1997; *Space Cowboys*, 2000; *The Last Castle*, 2001), an image sustained off screen in their directorial output (*The Horse Whisperer*, 1998; *Mystic River*, 2003; *Million Dollar Baby*; *Flags of Our Fathers*, 2006; *Lions for Lambs*, 2007). While aging may not be completely concealed, as Holmlund's reading of Eastwood indicates, defying old age is the ultimate goal. Morgan Freeman could also be considered as an 'aging hero', albeit as an actor for whom aging is central to his screen persona, rather than a persona that has adapted to accommodate his advancing years. While Freeman's acting career began in the 1960s, it was not until 1989 when the actor was in his early fifties that he made his breakthrough with *Lean on Me* and *Driving Miss Daisy*. His prolific film output in the 1990s and 2000s, in a variety of supporting, starring and voice-over roles, presents Freeman as a counterpoint to the privileging of youth in Hollywood.

More usually, the process of defying old age is closely linked to a denial of aging – a more extreme form of 'positive aging'. In this instance, youth is retained (or aging is reversed) through cosmetic surgery or treatments, extensive diet and exercise regimes; Sylvester Stallone's ever-solid physique once again made headlines with his reappearance as Rocky Balboa and John Rambo, thirty years after his 'hard body' was first launched onto screens.[10] Whether defying or denying aging, these men demonstrate that old age does not necessarily equate with physical, mental and social decline and create the possibility that aging men can be professional and successful like their younger counterparts.

Closer to Holmlund's 'despondent, rickety "rotting"' is the second image of aging proposed by Featherstone. Depicting the 'hidden and more disagreeable aspects of the aging process', this image presents growing old as decline – physical or mental – offering the elderly as 'subhuman' in contrast to the 'parahuman' aging heroes, exemplified by the 'aging curmudgeon' and 'dirty old man' stereotypes that abound in popular representation.[11] According to Jeff Hearn, this second category also includes the man 'moving on', or the 'aging king' who is on the brink of retirement or experiencing a similar change in occupational status. As with the 'heroes of aging', notions of power are fundamental to the construction of aging male identity. Instead of retaining youth-associated power through authoritative life roles, however, the 'aging king' demonstrates a *loss* of power, real or perceived, aligning aging with weakness and vulnerability. Hearn offers the films *Shadowlands* (1993), *The Remains of the Day* (1993) and *The Browning Version* (1994) as depictions of the 'sadness/status of the aging respectable man',[12] a theme Anthony Hopkins has revisited more recently in *The Human Stain* (2003) and *Proof* (2005). Images conforming to the 'aging king' model not only describe the men in a position of waning authority but also those men whose only source of power comes from the authority that a patriarchal culture offers. Al Pacino is a further example of an actor who has adopted this motif; his 'aging king' roles include the aging mafia soldier struggling to preserve his status in *Donnie Brasco* (1997) and the football coach whose advancing years cause him to reassess his career in *Any Given Sunday* (1999). In *Gran Torino* (2008), Clint Eastwood plays a variation on the aging king motif that sees him move closer to rickety than ripening. Eastwood's embittered Korean War veteran Walt Kowalski largely conforms to the 'grumpy old man' stereotype with his performance of old age reduced to a series of grunts, monosyllabic mumbling and curmudgeonly grousing.

While the aging hero motif potentially offers an example of successful aging, success is largely obtained by suppressing the negative associations of getting old; rather than directly addressing old age, it is concealed behind a façade of youthfulness. For Featherstone and others, this façade constitutes the male myths or 'masks' of aging, highlighting a conflict between the outer, aging appearance and the inner, youthful persona. The 'heroes of aging' mask the very processes of aging through their continuing performance of youth-associated activities or, in a more drastic attempt, reversing the aging process through cosmetic surgery. Conversely, with aging as decline, the body itself becomes a mask, 'misrepresenting and imprisoning the inner self'.[13] The limited number of major film roles for older men has contributed to this simplified idea of aging. As Hearn states, 'More usually older men figure as complements to the main characters, as exceptions to the general flow of the film narrative, as objects of fun, interest, and curiosity'.[14] The elderly have, according to Hearn, become a cinematic 'other', marginalised and ignored in a youth-oriented culture.

However, from books dedicated to the retiring baby boom phenomenon to market projections for a wide variety of consumer products, boomers are being hailed as a positive force that will 'revolutionise', 'transform', 'change', 'challenge', 'revitalise' and 'redefine' what it means to age and retire.[15] Colourfully referred to by some demographers and market theorists as 'the pig in the python', the baby boom generation (born between 1946 and 1964) is frequently credited with redefining every decade through which they have passed.[16] Their influence on society is explained not only through sheer demographic size but also due to their particular social attitudes and behaviours. As marketing theorist Marc Gobé describes:

> Baby Boomers are used to challenging America's assumptions and used to fighting for what they want. This generation's sheer size has empowered it like no other American generation. In the sixties and seventies, *their* mores, *their* music, *their* clothes, *their* politics were the forces that restructured America. ... As Boomers marched into the boardrooms and backrooms of the eighties, suddenly they were fighting for success and affluence, redefining success, materialism and the 'American Dream' in the process.[17]

Rather than deny or defy aging like Featherstone's aging heroes, it has become a truism in management literature that baby boomers will redefine aging by putting pressure on the market to change what it means to grow old. Baby boomers have been recognised as a potent economic and political market force; not only has the sheer size of the boomers affected consumer marketing approaches, market analysts also project that the boomers will be the most affluent elderly generation in history. The aging boomers have had an extensive effect on the market from restaurant menus and incontinence

products to recreational vehicles, college courses, and gym member-
ships. Rather than adapting to accommodate their aging and retirement years, then, the baby boomers are forcing marketers to 'rebrand
aging' and thus accommodate *them*.[18]

The baby boom generation has also had an extensive influence
on film production trends and marketing strategies in Hollywood.
Linda Ruth Williams and Michael Hammond go so far as to state
that the boomer generation is 'perhaps the most significant of the
underlying factors in the developments and shifts in the American
film industry since 1960'.[19] Indeed, major shifts in film production
have in many ways tracked the demographic significance of the
baby boom. Forming a large bulk of the cinema audience during the
1960s and early-1970s, boomers encouraged the focus on youth-
oriented, countercultural films, such as *Bonnie and Clyde* (1967), *Easy
Rider* (1969) and *Midnight Cowboy* (1969). When the baby boomers
became parents in the 1980s, and their children (the correspondingly named 'echo boom') became consumers, they created a vast
new audience for family entertainment, contributing to the rise of
the family film.[20]

Predictably, as the aging boomers have been identified as a prominent market power in other areas of the economy, cultural commentators and entertainment analysts predict that baby boomers
will have a significant effect on film industry output and cinematic
images of aging.[21] In the context of Hollywood's youth-oriented
blockbuster economy, however, the aging boomers no longer dictate
the major trends of film production, a function now assumed by the
echo boom. Yet they still play a significant role in the profitability of
the film industry, representing a sizeable market segment. As Thomas
Austin notes, 'The film business, like other industries, has a stake
in exploiting difference, insofar as its products can be successfully
targeted at distinct niche markets.'[22] With the 50-plus demographic
heading towards retirement, the aging baby boomers offer a substantial niche audience.

A number of films released in the early- to mid-2000s suggest that
the film industry is attempting to accommodate the interests of the
50-plus market segment, but instead of catering exclusively to the
aging boomers, these films are produced and marketed in a way
that seek out multiple niche audiences in order to maximise profit.
For example, *The Notebook* was the 'sleeper hit' of summer 2004,

grossing over $81 million at the US box office with more that $124 million in DVD sales. The film focuses on Duke (76-year-old James Garner), an old man reading a love story to an elderly woman suffering from Alzheimer's (74-year-old Gena Rowlands) in a nursing home, interspersed with flashback scenes of the two young lovers of the story, Noah and Allie (Ryan Gosling and Rachel McAdams). According to Matt Lasorsa, New Line Home Entertainment executive, *The Notebook* was aimed at women over 25 – not the demographic 'you look forward to' – yet the film proved to be successful with the younger, teen (female) market as well as the older, fifty-plus segment, suggested by the results at a number of 2005 film award ceremonies: *The Notebook* won the MTV Movie Award ceremony for 'Best Kiss' (between Gosling and McAdams, McAdams was also nominated for Best Actress) and eight Teen Choice Awards (including 'Choice Date Movie' and 'Choice Movie Liplock'), as well as being voted 'Best love story for grownups' at the Grownup Movie Awards, the awards ceremony run by the American Association for Retired Persons. With the DVD released strategically a week before Valentine's Day, *The Notebook* was also marketed at the male consumer, with the extras-laden disc dubbed 'the gift that keeps on giving'.[23] In the case of *The Notebook*, the film was primarily marketed at the teen/young adult female audience but maximised its appeal by incorporating 'older' or more 'mature' subject matter.

About Schmidt, a dark comedy about a newly retired 66-year-old curmudgeon, was another 'sleeper' hit, taking over $65 million at the US box office – nearly eight times the January opening weekend figure. *Something's Gotta Give*, a romantic comedy about a 63-year-old womaniser who falls in love with a 50-something, grossed just under $125 million at the domestic box office (with another $142 million at the foreign box office) to become the 16th biggest domestic box-office hit of the year and the 11th biggest worldwide (after blockbuster action films *The Matrix Revolutions*, *X2: X-Men United* and *Bad Boys II*). Thematically, both films incorporate and engage with contemporary debates around aging, in particular aging male identity, by addressing aging issues such as fears around retirement and the relationship between sexuality and growing old. Aging is a central concern, rather than a subplot as it was in *The Notebook*. Unlike *The Notebook*, *About Schmidt* and *Something's Gotta Give* visually foreground old age by providing the aging Jack Nicholson as the focal point in the poster campaigns; it is the younger stars (Keanu Reeves and Amanda Peet in *Something's Gotta Give* and Dermot Mulroney and Hope Davis in *About Schmidt*) who are contained in the small type.

Although not a baby boomer himself (he was born in 1937, nine years before the figurative start of the baby boom), Jack Nicholson, like the boomers, has been at the forefront of a number of social and cultural events as they have been played out cinematically. Whether demonstrating 'the ambivalent ideology of sixties individualism' in *Easy Rider*, or 'mid-seventies cultural pessimism' in *Chinatown* (1974), both Nicholson's characters and his films have been considered cultural markers, reflecting the contemporary mood and exhibiting a particular connection to American youth.[24] The actor's associations with youthfulness largely stem from his film choices in the earlier part of his career – in particular those films made in the 1960s and 1970s which held strong countercultural ties. With their celebration of nonconformity and dissidence, films such as *Easy Rider*, *Five Easy Pieces* (1970) and *One Flew Over the Cuckoo's Nest* (1975) saw Nicholson defy authority, reject social norms and exude youth in his rebelliousness, individualism and mischievous nature.

As a result of his performances of aging men in the early 2000s, Nicholson has once again been aligned with the boomer cohort. As in the 1960s and 1970s, Nicholson's relationship with the baby boomers has been highlighted by film reviewers, but also by social demographers, cultural theorists, market researchers, and even sociologists, psychologists and physicians. While in the earlier period, commentators emphasised Nicholson's affinity with the youthful baby boom, in the 2000s the emphasis is on Nicholson's affinity with the boomers as they near their retirement years. In *USA Today*, for example, Marilyn Elias asserted that 'Just as *The Big Chill* (1983) voiced older boomers' worries over ticking biological clocks and waning idealism in their 30s, *Something's Gotta Give* reflects new concerns as the generation heads towards 60'.[25] In viewing Nicholson as a 'boomer icon', the remainder of this chapter examines the actor's shifting persona and performances of old age. As a star performer who has bridged the gap between the young and the old, building his career around his ties with youth culture and, later firmly establishing his affinity with the older market, Jack Nicholson has played a central role in the imaging of aging men in contemporary cinema.

Ageless performer, performing aging

A stark contrast between positive and negative aging is revealed by the disparate images of Nicholson on the movie posters for *About Schmidt* and *Something's Gotta Give* (Figure 5.1). The *About Schmidt* poster shows a haggard, unkempt, sad-looking old man: dishevelled, with his hair uncombed, and in his pyjamas. His ruffled grey-white hair and stubble suggest he has just rolled out of bed. In his pyjamas, Nicholson's character looks like he may have recently escaped from a mental hospital, his vacant, glazed-over expression not unlike his post-electro-shock treatment appearance in *One Flew Over the Cuckoo's Nest*. Conversely, in the *Something's Gotta Give* poster, Nicholson has lost the double chin and sallow skin; his clean-shaven, radiant complexion complements his beaming smile. Even the receding hairline that threatens to give his age away is removed from view; the only age markers left are his crow's feet and the distinguished flecks of silver in his hair.

The film posters demonstrate the two masks of aging identified by Featherstone, Hearn and Holmlund, displaying the mask of agelessness or 'ripening' in *Something's Gotta Give* with only subtle allusions to old age, and the 'rotting' mask of explicit decline trapping the inner self in *About Schmidt*. While foregrounding the two extremes of aging in the posters, however, the films themselves negotiate the terms of aging and question stereotypes of old age, firstly, in placing Nicholson and his performances at the centre of such debates and representations and, secondly, through their engagement with social discourses of aging in America during the 1990s and 2000s.

Over 50 years since his acting debut in *The Cry Baby Killer* (1958) and despite being in his seventies, Nicholson continues to be one of the most financially successful, critically acclaimed and popular actors in contemporary American cinema. While certainly not unique for his endurance as an actor – one need only consider Clint Eastwood, Paul Newman or Robert Redford, or indeed James Garner and Gena Rowlands, to witness other actors still successful in their later years – Nicholson is markedly different from these other actors because of his strong ties with youth and youthfulness: key characteristics of his early screen persona.

Despite appearing in over 60 films, ranging from comedies to dramas, Hollywood blockbusters to independent art films, Nicholson is most recognised for the roguish, mischievous behaviour on display in *Batman* (1989), *The Shining* (1980), *One Flew Over the Cuckoo's Nest* and *The Witches of Eastwick* (1987). In a *Sight and Sound* profile of the actor, Danny Leigh asserts that 'Joker Jack', Nicholson's characters in these films, is 'perhaps the single most defined persona in film today'.[26] The combination of the 'killer smile' that first put him on the cover of *Time* in 1974, the perpetually arched 'Mephistophelean eyebrows', and his notorious reputation as a womaniser characterise Nicholson's public persona.[27] Dennis Bingham argues that Nicholson's distinct screen persona has become almost inseparable from his public persona so that his '"real personality" hinges on almost a parody of personality; his public image teases the very idea of knowing what Dyer calls "the star's private self"'.[28] While many actors endeavour to mask the creation of their performance, Nicholson considers acting a masquerade and his 'over-the-top' performances have become synonymous with the star. According to the actor, excessiveness is 'good for business' and is all part of the construction of his public persona – a persona Nicholson himself has referred to in numerous interviews as 'being Jack'.[29]

Both on and off the screen, Nicholson has generated a reputation for romantic involvements with much younger women. On screen, he has engaged in relationships with Ellen Barkin and Kathleen Turner (17 years his junior), Jerry Hall (19 years), and Michelle Pfeiffer (21 years). Off screen, his much publicised affair with Rebecca Broussard (26 years his junior), whilst apparently in a long-term relationship with Anjelica Huston (14 years), blurred the boundary between person and persona. Significantly, Nicholson's romantic escapades have earned him the title of 'The Great Seducer' (rather than Dirty Old Man), conforming to the myth of agelessness proposed by Mike Featherstone. His role in *As Good As it Gets* (1997) is a case in point. In the film, Nicholson plays Melvin Udall, a novelist with obsessive-compulsive disorder who wins over a single mother and waitress played by Helen Hunt. The considerable age gap between the two protagonists (Hunt is 26 years younger than Nicholson) is referred to only once, and fleetingly, to imply that age is not an issue. Ultimately, *As Good As it Gets* reinforces what Susan Sontag has termed the 'double standard' of aging that allows men to age while women are forced to stay young.[30]

Based on his performances in the 2000s, starting with *The Pledge* in 2001, it seems that even Jack Nicholson cannot escape the perils of aging. After a four-year break following his Academy Award-winning

Figure 5.1 Imaging old age as 'rotting' and 'ripening' in *About Schmidt* (New Line/Avery Pix/The Kobal Collection, 2002) and *Something's Gotta Give* (Columbia/TriStar/The Kobal Collection, 2003)

Figure 5.1 Continued

performance in *As Good As it Gets*, Nicholson returned to the screen significantly older. Described by director Sean Penn as a 'retirement-crisis story disguised as a thriller', *The Pledge* is an intense character study of recently retired homicide detective, Jerry Black, who is driven insane by his obsession with the murder of a young girl.[31] As Black, Nicholson performs aging as decline. Rather than bodily decline as a consequence of the aging process, however, Black's decline stems from the loss of power that comes from retirement. *The Pledge* clearly illustrates Jeff Hearn's 'aging king' thesis; the once successful and respected detective experiences instability and insecurity in retirement as the masculine identity that he formed as a cop is threatened. As *The Guardian*'s Peter Bradshaw observed: 'Above all, it is a movie about masculinity and men. ... Nicholson exudes a battered virility as the retired Reno cop, a frazzled, near-exhausted machismo and a pitiful yearning for redemption'.[32] Black's mental decline is presented as a direct consequence of the aging process; it is retirement that initiates Black's psychosis.

On its release, reviewers readily emphasised Nicholson's departure as Black from his 'Joker Jack' persona: 'We don't get the sleepy-lidded grin, the twangy drawl, the crazy laughing-man act, all those things indulged to the full in his previous outing, *As Good as It Gets*', asserted Peter Bradshaw; Jason Solomons of *The Sunday Observer* pointed out that *The Pledge* was not 'one of those big, show-offy performances from Nicholson'; *The Village Voice*'s Michael Atkinson called it 'Nicholson's least mannered performance in a decade and a half'.[33] Like *The Pledge*, much of the interest generated by *About Schmidt* and *Something's Gotta Give* came from Nicholson's apparent suppression of the mannerisms and quirks that so clearly defined 'Jack'. In *About Schmidt*, 'Audiences expecting the devilish 'Jack' to burst out are in for a surprise', declared David Ansen; 'Nicholson jettisons all his trademark bells and whistles', noted *Newsweek*'s Jeff Giles, 'and delivers a magnificently controlled ode to the ordinary'. Despite the foregrounding of Nicholson's 'Joker Jack' persona in the poster, a number of reviewers pointed out the 'subtlety' of his 'modest' performance in *Something's Gotta Give*. The words 'subtle', 'controlled', 'restrained' and 'understated' punctuate reviews of the films, reinforcing Nicholson's departure from the exaggerated and exuberant performances that were a staple part of his earlier film career and connecting his restrained acting to his performance of old age.[34]

The posters for *About Schmidt* and *Something's Gotta Give* encapsu-
late the problematic distinction between persona and performance.
It seems that the filmmakers have attempted to erase all traces of
'Jack' in their construction of Nicholson for the *About Schmidt* poster:
his raggedy eyebrows have lost their defining arch; his eyes, once
bursting with mischief, are dull and flaccid; the 'killer smile' has been
replaced by a depressive frown. His ever-present receding hairline is
made *more* visible, his loose jowls and chin create the impression
that he has no neck. Gone are the playful glint and cheeky grin, as
Newsweek's David Ansen rightly declared in his review for the film:
'This is not the Nicholson you are used to'.[35]

On the other hand, the marketing for *Something's Gotta Give* drew
heavily on the power of star branding to sell the film. Referred to,
simply, as 'Jack and Diane', the movie poster relies on the power of
celebrity, demonstrating a self-conscious awareness of 'Jack', a tactic
largely dependent upon the audience's prior knowledge of Nicholson's
star persona (as well as the John Cougar Mellencamp 1982 boomer
hit 'Jack and Diane'). Moreover, the romantic coupling of 'Jack and
Diane' insinuates a degree of familiarity similar to the classic two-
some Fred and Ginger, or perhaps Bogart and Bacall, Hepburn and
Tracey. This is rather premature bearing in mind *Something's Gotta
Give* is only the second film in which Nicholson and Keaton appear
together, and their first film, *Reds* (1981), was a political epic and
a long way from this light-hearted romantic comedy. At the same
time, the sole use of first names affirms Nicholson's star power and
reputation as generated by his 'Jack' persona.[36] Just as *About Schmidt*
depended upon the erasure of 'Jack' to create a sense of ordinariness
about the main protagonist, the *Something's Gotta Give* poster clearly
depicts Nicholson 'being Jack' – from the 'killer smile' to the trademark sunglasses the 'real' Jack is rarely seen without – leaving the
audience with no doubt as to what to expect.

One of the main issues for reviewers, however, was seeing Nicholson
'finally act his age'. Glenn Whipp of the *Los Angeles Daily News* recalls
the start of *About Schmidt*:

> We've just seen Jack Nicholson sitting by himself in a barren
> office, portraying an old man (Jack? Old?) counting down the
> final seconds of a career that has spanned his entire adult life.
> Next we see Nicholson's character, an insurance actuary named

Warren Schmidt, at his retirement party. Seated next to him is an old woman. At first you think, 'How nice. Schmidt's mother has come to her son's retirement party'. Then it hits you. That's not Schmidt's mother. That's his wife.[37]

Although Whipp registers surprise at Nicholson playing an old man, the biggest shock comes from the pairing of Nicholson with a woman his own age, not some lithe 20-something as might be expected, suggesting Nicholson's performance of aging is constructed in relation to the aging of those around him.[38] Whipp's choice of words here – '*portraying* an old man' – warrant further exploration, particularly when taking into account the construction of Nicholson's persona as the very antithesis of aging, not forgetting that at 66 when he filmed *About Schmidt* Nicholson *was* an old man according to chronological definitions. How, then, *does* Nicholson portray an old man and what happens to old age as performance when the actor is already 'old'?

As the image of Warren Schmidt in the film poster attests, Nicholson's physical appearance in *About Schmidt* conforms to conventional codes for portraying old age: Nicholson's hair is thinning and grey with a comb-over unsuccessfully hiding his sizeable bald patch; his skin is wrinkled and saggy; his protruding paunch and flaccid chest indicate passivity and a lack of fitness, contrasting the energetic associations of youth. The physical markers of old age extend to Nicholson's facial and bodily performance in the film: his face displays a perpetual frown; the concave expression accentuating his sagging jowls and hollow, drooping eyes; his shoulders stoop from the weight of his plodding frame; the slowness of his movements. Old age is further created through props and costume: glasses perched on the end of his nose; a shirt collar buttoned to the top so that the skin on his wrinkled neck folds over; cardigans, high-waisted trousers and a flat cap. In line with aging as a mask trapping a youthful interior, Schmidt despairs at his diminishing exterior: 'when I look in the mirror and see the wrinkles around my eyes and the sagging skin on my neck and the hair in my ears and the veins on my ankles, I can't believe it's really me'. Close-ups of Schmidt's body accompany his resigned voice-over confession, presenting the aging body as fragments of deterioration and decay.

As Harry Sanborn in *Something's Gotta Give*, Nicholson's presentation of old age initially appears to correspond with Mike Featherstone's 'heroes of aging' – the men who deny their age and seek eternal youth. At 63, Harry is, according to the film's promotional description, a 'perennial playboy'. Chain-smoking cigars, drinking copious amounts of champagne, throwing wild parties, dating women half his age and taking Viagra, Harry appears to be on a relentless quest for agelessness. While he has some of the same markers of old age as Schmidt – wrinkles, greying hair, paunch and flaccid chest – these are toned down and more subtle in *Something's Gotta Give*, his eyes often hidden by sunglasses.[39] Rather than cardigans and slippers, Harry wears clothes that do not explicitly mark him as 'old', such as open neck shirts, khaki slacks and bright polo-shirts. Schmidt's stoop and plod are also gone and his frown has been replaced with an omnipresent grin, lifting and animating his face. Following a heart attack, however, his doctor (Keanu Reeves) informs Harry that he must restrain his excessive behaviour before it kills him. He must, in other words, start 'acting his age'. Aging is portrayed less as a bodily performance than a series of restrictions caused by getting older: waning eyesight, failing sex drive, weakened heart. Jokes centre on Harry's inability to see without glasses; his need to take Viagra and check his blood pressure before having sex; his desperate attempts to climb a flight of stairs without collapsing; his increased sensitivity and random bouts of crying after his heart attack.

In sum, aging in *About Schmidt* is more of a physical portrayal whereas *Something's Gotta Give* presents aging as a social performance. In contrast to Whipp's commendation for Nicholson 'acting his age' in *About Schmidt*, however, Kathleen Woodward has suggested that Nicholson 'acts too old', adamantly asserting that the presentation of old age is 'mockery, not mimicry':

> [O]lder age is performed in the way we would say gender might self-consciously be performed, albeit in a consistently negative register. It is something that is put on, like weight, in the case of Nicholson, or something emphasized, like a shapeless gray haircut, in the case of Squibb. Something captured in a gesture of movement, like shuffling. Something subtracted, like muscle tone.[40]

Woodward's comments identify a problem in defining 'old age', suggesting that Nicholson's portrayal of a 66-year-old in *About Schmidt* is too pronounced and, therefore, inauthentic. A significant issue is also raised in Woodward's proposition that Nicholson 'acts too old', essentially doing too much in his construction of old age and thus distinguishing between the performance of old age as 'doing' and the performance of old age as 'being', as seems to be the case in *Something's Gotta Give*. In other words, Nicholson demonstrates a much more active performance of old age in *About Schmidt* in comparison with his portrayal as Harry Sanborn. This is further complicated by the fact that Nicholson was approximately the same age as Warren Schmidt when he filmed *About Schmidt* whereas he was 67 when he portrayed 63-year-old Harry; as Schmidt, Nicholson acted 'too old' despite being the same age as his character but, as Sanborn, Nicholson foregrounded or 'keyed' his youthful persona in order to play a character four years his junior.[41]

This tactic can be partly explained as the difference between Nicholson playing an 'average' retired man in *About Schmidt* and the millionaire owner of a hip-hop label in *Something's Gotta Give*. By trying to remove all possible traces of 'Jack' in the construction of Warren Schmidt, the filmmakers of *About Schmidt* aimed to create an 'ordinary Everyman' that would not be possible if Nicholson's 'larger-than-life' persona were detectable. In an interview with *Entertainment Weekly*, Nicholson recalls his performance:

> [Panye] only gave me one major direction. He said, 'Jack, I want you to play a small man'. ... So I found myself standing on the set being Buster Keaton a lot of the time. ... I un-Jacked myself. Because it's easier to involve an audience if they don't already know who you are – or think they know who you are ... I've always liked that there were two of me – the person people think I am and the person I actually am.[42]

The achievement of the 'ordinary' resides in the removal (un-Jacking) of the 'Jack' star persona from Nicholson's performances, eradicating the sense of familiarity that knowledge of his persona provides. By playing the part of Warren 'small', Nicholson departs from the grandeur and distinction that being a major Hollywood player generates and describes a similar process to that of Michael Douglas 'wiping off' his star persona to play an American Everyman (see Chapter 2). Nicholson curtailed the excessive 'over-the-top' gestures and actions that characterised his earlier roles; his body is noticeably rigid, his eyes are glazed over and he wears a fixed frown throughout.

Nonetheless, 'Jack' is not entirely absent from Nicholson's performance. In a self-reflexive nod to 'The Great Seducer' who is renowned
for only dating younger women, Schmidt moans: 'Lately, every night,
I find myself asking the same question: who is this old woman that
lives in my house?' Nicholson voiced his fear of aging women in a
2006 *Rolling Stone* interview when he professed his fear of old and
wrinkled skin. Rather than implying his own fears of aging, he admitted he was more concerned with coming into contact with the 'crepe'
skin of old women, suggesting that while *About Schmidt* may reveal
a visually different Nicholson, the essence of 'Jack' has managed to
filter into the character.[43]

Conversely, *Something's Gotta Give* brings 'Jack' to the forefront.
Playing precisely to the audience's familiarity with the actor and
authenticating his demonstration of aging, it appears that Nicholson
is not 'performing' but merely '*being* himself'. In this instance,
Nicholson's ability to 'act his age' is largely dependent upon Nicholson
remaining faithful to his established persona which, in turn, relies
on the audience's awareness of his persona, leading one reviewer to
point out, 'Jack Nicholson is acting his age again in the romantic
comedy *Something's Gotta Give*. But this time, he's doing it as Jack.'[44]
In 'being Jack', Nicholson is not enacting conventional codes for performing age but relies on a 'biological performance' that makes use of
the markers of age 67-year-old Nicholson already has.

In both cases, the performance of old age is a process; it is something that is 'put on' either actively, by foregrounding and accentuating tropes of aging, or passively, by only subtly calling attention
to aging. In *About Schmidt*, Nicholson speeds up the aging process in
the same way Mel Gibson 'puts on' old age in *Forever Young* (1992)
or Brad Pitt 'puts on' old age in *The Curious Case of Benjamin Button*
(2008). *Something's Gotta Give* combines both active and passive portrayals of aging, actively portraying social characteristics of aging yet
passively portraying the physical appearance of aging. Considering
aging as an active or passive process problematises the potential to
present aging on screen as what James Naremore's terms 'pure biological performance'.[45] Aging, he notes, is an 'involuntary biological
process' to the extent that we cannot stop the process of growing
old (although it can, as Sylvester Stallone demonstrates, be delayed
or reversed via health care regimes and surgery). Nicholson's performance in *About Schmidt* is too contrived to be a *pure* biological

performance; the actor 'acts *too* old', despite being the same physical age as his character. Aging in *Something's Gotta Give*, on the other hand, alternates between unforgiving camera angles and a youthful tint that naturalises aging and gives the impression of Nicholson 'being' himself.[46]

In their most comedic moments, both films offer examples where film 'exploits the decay of celebrity players',[47] yet it is also a ploy to emphasise Schmidt and Harry's growing maturity. The films may depict stereotypes of aging in some respects but do so to highlight the restrictive nature of masculinity that is traditionally defined in relation to youth. Both protagonists go on journeys to reassess their male identities as they age. Schmidt, who defines himself in relation to his job as an actuary, as a husband and as a father, embarks on a road trip in his 35-foot Winnebago Adventurer to discover his 'place in the world' after he retires, his wife dies and his daughter announces her wedding. Harry Sanborn defines himself in relation to youth until his heart attack and relationship with a woman closer to his own age prompts him to visit past girlfriends to find out how to be a better man. 'Acting his age', therefore, not only refers to Nicholson's screen performances of old age but also his characters' respective steps towards maturity; both films show that not only is aging a process whereby old age is 'put on' but it is also a maturation process requiring a renegotiation of the terms of masculinity in accordance with a new life phase.

About Schmidt and *Something's Gotta Give* have been considered as films that 'tap into' or comment on contemporary perceptions of old age. For example, *Technology and Business Weekly* considered *About Schmidt* representative of the treatment of retirement in the workplace, suggesting that businesses could learn from Nicholson's character in order to 'reflect on the changing demographics of the workplace'; in *The New York Times*, *Something's Gotta Give* was used as an example to demonstrate the humorous consequences of age-related eye problems; in *United Press International*, Nicholson's alcohol abuse in *About Schmidt* was cited as a common problem with the elderly; and in the *Times Colonist* Nicholson's Viagra consumption in *Something's Gotta Give* was used as a cautionary warning: 'as Jack Nicholson showed ... the wonder drug of the twenty-first century is of little help to a man with a weak heart. (Lest any men are reading this: On no account should you take Viagra if you are using nitrates to control your angina attacks.)'[48] In constructing aging as a central concern, *About Schmidt, Something's Gotta Give* and *The Pledge* assimilate and articulate aging debates such as those around retirement, sexuality, and the conflict between positive and negative images of aging.

The critical and cultural reception the two films received suggest Nicholson's performances of aging are closer to mimicry rather than the mockery Woodward proposes; many critics applauded *About Schmidt* and *Something's Gotta Give* for their realistic portrayal of aging. The American Association for Retired Persons (AARP) voted *About Schmidt* the 'best movie for grownups' and, in 2004, *Something's Gotta Give* won the award for 'best grownup love story'. According to AARP magazine, both films not only addressed 'the concerns and dreams of people fifty and over', they also offered 'an authentic image of the second half of life [and] celebrated the differences among age groups, rather than exploit them'.[49] Nicholson and the films achieve this by directly engaging with recent social and cultural discourse around aging Americans. In July 2005, for example, PBS aired a documentary dedicated to the retiring baby boom and America's relationship with aging. In *The Open Road: America Looks at Aging*, four 'experts on aging' discussed how the 'profound change in the American lifespan' would revitalise, redefine and reassess how America considers retirement and growing older. Featured stories included a group of 55- to 75-year-old manual labourers at a National Park, a 69-year-old retired surgeon who volunteered in a clinic instead of giving up work and an 80-year-old who, like Warren Schmidt, spends his retirement travelling the country in his RV.[50]

The two images presented by Nicholson seemingly reiterate the male masks of aging: the youthful exterior let down by aging bodily organs in *Something's Gotta Give* and the aging exterior trapping the inner child in *About Schmidt*. In both films, aging is presented as loss – of physical features, social characteristics, personality traits and emotions. Yet in foregrounding aging as a process, both films also call attention to cultural fears around aging and the effects of aging on male identity. As a result of his boomer ties, Nicholson has direct links to the social discourse on aging in America during the 1990s and 2000s and it is ultimately the casting of Nicholson in both roles that has the most significant impact on the imaging of aging offered by these films. As the observations from film reviewers and social commentators demonstrate, in the 2000s, as in the 1960s, 1970s and 1980s, Nicholson has become a cinematic spokesperson for the baby boomers, playing out their concerns and realities. By drawing attention to processes of aging, Nicholson's performances demonstrate a self-consciousness that presents old age as a viable social category, rather than relegating it to the margins. Moreover, Nicholson revitalises aging precisely *because* of his youthful persona – 'Jack' – the very antithesis of getting old. Through his strong ties with the baby boom generation, Nicholson is able to present aging as decline, but still retain an element of youthfulness that undermines the more negative associations of growing old. Older audiences may well identify with *About Schmidt* and *Something's Gotta Give* because they address aging issues but also, and most importantly, because Jack Nicholson is the performer.

Conclusion: Returns, Renewals, Departures

Through the actor and film case studies examined in this book, 'male angst' is presented as a performance on two levels. First, angst is revealed as a frown, a concave expression, sad eyes, trembling hands, or a contorted face: a gesture, a series of movements, a sequence of sounds. Second, angst is evident as the breakdown of 'male' social roles: the failure to be a 'traditional' father and the necessary revision of the father image; the acknowledgement that men can be both 'hard' and 'soft'; or the realisation that the aging process calls for a reassessment of what it means to be a man. The chapters examine the performative nature of male identity by exploring the images and enactments of male angst that have frequently appeared in American films in the last two decades. The book not only considers the ways in which male instability has been performed both on and off screen but also reveals the constructedness of normative masculinity – itself an image consolidated and disseminated by the media. Overall, this book problematises notions of a quintessential 'crisis of masculinity' as epitomised by a select handful of actors or encapsulated by a specific film. Instead, the films and actors I discuss offer a miscellany of performance styles and demonstrate multiple tropes of male angst.

Throughout, the book 'performance' has been considered in three main ways. First, performance describes the overall presentation of actions, whether via a film in a variety of contexts, an appearance on a talk show, or the delivery of a political statement to an audience. Second, performance refers to specific enactments, the methods used to present a character, the sign vehicles, physical and vocal gestures employed to create meaning. Finally, I have considered performance as a gendered enactment, perceiving masculinity as that which is put on – a social role that is informed by cultural expectations. All three elements highlight the need to contextualise performances, locating them in social, cultural and historical terms, in order to make sense of the actions presented. The chapters illustrate how on-screen performances of male instability not only reflect the social and cultural moment in which they are situated but also feed back into the discourse, becoming part of the mediated process through which understandings of gendered identity are constructed.

Andrew Klevan has argued that it is only in the detailed investigation of select sequences in films that real meaning can be revealed. 'Concentrating on a sequence or a succession of sequences from each film', he observes, 'directs our attention to the moment-by-moment development of the performances', and he argues that a comprehensive analysis of sequences 'brings out the relationship between appreciating a performance and understanding a film's meaning as it develops'.[1] Yet this intensive and highly subjective approach does little to reveal the cultural significance of performance. Criticising James Naremore's analysis for its attempts to contextualise gestures and movements in relation to the cultural moment in which they take place, Klevan argues that such an approach 'fails to illuminate the significance of a whole film' and that Naremore's study is, in fact, *'restricted* by context'.[2] To watch Bill Murray's face or listen to William H. Macy's voice in isolation, without regard for the decade in which they are located, the social discourses circulating at that particular moment, the persona that has been constructed by the actor and his films, or the news headlines circulating at that point in time, is to ignore the role of performance in the wider culture. It is only by placing the performances in relation to these various elements that meaning can be attributed to an actor or film. Contextualising performance in this way – considering performances in relation to processes of reception and consumption and examining how they are received and how they have been discussed – limits the inevitable subjectivity of gestural interpretation. Furthermore, it is highly likely that fifty years from now, or in another culture, Murray's face and Macy's voice would be read differently; performance codes of the future, or another culture may indicate a different emotion to 'angst', a possibility that Klevan, writing in 2005 about screen performances of the 1950s, fails to acknowledge. He concludes by asserting that 'Understandings of performance emerge simultaneously during an account of what happens *on the screen*'.[3] This book, on the other hand, recognises the cinema screen as only the starting point in understanding performance.

The films and actors discussed in the book problematise the proposition that male power operates according to cycles of crisis and resolution, emphasising crisis over resolution or wholly denying the possibility of stability. At the end of *About Schmidt*, for example, it is implied that Schmidt has decided to take responsibility for himself and 'grow up'. Yet Schmidt's unreliable narration throughout the film – making repeated claims for change that he fails to follow through – suggests a resolution to his crisis is far from imminent. However, Schmidt *has* learned how to perform; realising the futility of his persistent complaining, he learns to appease his daughter by pretending to accept his new in-laws. Part of the process of Schmidt 'acting his age' involves recognising how a father should perform when giving his daughter away at her wedding, even if the speciousness of his performance is clearly perceptible.

Similarly unresolved, in *Lost in Translation* Bob Harris returns home, leaving Charlotte in Tokyo and their blossoming romance unconsummated, to resume his life as a father who forgets his children's birthdays, puts his work commitments before his family and remains detached from his wife. Bob's trivial attempts to change – requesting 'light meals' at home instead of takeaways – are too inconsequential to suggest his identity crisis will be resolved any time in the near future. In *Broken Flowers*, after his unsuccessful attempts to find his son, Don Johnston returns to the solitude of his sofa, no closer to revealing the identity of the person who sent him the letter informing him he is a father. A close-up of a bunch of wilted roses underscores his inability to take care of himself, not to mention a dependent. The ending of *Magnolia* offers only a provisional solution to Frank Mackey's angst. Cruise's character does finally manage to weep for his father and, in going to meet his stepmother for the first time, the film suggests that Mackey might now be able to forge a 'normal' connection with the opposite sex. But the strength of his misogyny – as displayed in the 'Seduce and Destroy' seminars – undermines the possibility of change. There is no indication that he understands the destructive nature of his misogynistic identity, and no way to tell whether he will now attempt to adapt or reject this restrictive personality.

Even in the films that offer a more tangible resolution to the men's crises, the possibility of a re-stabilised, normative masculinity remains ambiguous. *Pleasantville*'s George Parker, who has defined himself in relation to his homemaker wife, faces an uncertain future after she leaves. In *Far from Heaven*, Frank Whitaker's new identity as a divorced homosexual no longer fits the 'family man' image promoted by Magnatech. Chris Gardner's work success in *The Pursuit of Happyness* may mean he is able to provide for his son financially, but he must do so as a single father, independently juggling his work and family commitments. Even *John Q.*'s 'happy ending', which sees John Archibald's son restored to good health, masks the fact that John's actions have not solved the other difficulties he and his family encountered prior to Mike's illness, specifically John's underemployment and insufficient health insurance. In each case, the new departures the male protagonists make call for them to reassess their previously held notions of male identity and force them to adapt.[4]

Many of the actors discussed have continued to play angst-ridden characters in Hollywood, underscoring the importance of considering screen persona alongside screen performance. In *Edmond* (2005), the film version of David Mamet's stage play, the eponymous protagonist is again played by William H. Macy who builds on John's verbal and physical implosion in *Oleanna*. Macy portrays a nervy businessman who, after being told by a tarot card reader 'You are not where you belong', leaves his wife and viciously murders a young waitress after they have sex. In *The Bucket List* (2007), cancer patients Jack Nicholson and Morgan Freeman refuse to equate aging with decay and deterioration by doing all the things they wished they had done in their youth. The conclusion sees Nicholson's womanising character decide to 'act his age' and attempt to rebuild his relationship with his estranged daughter. In May 2008, the importance of family values, and the father as role model, once again became a contested topic of debate in Hollywood, when Bill Murray's wife and the mother of four of his children filed for divorce, citing abusive behaviour, adultery, family abandonment and drug addiction. Days later on *The Ellen DeGeneres Show*, Will Smith's performance of responsible fatherhood in *The Pursuit of Happyness* extended past the cinematic stage when he emphasised the importance of the two-parent family unit, stating that for him and wife Jada Pinkett Smith, 'Divorce is not an option'. In each case, the performance of male angst – as both physical expression and social role – involves more than an isolated screen performance and blurs the line between person and persona, actor and character.

Referring to the complex and ambiguous nature of performance signs and the differing ways the term has been adopted by a variety of academic disciplines, Marvin Carlson has argued that 'performance by its nature resists conclusions'.[5] Indeed, the boundaries of performance appear to be limitless, crossing multiple media platforms, genres, actors, and personalities. However, there is also much to gain by considering films and actors in terms of performance, that is, in conceiving performance as a multifaceted idiom comprised of discrete yet interrelated elements. Performance, as I have shown, can be a style, a gendered act, a social action, with or without intention, practice or repetition, enmeshed in the fabric of the wider culture, not separate from it. This book establishes that meaning is most fully realised when taking into account the complex and often contradictory network of factors affecting performance, presenting 'performance' as much more than a sequence of gestures and sounds.

In focussing on specific performances of male angst, the film and actor case studies presented here not only comment on socio-cultural discourses of 'masculinity crisis' circulating during the 1990s and 2000s but also have significant implications for images of masculinity in general and the production and diffusion of notions of 'maleness' in American culture. Images of angst-ridden men immediately challenge the idea of a 'true' masculinity (Butler) or 'dominant masculine' (Buchbinder), no more so than when their narratives fail to be resolved or, if resolved, fail to re-establish gender binaries that reinforce male power and domination. Furthermore, the 'unmasked' men examined here exhibit the damaging effect of a 'true' masculinity and imply that it is only in attaining a particular standard of maleness that they can be considered successful 'men'. Their failure to achieve such a standard can be seen as the crux of their downfall; the men who realise the myth of 'true' masculinity move closer to rejecting the restrictive model to which they aspire. The actors and films examined here ultimately demonstrate that it is in the performances of male angst that the performance of 'normative' masculinity is most fully realised.

Notes

Introduction: Being a Man

1. J. M. Blanchard (1992) '"Glengarry" hits the screen with the joys of male angst', *The Washington Times*, Arts (27 September), D1.
2. A. Solomon-Godeau (1997) *Male Trouble: A Crisis in Representation* (London: Thames and Hudson), p. 35; T. Modleski (1991) *Feminism Without Women: Culture and Criticism in a 'Postfeminist' Age* (New York: Routledge), p. 7.
3. M. Kimmel (1987) 'The Contemporary "Crisis" of Masculinity in Historical Perspective' in H. Brod (ed.) *The Making of Masculinities: The New Men's Studies* (Boston, MA: Unwin and Hyman), pp. 121–53.
4. S. Faludi (1991) *Backlash: The Undeclared War Against Women* (London: Chatto and Windus), p. 9.
5. S. Faludi (1999) *Stiffed: The Betrayal of the Modern Man* (London: Chatto and Windus), p. 10.
6. Faludi, *Stiffed*, pp. 38–9.
7. Faludi, *Stiffed*, p. 608.
8. The example of prominent profeminist-turned-promale author Warren Farrell is also a case in point. See W. Farrell (1978) *The Liberated Man. Beyond Masculinity: Freeing Men and Their Relationship With Women* (New York: Bantam); and W. Farrell (1993) *The Myth of Male Power* (New York: Simon and Schuster).
9. The broad and interdisciplinary field of whiteness studies is comprised of works such as D. Roediger (1994) *Towards the Abolition of Whiteness: Essays on Race, Class and Politics* (New York: Verso) and bell hooks (1992) *Black Looks: Race and Representation* (London: Turnaround), pp. 165–78 in particular. See also, R. Frankenberg (1993) *White Women, Race Matters: The Social Construction of Whiteness* (New York: Routledge) and T. Morrison (1993) *Playing in the Dark: Whiteness and the Literary Imagination* (London: Pan).
10. S. Robinson (2000) *Marked Men: White Masculinity in Crisis* (New York: Columbia University Press), pp. 2–3.
11. Robinson, *Marked Men*, pp. 10–11.
12. See A. Wierzbicka (1999) *Emotions Across Languages and Cultures* (Cambridge: Cambridge University Press).
13. C. K. Bellinger (2001) *The Genealogy of Violence: Reflections on Creation, Freedom, and Evil* (Oxford: Oxford University Press), p. 38.
14. Wierzbicka, *Emotions Across Languages and Cultures*, p. 127.
15. S. Cohan (1997) *Masked Men: Masculinity and the Movies in the Fifties* (Bloomington, IN: Indiana University Press); D. Bingham (1994) *Acting Male: Masculinities in the Films of James Stewart, Jack Nicholson and Clint Eastwood* (New Brunswick, NJ: Rutgers University Press); R. Sklar (1992)

City Boys: Cagney, Bogart, Garfield (Princeton, NJ: Princeton University Press).

16. B. Malin (2005) *American Masculinity under Clinton: Popular Media and the Nineties 'Crisis of Masculinity'* (New York: Peter Lang); P. Gates (2006) *Detecting Men: Masculinity and the Hollywood Detective Film* (New York: State University of New York Press); P. Powrie, A. Davis and B. Babington (eds) (2004) *The Trouble with Men: Masculinities in European and Hollywood Cinema* (London: Wallflower Press); P. Lehman (ed.) (2001) *Masculinity: Bodies, Movies, Culture* (London and New York: Routledge); A. Klevan (2005) *Film Performance: From Achievement to Appreciation* (London: Wallflower Press); K. Hollinger (2006) *The Actress: Hollywood Acting and the Female Star* (London and New York: Routledge).

17. B. King (1985) 'Articulating Stardom', *Screen*, 26 (5), 31.

18. V. Turner (1982) *From Ritual to Theatre: The Human Seriousness of Play* (New York: PAJ Publications), p. 122.

19. See G. Studlar (2001) 'Cruise-ing into the Millennium: Performative Masculinity, Stardom, and the All-American Boy's Body' in M. Pomerance (ed.) *Ladies and Gentlemen, Boys and Girls: Gender in Film at the End of the Twentieth Century* (New York: State University of New York Press), p. 176.

20. P. Drake (2006) 'Reconceptualizing Screen Performance', special issue on Screen Performance, *Journal of Film and Video*, 58 (1–2) (Spring/Summer), 93.

21. N. Gabler (1998) *Life: The Movie: How Entertainment Conquered Reality* (New York: Vintage), p. 5.

22. J. Naremore (1990) *Acting in the Cinema* (Berkeley, CA: University of California Press), pp. 5–6.

1   Performance and Masculinity

1. M. Carlson (1996) *Performance: A Critical Introduction* (London: Routledge), p. 2.

2. Carlson, *Performance*, p. 4.

3. R. Bauman (1977) *Verbal Art as Performance* (Rowley, MA: Newbury House), p. 4.

4. H. Bial (2007) 'What is Performance?' in H. Bial (ed.) *The Performance Studies Reader*, Second Edition (Abingdon: Routledge), p. 57.

5. R. Schechner (2007) 'Performance Studies: The Broad Spectrum Approach' in Bial (ed.) *The Performance Studies Reader*, Second Edition (Abingdon: Routledge), pp. 7–9. See also, B. Kirschenblatt-Gimblett (2007) 'Performance Studies' in Bial (ed.) *The Performance Studies Reader*, Second Edition (Abingdon: Routledge), pp. 26–31.

6. E. Goffman (1959) *The Presentation of Self in Everyday Life* (New York: Anchor), p. 81.

7. Goffman, *The Presentation of Self in Everyday Life*, p. 32.

8. Goffman, *The Presentation of Self in Everyday Life*, pp. 32–4, 59.

9. Goffman, *The Presentation of Self in Everyday Life*, pp. 37–8.

10. See R. Dyer (1993) 'The Role of Stereotypes' in *The Matter of Images: Essays on Representation* (London: Routledge), pp. 11–18.
11. Bauman, *Verbal Art as Performance*, p. 31.
12. J. Naremore (1990) *Acting in the Cinema* (Berkeley, CA: University of California Press), p. 70.
13. See P. R. Wojcik (2004) 'Typecasting' in Wojcik (ed.) *Movie Acting: The Film Reader* (New York: Routledge), pp. 169–90.
14. For a discussion of Pacino's destabilised identity in *Cruising* see, G. Davidson (2005) '"Contagious Relations": Simulation, Paranoia, and the Postmodern Condition in William Friedkin's *Cruising* and Felice Picano's *The Lure*', *GLQ: A Journal of Lesbian and Gay Studies* 11(1), 23–64.
15. Goffman, *The Presentation of Self in Everyday Life*, p. 77.
16. R. Schechner (2006) *Performance Studies*, Second Edition (New York: Routledge), p. 43.
17. V. Turner (1982) *From Ritual to Theatre: The Human Seriousness of Play* (New York: PAJ Publications), p. 122.
18. M. Kirby (1972) 'On Acting and Not Acting', *The Drama Review* 16(1) (March), 3–15.
19. Goffman, *The Presentation of Self in Everyday Life*, p. 34.
20. Passing refers to the process whereby a person of one identity (most often applied to race, sexuality and religion), takes on or acts out a different identity or, as M. C. Sanchez and L. Schlossberg describe, 'passing for what you are not'. M. C. Sanchez and L. Schlossberg (2001) *Passing: Identity and Interpretation in Sexuality, Race and Religion* (New York: New York University Press). See also E. K. Ginsberg (ed.) (1996) *Passing and the Fictions of Identity* (Durham, NC: Duke University Press); G. Wald (2000) *Crossing the Line: Racial Passing in Twentieth Century US Literature and Culture* (Durham, NC: Duke University Press).
21. J. Butler (1990) *Gender Trouble: Feminism and the Subversion of Identity* (New York: Routledge), pp. 173, 176; J. L. Austin (1955) 'How To Do Things With Words', The William James Lectures, Harvard University, reprinted in J. O. Urmson and M. Sbisà (eds) (1962) *How To Do Things With Words: J. L. Austin* (Cambridge, MA: Harvard University Press). Butler's consideration of gender performativity is central to a position taken by a number of feminist critics including Marjorie Garber and Eve Kosofsky Sedgwick. See M. Garber (1992) *Vested Interests: Cross-Dressing and Cultural Anxiety* (New York: Routledge); E. K. Sedgwick (1990) *Epistemology of the Closet* (Berkeley and Los Angeles: University of California Press); E. K. Sedgwick and Andrew Parker (eds) (1995) *Performativity and Performance* (New York: Routledge).
22. Butler, *Gender Trouble*, pp. 178–9.
23. J. Butler (1999) 'Preface 1999' in *Gender Trouble: Feminism and the Subversion of Identity*, 10th Anniversary Edition (New York: Routledge), p. xxii.
24. Butler, *Gender Trouble*, pp. 173–8.
25. J. Butler (1993) *Bodies that Matter: On the Discursive Limits of 'Sex'* (New York, Routledge), p. 94.
26. Butler, Preface 1999, p. xxiii.

27. T. Modleski (1991) *Feminism Without Women: Culture and Criticism in a 'Postfeminist' Age* (New York: Routledge).
28. Butler, *Gender Trouble*, p. 180.
29. D. Buchbinder (1998) *Performance Anxieties: Re-Producing Masculinity* (St. Leonards, NSW: Allen and Unwin), pp. vii, ix.
30. Buchbinder, *Performance Anxieties*, p. 29.
31. Buchbinder, *Performance Anxieties*, p. 122.
32. S. Robinson (2000) *Marked Men: White Masculinity in Crisis* (New York: Columbia University Press), p. 9.
33. S. Cohan (1997) *Masked Men: Masculinity and the Movies in the Fifties* (Bloomington and Indianapolis: Indiana University Press), p. x.
34. Cohan, *Masked Men*, p. 23.
35. Butler, *Gender Trouble*, p. 175.
36. Cohan, *Masked Men*, p. 33.
37. Naremore, *Acting in the Cinema*, p. 1.
38. P. Drake (2006) 'Reconceptualizing Screen Performance', *Journal of Film and Video* 58 (1–2) (Spring/Summer), 93.
39. B. King (1985) 'Articulating Stardom', *Screen* 26 (5), 27–50; A. Higson (1986) 'Film Acting and Independent Cinema', *Screen* 27 (3), 110–32; Naremore, *Acting in the Cinema*; R. Pearson (1992) *Eloquent Gestures: The Transformation of Performance Style in the Griffith Biograph Films* (Berkeley, CA: California University Press); V. W. Wexman (1993) *Creating the Couple: Love, Marriage, and Hollywood Performance* (Princeton, NJ: Princeton University Press); P. Krämer and A. Lovell (eds) (1999) *Screen Acting* (London and New York: Routledge); C. Baron, D. Carson and F. P. Tomasulo (eds) (2004) *More Than a Method: Trends and Traditions in Contemporary Film Performance* (Detroit, MI: Wayne State University Press).
40. P. Krämer and A. Lovell (1999) 'Introduction' in Krämer and Lovell (eds) *Screen Acting*, p. 4.
41. C. Geraghty (2000) 'Re-Examining Stardom: Questions of Texts, Bodies and Performance' in Christine Gledhill and Linda Williams (eds) *Reinventing Film Studies* (London: Arnold), pp. 187–195.
42. Geraghty, 'Re-Examining Stardom', p. 195.
43. R. Dyer (1979) *Stars* (London: British Film Institute), p. 134.
44. P. R. Wojcik (2006) 'The Sound of Film Acting', *Journal of Film and Video* 58 (1–2) (Spring/Summer), 73.
45. Cited in S. Prince and W. E. Hensley (1992) 'The Kuleshov Effect: Recreating the Classic Experiment', *Cinema Journal* 31 (2) (Winter), 59.
46. Prince and Hensley, The Kuleshov Effect, 73.
47. C. Baron (2007) 'Acting Choices/Filmic Choices: Rethinking Montage and Performance', *Journal of Film and Video* 59 (2) (Summer), 32. Emphasis added.
48. Dyer, *Stars*, pp. 119–20.
49. L. Stern and G. Kouvaros (eds) (1999) *Falling for You: Essays on Cinema and Performance* (Sydney: Power Publications), p. 5.
50. P. McDonald (2004) 'Why Study Film Acting? Some Opening Reflections' in C. Baron, D. Carson and F. Tomasulo (eds) *More Than a Method: Trends*

and Traditions in Contemporary Film Performance (Detroit: Wayne State University Press), pp. 39–40, 32.

51. A. Klevan (2005) *Film Performance: From Achievement to Appreciation* (London: Wallflower), p. 7.

52. F. Hirsch (1991) *Acting Hollywood Style* (New York: Harry N. Abrams Publishers/AFI Press), p. 12.

53. J. O. Thompson (1978) 'Screen Acting and the Commutation Test', *Screen* 19 (2), 55.

54. R. E. Pearson (1999) 'A Star Performs: Mr March, Mr Mason and Mr Maine' in P. Krämer and A. Lovell (eds) *Screen Acting* (London: Routledge), pp. 59–74; McDonald, Why Study Film Acting? pp. 26–32.

55. McDonald, Why Study Film Acting? p. 27; Pearson, A Star Performs, 72–3.

56. Wexman, *Creating the Couple*, pp. 20–1.

57. Pearson, *Eloquent Gestures*, p. 43.

58. For a discussion of how such techniques impact on and work with film noir performance, see D. Peberdy (2013) 'Acting and Performance in Film Noir' forthcoming in H. Hanson and A. Spicer (eds) *The Blackwell Companion to Film Noir* (Oxford: Blackwell).

59. King, Articulating Stardom, 45.

60. King, Articulating Stardom, 44.

61. Higson, Film Acting and Independent Cinema, 121.

62. Higson, Film Acting and Independent Cinema, 113.

63. J. M. Blanchard (1992) '"Glengarry" hits the screens with the joys of male angst', *The Washington Times*, Arts (27 September), D1.

64. A selection of the photographs are available at: http://www.vanityfair.com/culture/features/2006/05/actorsacting_portfolio200605#intro, date accessed July 2010.

65. http://www.vanityfair.com/culture/features/incharacter-slideshow#slide=19, date accessed July 2010.

66. http://www.vanityfair.com/culture/features/2006/05/actorsacting_portfolio200605#slide=5, date accessed July 2010.

67. Klevan, *Film Performance*, p. 103.

68. Pearson, *Eloquent Gestures*, p. 16.

69. Turner, *From Ritual to Theatre*, p. 108.

70. S. Cavell (2004) 'Reflections on the Ontology of Film' reprinted in Wojcik (ed.) *Movie Acting: The Film Reader* (Routledge: London and New York), p. 31.

2 Performing Angst

1. A. Klevan (2005) *Film Performance: From Achievement to Appreciation* (London: Wallflower), p. ii, 7; see also C. Affron (1977) *Star Acting: Gish, Garbo, Davis* (New York: E. P. Dutton), p. 7.

2. P. McDonald (2004) 'Why Study Film Acting?: Some Opening Reflections' in C. Baron, D. Carson and F. Tomasulo (eds) *More Than a Method: Trends*

and Traditions in Contemporary Film Performance (Detroit: Wayne State University Press), p. 32.

3. J. Naremore (1990) *Acting in the Cinema* (Berkeley, CA: University of California Press), p. 4.

4. L. R. Williams (2005) *The Erotic Thriller in Contemporary Cinema* (Edinburgh: Edinburgh University Press), p. 177; M. Kimmel (1996) *Manhood in America: A Cultural History* (New York: Free Press), p. 309; C. Deleyto (1997) 'The Margins of Pleasure: Female Monstrosity and Male Paranoia in *Basic Instinct'*, *Film Criticism*, 21 (3) (Spring), 20.

5. See, for example, J. Davies (1995) 'Gender, Ethnicity and Cultural Crisis in *Falling Down* and *Groundhog Day'*, *Screen*, 36 (3), 214–32; J. Davies (1995) ' "I'm the bad guy?" *Falling Down* and White Masculinity in 1990s Hollywood', *Journal of Gender Studies*, 4 (2), 145–52; D. Savran (1996) 'The Sadomasochist in the Closet: White Masculinity and the Culture of Victimization', *Differences*, 8 (2), 127–52; J. Gabriel (1996) 'What Do You Do When Minority Means You? *Falling Down* and the Construction of "Whiteness"', *Screen*, 37, 129–52.

6. B. Weinraub (1992) 'The talk of Hollywood: A movie of one man's riot exploding from the inside out', *The New York Times* (9 June), C11; A. Harmetz (1993) '*Falling Down* takes its cue from the headlines', *The New York Times* (21 February), 28; M. Eng (1993) 'Shaking things up with *Falling Down*', *Chicago Sun-Times* (21 February), 8; M. LeSalle (1993) 'So what if the movie isn't PC?' *The San Francisco Chronicle* (2 March), E1; K. Honeycutt (1993) ' "Falling" comes under fire: Warners' LA story angers some Koreans, Latinos, defense workers', *The Hollywood Reporter* (2 March); G. Will (1993) ' "Catharsis cinema": audience indulges guilty pleasure', *Seattle Post-Intelligencer* (1 April); R. Reinhold (1993) 'Horror for Hollywood: film hits a nerve with its grim view of Hometown', *The New York Times* (29 March), A11.

7. S. Saroyan (2004) 'Douglas on Douglas', *Daily Variety*, special section (9 January), 34; H. Hinson (1993) 'Falling Down: the last straw', *The Washington Post*, Style (26 February), C1; P. Green (1998) *Cracks in the Pedestal: Ideology and Gender in Hollywood* (Amherst, MA: University of Massachusetts Press), p. 195.

8. Y. Tasker (1998) *Working Girls: Gender and Sexuality in Popular Cinema* (London: Routledge), p. 132.

9. Davies, Gender, Ethnicity and Cultural Crisis, 216; Williams, *The Erotic Thriller in Contemporary Cinema*, p. 194.

10. B. King (2003) 'Embodying an Elastic Self', in T. Austin and M. Barker (eds) *Contemporary Hollywood Stardom* (Oxford: Hodder and Arnold), p. 47.

11. In *The Game*, CRS (a company that creates real-life games for wealthy patrons) is ultimately the source of manipulation.

12. Davies, Gender, Ethnicity and Cultural Crisis, 216.

13. C. James (1993) 'Using one's head: the bad haircut as star turn', *The New York Times* (21 March); M. Fine (1993) 'Buzzcut sends Michael Douglas "Falling Down"', *Chicago Sun-Times* (7 March).

14. P. Keough (2000) 'Boys don't try: Curtis Hanson wanders far from LA', *The Boston Phoenix* (24 February), emphasis added; A. O'Hehir (2000) 'Wonder Boys', *The Salon* (25 February).
15. Naremore, *Acting in the Cinema*, p. 14.
16. J. Ellis (1992) 'Stars as Cinematic Phenomenon' in *Visible Fictions: Cinema, Television, Fiction* (London: Routledge), p. 104. Emphasis added.
17. F. Pfeil (1995) *White Guys: Studies in Postmodern Domination and Difference* (New York: Verso), pp. 239–40.
18. P. Gormley (2005) *The New-Brutality Film: Race and Affect in Contemporary Hollywood Cinema* (Bristol: Intellect), p. 45. See also Davies, Gender, Ethnicity and Cultural Crisis, 217; C. Clover (1993) 'White Noise', *Sight and Sound* (May), 6–9.
19. M. A. Doane (2003) 'The Close-Up: Scale and Detail in the Cinema', *Differences: A Journal of Feminist Cultural Studies*, 14 (3), 93.
20. C. Baron (2007) 'Acting Choices/Filmic Choices: Rethinking Montage and Performance', *Journal of Film and Video*, 59 (2) (Summer), 32.
21. E. Goffman (1981) *Forms of Talk* (Philadelphia: University of Pennsylvania Press).
22. A. Higson (1986) 'Film Acting and Independent Cinema', *Screen*, 27 (3–4), 116.
23. Higson, Film Acting and Independent Cinema, 113.
24. Naremore, *Acting in the Cinema*, pp. 83–8.
25. Quoted in *Movieline* (December 2000/January 2001).
26. A. McKay (2003) '*The In-Laws*', *The Scotsman* (10 July), 18; W. Morris (2000) 'A graceful "Wonder"', *San Francisco Examiner* (25 February), C1.
27. 'Remembering Fatal Attraction' documentary, *Fatal Attraction* (1987), Paramount Pictures, 2002 DVD.
28. B. King (1985) 'Articulating Stardom', *Screen* 26 (5), 30.
29. Ellis, Stars as Cinematic Phenomenon, 91. The paradoxical function of the ordinary and extraordinary in relation to stardom has been well documented, developed more recently in the burgeoning field of research around television stardom and celebrity. See S. Holmes (2004) ' "All you've got to worry about is the task, having a cup of tea, and doing a bit of sunbathing": Approaching Celebrity in *Big Brother*' in S. Holmes and S. Redmond (eds) *Understanding Reality Television* (London: Routledge), pp. 111–35; J. Corner (2002) 'Performing the Real: Documentary Diversions', *Television & New Media*, 3 (3), 255–69.
30. Despite categorically denying his ex-wife's claims, stating that he was being treated at the clinic for an alcohol dependency problem, Douglas is still widely referred to as a 'self-confessed sex addict' reinforcing the power of celebrity gossip in determining star identity.
31. M. Fine (2000) 'Douglas' real story imitated *Wonder Boys* elements' (*The Seattle Times*, 25 February). Elsewhere, Douglas has made a distinction between his 'Prince of Darkness' roles (*Fatal Attraction, Basic Instinct, Disclosure*) and 'quirk' films (*Falling Down* and *Wonder Boys*), also including *The War of the Roses* (1989) in the latter category. C. Rickey (2000) 'Wonderful Mr Douglas' *The Advertiser* (20 July).

32. J. Naremore (1984) 'Film and the Performance Frame', *Film Quarterly*, 38 (2) (Winter), 8–15.

33. W. Arnold (2004) 'Bill Murray's deadpan shtick keeps this goofy ship from sinking', *Seattle Post-Intelligencer* (24 December), 23; H. Barlow (2005) 'Midlife crisis? I have crises all the time', *The Advertiser*, Magazine (17 December), W22; J. Tyrangiel (2005) 'The many faces of Bill', *Time*, 165 (2) (3 January).

34. J. Senior (2006) 'Can't get no satisfaction', *New York Magazine* (4 December), 26–31; 'What Hollywood doesn't tell you about male menopause; more than just convertibles and younger women' (2005) *Business Wire* (21 September). At Cannes Film Festival a reporter asked Murray if he could 'relate to playing a man in a midlife crisis?' Murray's reply blurred the boundary between person and persona: 'I'm just getting to my midlife crisis, ma'am, so stick around. But I have crises all the time, not how long I've been living, but the type of life I've been living. It's been a real problem.'

35. King, Articulating Stardom, 31.

36. See Jonathan Gray's excellent study of the significance of paratexts in film, television and 'off-screen studies' in J. Gray (2010) *Show Sold Separately: Promos, Spoilers and Other Media Paratexts* (New York: New York University Press).

37. S. Cohan (1997) *Masked Men: Masculinity and the Movies in the Fifties* (Bloomington and Indianapolis: Indiana University Press), p. 1.

38. Cohan, *Masked Men*, p. 4.

39. A. Sarris (2003) 'Lonely souls in a strange land: *Lost in Translation* maps the way', *New York Observer* (28 September), 29.

40. J. Winter (2004) 'The Tao of Bill', *The Village Voice* (30 March), 1; G. Seymour (2005) 'The evolution of Bill Murray', *Newsday* (22 August).

41. R. Dyer (1979) *Stars* (London: British Film Institute), p. 98. 'In a role unlike anything he's ever done before', the theatrical trailer asserted, *The Razor's Edge* made back just half of its production budget in box-office receipts.

42. H. Hinson (1993) 'Groundhog Day: Bill Murray burrows into Foreverland', *The Washington Post* (12 February), C1.

43. Winter, The Tao of Bill, 1.

44. L. Hirschberg (1999) 'Bill Murray: in all seriousness', *The New York Times Magazine* (31 January), 18.

45. L. Hirschberg (2005) 'The last of the indies', *The New York Times*, Magazine (31 July), 18.

46. R. Ebert (2005) 'A big stir about three quiet films and journeys', *Chicago Sun-Times*, Features (18 May), 75. Emphasis added.

47. M. Kirby (1972) 'On Acting and Not Acting', *The Drama Review*, 16 (1) (March), 5.

48. G. King (2010) *Lost in Translation* (Edinburgh: Edinburgh University Press), pp. 31–47.

49. Higson, Film Acting and Independent Cinema, p. 153.

50. Murray, quoted in Barlow, Midlife crisis? I have crises all the time, W22.

51. Murray, quoted in J. Stone (2005) 'Murray's soul: the star of Broken Flowers on unanswered questions, his family life and what's next', *The Vancouver Sun*, Arts and Life (12 August), H1.
52. E. Porter (2005) 'Master of the minimal', *The Sunday Times*, Culture (23 October), 11; Winter, The Tao of Bill, 1; C. Rickey (2005) 'Broken Flowers', *Philadelphia Enquirer* (5 August), W04; A. O. Scott (2003) 'Murray's art of losing', *The New York Times* (14 September), 1.
53. Doane, The Close-Up, 94, 96.
54. J. Staiger (1985) ' "The eyes are really the focus": Photoplay Acting and Film Form and Style', *Wide Angle*, 6 (4), 20.
55. L. Shaffer (1977) 'Reflections on the Face in Film', *Film Quarterly*, 31 (2) (Winter), 3, 5; R. Barthes (1972) 'The Face of Garbo' in *Mythologies*, trans. Annette Lavers (New York: Hill and Wang), pp. 56–7.
56. As Tom Gunning has observed, physiognomy has a long and complex history. On the one hand, physiognomy means the science of facial classification that has evolved from a form of divination derived from Aristotle and Pythagoras who linked the composition of the face to cosmic inner being, to comparisons with animals, to the study of the face as the aesthetic signification of character. Here, I use 'physiognomy' according to its simpler definition: as a person's specific facial composition or typography. See T. Gunning (1997) 'In Your Face: Physiognomy, Photography and the Gnostic Mission in Early Sound Film', *Modernism/ Modernity*, 4 (1), 1–29.
57. C. Aubert (2003 [1851]) *The Art of Pantomime*, trans. Edith Sears (Mineola, NY: Dover Publications), pp. 58–77. See Naremore, *Acting in the Cinema*, pp. 56–60 for a critique of the problems with Aubert's approach.
58. Reprinted in E. V. Demos (ed.) (1995) *Exploring Affect: The Selected Writings of Silvan S. Tomkins* (Cambridge: Cambridge University Press), pp. 218–91. See also S. Tomkins (1963) *Affect, Imagery, Consciousness: The Positive Affects (Vol. I)* (New York: Springer) and *Affect, Imagery, Consciousness: The Negative Affects (Vol. III)* (New York: Springer).
59. King, Articulating Stardom, 41.
60. C. Fitzgerald (2004) 'The top 10 ways to take Bill Murray home with you', *The Austin Chronicle* (2 January); S. Watson (2004) 'Lust is blind', *The Sunday Times*, Style (28 March), 58.
61. K. Turan (2003) 'Lost in Translation', *Los Angeles Times* (12 September).
62. P. Travers (2005) 'Broken Flowers', *Rolling Stone* (22 July).
63. C. Bishop (1958) 'The Great Stone Face', *Film Quarterly* 12 (1) (Autumn), 10; G. Pearce (2005) 'Old stone face cracks', *The Guardian*, Weekend (22 October), 91–4.
64. Ebert, A big stir about three quiet films and journeys, 75; Scott, Murray's art of losing, 1.
65. R. Corliss (2003) 'A victory for lonely hearts', *Time* (8 September).
66. Wes Anderson commenting on Murray's performance in *Rushmore*, quoted in M. Bertin (1998) 'Academy leader', *The Austin Chronicle* 18 (23) (8 February). Anderson went on to direct Murray in *The Royal Tenenbaums, The Life Aquatic with Steve Zissou* and *The Darjeeling Limited* (2007).

67. J. Sconce (2002) 'Irony, Nihilism and the New American "Smart" Film', *Screen*, 43 (4) (Winter), 351.
68. Anon (2005) 'Bill Murray', *The Times* (13 February).
69. D. Bordwell (2002) 'Intensified Continuity: Visual Style in Contemporary American Film', *Film Quarterly*, 55 (3), 21.
70. Sconce, Irony, Nihilism and the New American 'Smart' Film, 364.
71. R. Pearson (1992) *Eloquent Gestures: The Transformation of Performance Style in the Griffith Biograph Films* (Berkeley, CA: California University Press), p. 9.
72. See V. W. Wexman (2004) 'Masculinity in Crisis: Method Acting in Hollywood' in P. R. Wojcik (ed.) *Movie Acting: The Film Reader* (London and New York: Routledge), pp. 127–44.
73. M. A. Doane (1980) 'The Voice in the Cinema: The Articulation of Body and Space', *Yale French Studies*, 60, Cinema/Sound, 33–50; M. Chion (1999 [1982]) *The Voice in Cinema*, trans. Claudia Gorbman (New York: Columbia University Press). Two notable recent studies include J. Smith (2008) *Vocal Tracks: Performance and Sound Media* (Los Angeles, CA: University of California Press) and S. Smith (2007) 'Voices in Film' in *Close-Up 02* (London: Wallflower), pp. 159–235.
74. A. Dean (1990) *David Mamet: Language as Dramatic Action* (London and Toronto: Associated University Presses), p. 15. Emphasis added.
75. R. Bechtel (1996) 'PC Power Play: Language and Representation in David Mamet's *Oleanna*', *Theatre Studies*, 41, 29–48; Dean, *David Mamet: Language as Dramatic Action*; P. McDonald (1998) 'The 'Unmanning' Word: Language, Masculinity and Political Correctness in the Work of David Mamet and Philip Roth', *Journal of American Studies of Turkey*, 7, 23–30; B. Richardson (2001) 'Voice and Narration in Postmodern Drama', *New Literary History*, 32, 681–94; T. S. Zinman (1992) 'Jewish Aporia: The Rhythm of Talking in Mamet', *Theatre Journal*, 44 (2), American Scenes, 207–15; B. Murphy (2004) '*Oleanna*: Language and Power' in C. Bigsby (ed.) *The Cambridge Companion to David Mamet* (Cambridge: Cambridge University Press), pp. 124–37.
76. M. Shingler (2006) 'Fasten Your Seatbelts and Prick Up Your Ears: The Dramatic Human Voice in Film', *Scope: An Online Journal of Film Studies*, 5, Sound: Special Issue (June).
77. G. Sergi (1999) 'Actors and the Sound Gang' in P. Krämer and A. Lovell (eds) *Screen Acting* (London: Routledge), pp. 131–2.
78. Naremore, *Acting in the Cinema*, p. 46.
79. Sergi, Actors and the Sound Gang, pp. 131–2.
80. Chion, *The Voice in Cinema*, p. 166.
81. Chion, *The Voice in Cinema*, p. 166.
82. D. Mamet (1991) *On Directing Film* (New York: Penguin), pp. 70–1, original italics.
83. Other non-fiction works include: *True and False: Heresy and Common Sense for the Actor* (London: Faber and Faber, 1998); *3 Uses of the Knife: On the Nature and Purpose of Drama* (New York: Columbia University Press, 1998); *Make-Believe Town: Essays and Remembrances* (London: Faber and Faber, 1996); *Writing in Restaurants* (New York: Penguin, 1987).

84. D. Mamet (1993) 'Realism' in *Oleanna* (London: Methuen Drama), p. iii. For more on Stanislavsky and theatre acting see J. Martin (1991) *Voice in Modern Theatre* (London and New York: Routledge); Mamet, *On Directing Film*, pp. 70–1, 76.

85. C. McDonough (1997) *Staging Masculinity: Male Identity in Contemporary American Drama* (Jefferson, NC: McFarland), p. 99.

86. I explore the relationship between film and theatre voices in an earlier version of this section. See, D. Peberdy (2007) 'Tongue-tied: Film and Theatre Voices in David Mamet's *Oleanna*', *Screening the Past*, Special Issue: Cinema/Theatre/Adaptation (Spring/Summer).

87. Chion, *The Voice in Cinema*, p. 78.

88. Sergi, Actors and the Sound Gang, p. 130.

89. K. Bean (2001) 'A Few Good Men: Collusion and Violence in Oleanna' in C. Hudgins and L. Kane (eds) *Gender and Genre: Essays on David Mamet* (New York: St. Martin's), pp. 121, 123.

90. Bean, A Few Good Men, p. 120.

91. J. Vallely (1980) 'David Mamet makes a play for Hollywood', *Rolling Stone* (April), 44.

92. Mamet, Realism, p. ii.

93. William H. Macy cited in D. B. Wilmeth (2004) 'Mamet and the Actor' in C. Bigsby (ed.) *The Cambridge Companion to David Mamet* (Cambridge: Cambridge University Press), p. 148.

94. S. Kozloff (2000) *Overhearing Film Dialogue* (Berkeley: University of California Press), p. 44.

95. S. M. Carnicke (2004) 'Screen Performance and Directors' Visions' in C. Baron, D. Carson and F. P. Tomasulo (eds) *More Than a Method: Trends and Traditions in Contemporary Film Performance* (Detroit, MI: Wayne State University Press), p. 63.

96. Cited in J. M. Blanchard (1992) ' "Glengarry" hits the screens with the joys of male angst', *The Washington Times*, Arts (27 September), D1.

97. R. Barthes (1977) 'The Grain of the Voice' in *Image, Music, Text*, trans. Stephen Heath (New York: Hill and Wang).

98. A. Quinn (2000) 'The big picture: Into the valley of the damned', *The Independent* (17 March), 10; C. Isherwood (2000) 'American Buffalo', *Daily Variety* (17 March).

99. For more on the relationship between vocal affectations and masculinity, see D. Peberdy (2013) 'Male Sounds and Speech Affectations: Voicing Masculinity' forthcoming in J. Jaeckle (ed.) *Film Dialogue* (London: Wallflower).

100. See D. Peberdy (2012) 'Acting and Performance in Film Noir' forthcoming in H. Hanson and A. Spicer (eds) *The Blackwell Companion to Film Noir* (Oxford: Blackwell); C. Baron (2010) 'Film Noir: Gesture Under Pressure' in C. Cornea (ed.) *Genre and Performance: Film and Television* (Manchester: Manchester University Press).

101. Doane, The Voice in the Cinema, 49.

102. E. Goffman (1959) *The Presentation of Self in Everyday Life* (New York: Anchor), p. 34.

103. See, for example, H. Jenkins (2006) *Convergence Culture: Where Old and New Media Collide* (New York: New York University Press); J. P. Jones (2004) *Entertaining Politics: New Political Television and Civic Culture* (Lanham, MD: Rowman and Littlefield).
104. V. Turner (1982) *From Ritual to Theatre: The Human Seriousness of Play* (New York: PAJ Publications), p. 122.
105. Dyer, *Stars*, pp. 71–2.

3   From Wimps to Wild Men: Bipolar Masculinity and the Paradoxical Performances of Tom Cruise

1. Bridges' appearance on the *Esquire* cover coincided with the release *The Fisher King* (1991) in which Bridges plays Jack Lucas, a suicidal radio talk show host, who befriends a mentally unstable homeless man Parry (Robin Williams).
2. S. Jeffords (1994) *Hard Bodies: Hollywood Masculinity in the Reagan Era* (New Brunswick, NJ: Rutgers University Press); F. Pfeil (1995) *White Guys: Studies in Postmodern Domination and Difference* (London: Verso).
3. K. L. Ashcraft and L. A. Flores (2003) ' "Slaves with white collars": Persistent Performance of Masculinity in Crisis', *Text and Performance Quarterly* 23 (1) (January), 5.
4. E. Gilbert (2002) *The Last American Man* (New York: Penguin), p. 4.
5. R. Slotkin (1973) *Regeneration through Violence: The Mythology of the American Frontier 1600–1860* (Norman: University of Oklahoma Press); Slotkin (1985) *The Fatal Environment: The Myth of the Frontier in the Age of Industrialization 1800–1890* (New York: Atheneum); Slotkin (1992) *Gunfighter Nation: The Myth of the Frontier in Twentieth Century America* (New York: Atheneum).
6. S. Bliss (1987) 'Revisioning Masculinity', *In Context: A Quarterly of Humane Sustainable Culture*, 16 (Spring), 21.
7. W. Farrell (1993) *The Myth of Male Power* (New York: Simon and Schuster); S. Keen (1992) *Fire in the Belly: On Being a Man* (London: Piatkus).
8. M. Kimmel (1996) 'Wimps, Whiners, and Weekend Warriors: The Contemporary Crisis of Masculinity and Beyond' in *Manhood in America* (New York: The Free Press), p. 321.
9. See, for example, Kimmel (1996) 'Wimps, Whiners and Weekend Warriors'; J. K. Gardiner (2002) 'Theorizing Age with Gender: Bly's Boys, Feminism, and Maturity Masculinity' in Gardiner (ed.) *Masculinity Studies and Feminist Theory: New Directions* (New York: Columbia University Press); K. Clatterbaugh (1990) 'The Mythopoetic Movement: Men in Search of Spiritual Growth', in *Contemporary Perspectives on Masculinity: Men, Women, and Politics in Modern Society* (Oxford: Westview Press).
10. R. Bly (1990) *Iron John: A Book About Men* (Shaftesbury: Element), p. 6.
11. Bly, *Iron John*, p. 21.
12. R. W. Connell (1993) 'The Big Picture: Masculinities in Recent World History', *Theory and Society* 22 (5), Special Issue: Masculinities (October), 619.

13. Bly, *Iron John*, p. x.
14. S. Faludi (1991) *Backlash: The Undeclared War Against Women* (London: Chatto and Windus), p. 345.
15. Jeffords (1994) *Hard Bodies*; Pfeil (1995) *White Guys*; S. Jeffords (1993) 'The Big Switch: Hollywood Masculinity in the Nineties' in J. Collins, H. Radner and A. P. Collins (eds) *Film Theory Goes to the Movies* (London: Routledge); J. Rutherford (1988) 'Who's That Man?' in R. Chapman and J. Rutherford (eds) *Male Order: Unwrapping Masculinity* (London: Lawrence and Wishart).
16. Jeffords, *Hard Bodies*, p. 153; Jeffords, The Big Switch, 198.
17. Pfeil, *White Guys*, pp. 37–70.
18. Rutherford, Who's that Man? pp. 28, 32.
19. K. T. Walsh (1993) 'Clinton's Journey Inward', *US News and World Report*, 115 (23) (13 December), 40. In numerous newspaper cartoons, Clinton was depicted wearing a dress with Hillary Clinton in trousers, although the name-calling subsided after Clinton ordered the missile attack on Iraqi intelligence headquarters in 1993. See also, P. Cockburn (1993) 'Texas bully-girl tactics hand the first round to Clinton's wimp', *The Independent* (2 May), 18; B. Marotte (1993) 'Clinton fights "wimp factor," ' *Vancouver Sun* (28 June), A8; C. Krauthammer (1999) 'Triumph of the wimp', *The Washington Post* (19 February), A23; R. Givhan (2000) 'Voters seek candidate who is fit, sexy, confident: wimps need not apply', *The Washington Post* (4 March), C01.
20. R. W. Connell (1995) *Masculinities* (Cambridge: Polity Press).
21. Y. Tasker (1993) *Spectacular Bodies: Gender, Genre and the Action Cinema* (London: Routledge), p. 129.
22. D. Stanton (1991) 'Inward, Ho!' Wild Men and Wimps: A Special Issue, *Esquire* 116 (4) (October), 113.
23. G. Crowdus (2000) 'Getting exercised over Fight Club', *Cineaste* (22 September).
24. *Fight Club*, dir: David Fincher, Twentieth-Century Fox, 1999.
25. Connell, The Big Picture, 619. Emphasis added.
26. G. J. Broude (1990) 'Protest Masculinity: A Further Look at the Causes and the Concept', *Ethos* 18 (1) (March), 103.
27. R.W. Connell, *Masculinities*, p. 111.
28. G. Studlar (2001) 'Cruise-ing into the Millennium: Performative Masculinity, Stardom, and the All-American Boy's Body' in Murray Pomerance (ed.) *Ladies and Gentlemen, Boys and Girls: Gender in Film at the End of the Twentieth Century* (New York: State University of New York Press), p. 176.
29. Bly, *Iron John*, p. 21.
30. Studlar, Cruise-ing into the Millennium, p. 176.
31. L. Hirschberg (1999) 'His way', *New York Times Magazine* (19 December), 52.
32. C. Puig (2000) ' "Life and love and death" and genius: "dangerous ground" is Paul Thomas Anderson's turf', *USA Today*, Life (7 January), 10E.

33. D. Bingham (2004) 'Kidman, Cruise and Kubrick: A Brechtian Pastiche' in C. Baron, D. Carson and F. P. Tomasulo (eds) *More Than a Method: Trends and Traditions in Contemporary Film Performance* (Detroit: Wayne State University Press), p. 253.
34. J. Hoberman (1999) 'Your show of shows', *Village Voice* (21 December), 143; J. Rosenbaum (1999) 'Magnolia', *Chicago Reader* (3 January).
35. Alec Baldwin on *The Charlie Rose Show*, 11:00PM EST (9 January 2004). Emphasis added.
36. Bingham, Kidman, Cruise and Kubrick, p. 273.
37. S. Smith and J. L. Roberts (2006) 'Risky business: Can Tom Cruise survive a studio snub?' *Newsweek* (4 September), 73. See also K. Smith (2005) 'Crazed Cruise needs PR shock treatment', *The New York Post* (25 May), 45; G. Hernandez (2005) 'Star's popularity may not always be boon at the box office', *Daily News* (3 June); R. Roeper (2005) 'Admit it, you're curious: is Tom Cruise nuts or what?' *Chicago Sun-Times* (7 June), 11; J. Portman (2006) 'Is Cruise out of control? Critics writing with mockery and derision', *Ottawa Citizen* (16 June).
38. S. Smith (2005) 'Celebs: Tom Cruise goes crazy', *Newsweek* (26 December), 34.
39. J. Naremore (1990) *Acting in the Cinema* (Berkeley, CA: University of California Press), p. 220.
40. A further example is Cruise's unconventional response when he was squirted with a water pistol disguised as a microphone by a 'fake' British reporter at the London premiere for *War of the Worlds*. As with 'Oprah', the incident made more news headlines than the film premiere. N. Lampert (2005) 'Cruise loses his cool over soaking in the square', *The Daily Mail* (21 June), 23; S. Brook (2005) 'Cruising for a bruising: actor rounds on water pistol pranksters', *The Guardian* (21 June), 6; S. McKay (2005) 'Call that funny? Don't be so wet', *The Daily Telegraph* (22 June), 015.
41. T. Brown (2005) 'It's only publicity love', *The Washington Post* (26 May).
42. E. Goffman (1959) *The Presentation of Self in Everyday Life* (New York: Anchor), p. 59.
43. P. D. Marshall (1997) *Celebrity and Power: Fame in Contemporary Culture* (Minneapolis, MN: University of Minnesota Press), pp. 105–6.
44. Goffman, *The Presentation of Self in Everyday Life*, p. 60.
45. Allegations of falseness were once again levelled at the actor when Oprah interviewed Cruise in the actor's home in 2008, asking the actor to comment on his strident attacks on psychiatry and anti-depressants. Viewers posted scathing comments on the Oprah.com message boards regarding Cruise's 'fake' performance and criticised Oprah for not sufficiently challenging the actor, thus validating his forged behaviour.
46. The notion of expressive *in*coherence takes on a dual meaning in this regard. Numerous Oprah viewers posted comments on the show's website about the actor's inability to form proper sentences and articulate an argument in his Telluride home interview.

47. G. Gómez-Peña (2007) 'Culturas-in-extremis: Performing Against the Cultural Backdrop of the Mainstream Bizarre' in H. Bial (ed.) *The Performance Studies Reader*, Second Edition (London: Routledge), p. 345.
48. D. Negra and S. Holmes (2008) 'Introduction', *Genders*, 48, special issue: Going Cheap? Female Celebrity in Reality, Tabloid and Scandal Genres, 2.
49. Negra and Holmes, Introduction, 12.

4   Performing Paternity: Clinton, Nostalgia and the Racial Politics of Fatherhood

1. 'The American Family' (2001) *US Society and Values: An Electronic Journal of the US Department of State* 6 (1) (January), 1. http://www.4uth.gov.ua/usa/english/facts/ijse0101/ijse0101.htm accessed February 2007.
2. See for example, S. Waldman (1992) 'Deadbeat dads', *Newsweek*, life/style (4 May), 46; N. J. Easton (1992) 'Life without father', *Los Angeles Times Magazine* (14 June), 14; "America's deadbeat dad" (1992) *The Economist* (15 August), 11; D. Fost (1996) 'The lost art of fatherhood', *American Demographics* (March), 16.
3. D. Blankenhorn (1995) 'Pay, papa, pay: where have all the fathers gone?' *National Review*, 47 (3 April), 34. See also, Blankenhorn (1995) *Fatherless America: Confronting Our Most Urgent Social Problem* (New York: Basic Books); D. Popenoe (1996) *Life Without Father* (New York: Free Press); C. R. Daniels (ed.) (1998) *Lost Fathers: The Politics of Fatherlessness in America* (New York: St. Martin's Press).
4. USA Census Bureau statistics suggest there has been a steady decline in the number of married-couple households with only the husband in employment. Between 1986 and 1998, the percentage of dual-earning couples increased from 59 per cent to 68 per cent. During the same period, families with only the husband in employment declined from 36 per cent to 21 per cent. In 1975, the traditional family (defined as the breadwinner father, at-home mother and children younger than eighteen) constituted 46 per cent of American families. In 1998, this figure had dropped to around 26 per cent. While these statistics indicate a decrease in 'traditional' families – that is, married-couple households where only the husband works (and the wife is, presumably, the homemaker) – the USA Census Bureau do not collect statistics on what percentage of dual-earning couples feature husbands earning more than their wives which would effectively still constitute male breadwinners, though not in the 'traditional' sense. Census Bureau statistics showed a 50 percent increase in full-time fathers from 98,000 in 2003 to 147,000 in 2004, although such statistics exclude unmarried, gay, and single fathers. 'By the numbers' (2001) 'The American family', *US Society and Values: An Electronic Journal of the US Department of State* 6 (1) (January), 8–10.
5. W. J. Clinton (1995) 'On Race Relations; Liz Sutherland Carpenter Distinguished Lectureship in the Humanities and Sciences, University of Texas Austin (16 October).

6. Quayle cited a 20 per cent decrease in the number of black families headed by married couples from 1967 to 1991 and a 37 per cent increase in the illegitimacy rate among black families between 1965 and 1989. Quayle's now infamous speech is better known as the 'Murphy Brown speech' in which Quayle cited the popular prime time television show as evidence of the demise of family values and argued that single-mother Brown was 'mocking the importance of fathers, by bearing a child alone, and calling it just another "lifestyle choice"'. Address to the Commonwealth Club of California (19 May 1992). Full transcript available at http://www.vicepresidentdanquayle.com/speeches_StandingFirm_CCC_1.html accessed March 2008.

7. J. D. Hunter (1991) *Culture Wars: The Struggle to Define America* (New York: Basic Books), pp. 173, 176.

8. W. F. Horn (2000) 'Fathers increasingly devalued in families', *The Washington Times* (4 January), E2.

9. J. Stacey (1996) *In the Name of the Family: Rethinking Family Values in the Postmodern Age* (Boston, MA: Beacon Press); S. Coontz (1992) *The Way We Never Were: American Families and the Nostalgia Trap* (New York: Basic Books); Coontz (1998) *The Way We Really Are: Coming to Terms with America's Changing Families* (New York: Basic Books).

10. S. A. Hewlett and C. West (1998) *The War Against Parents: What Can We Do for America's Beleaguered Moms and Dad* (Boston and New York: Houghton Mifflin), p. 173.

11. Stacey, *In the Name of the Family*, p. 77.

12. In one of the more memorable celebrity commentaries on fatherhood during the 2000s, Bill Cosby made the headlines for his criticism of the problem with fathers in the black community in his address to the National Association for the Advancement of Colored People (NAACP) in 2004 (since referred to as his 'Pound Cake Speech'), almost 20 years after the publication of his best-selling *Fatherhood* (New York: Doubleday, 1986).

13. See for example, T. Brokow (1998) *The Greatest Generation* (New York: Random House). As I discuss in the following chapter, the large cohort that is the baby boomer generation are frequently credited as redefining every decade through which they pass, giving rise to the colourful phrase 'pig in the python' to describe the impact of this demographic bulge on American culture.

14. R. Brownstein (1992) 'Bush and Clinton: cold warrior vs. baby boomer', *The Record* (25 April), A7. Also: S. Piccoli (1993) 'The boomer bomb: some say passing the torch might just light the fuse of a generation grenade', *The Washington Times*, Life (1 March), D1; K. Miller and K Ode (1992) 'BOOMERANGST! Suddenly, baby boomers realize that they're the grownups now', *Star Tribune* (10 November), 1E; P. Edmonds (1993) 'A new generation: baby boomers rock into the White House', *USA Today* (20 January), 5A.

15. P. C. Roberts (1993) 'Contradiction of reinvention terms', *The Washington Times* (15 September), A18; W. Shapiro (1998) 'President could be perfect

spokesman for Contradiction', *USA Today* (2 September), 5A; G. Marcus (2000) *Double Trouble: Bill Clinton and Elvis Presley in a Land of No Alternatives* (New York: Picador), p. xvii.

16. A. Ferguson (1998) 'The feminist Lothario', *Time* (21 September). See also, P. Rubin (1998) 'Family man', *New Republic* (27 April), 14.

17. K. T. Walsh (1995) 'The times are not the only thing a-changin'': the protean president', *US News and World Report* 119 (21) (27 November), 36; K. T. Walsh and M. Copper (1995) 'Clinton's many faces', *US News and World Report* 118 (4) (30 January), 24. Also: T. B. Edsall (1996) 'The protean president', *The Atlantic* (May).

18. R. Roberts (2004) 'The Clinton Show: Notes on a Postmodern President' in T. G. Shields, J. M. Whayne and D. R. Kelley (eds) *The Clinton Riddle: Perspectives on the Forty-Second President* (Fayetteville: University of Arkansas Press), p. 212.

19. W. J. Clinton (1994) 'Remarks to the National Baptist Convention', Ernest N. Morial Convention Center, New Orleans, Louisiana on 9 September 1994 (Transcript) *Weekly Compilation of Presidential Documents* (12 September); W. J. Clinton (1995) 'On Race Relations', Liz Sutherland Carpenter Distinguished Lectureship in the Humanities and Sciences, University of Texas Austin (16 October). Complete transcript available at http://clinton4.nara.gov/textonly/Initiatives/OneAmerica/19970610-839. html accessed February 2006.

20. S. Cohan (1997) *Masked Men: Masculinity and the Movies in the Fifties* (Bloomington and Indianapolis: Indiana University Press), pp. 38, 175.

21. B. Ehrenreich (1983) *The Hearts of Men: American Dreams and the Flight from Commitment* (New York: Pluto Press), p. 20.

22. R. Griswold (1993) *Fatherhood in America: A History* (New York: Basic Books), p. 2.

23. In *Hollywood vs. America*, conservative critic Michael Medved is much more cynical about looking to the 1950s sitcom family as an American model. 'In today's climate', he notes, 'a television series called "Father Knows Best" would be absolutely unthinkable – it would be deemed too judgmental, authoritarian, patriarchal, and perhaps even sexist. A program entitled "Father Knows Nothing" would stand a far better chance'. M. Medved (1992) *Hollywood vs. America: Popular Culture and the War on Traditional Values* (New York: HarperCollins), p. 148.

24. According to Greg Dickinson, for example, *Pleasantville* and *The Truman Show* (1998) revise the suburban image through 'nostalgic invocations of the past'. G. Dickinson (2006) 'The Pleasantville Effect: Nostalgia and the Visual Framing of (White) Suburbia', *Western Journal of Communication* (1 July), 212–33; Similarly, Stella Bruzzi suggests that *Far from Heaven*, along with films such as *The Road to Perdition* (2002) and *Catch Me If You Can* (2002), offer 'scenarios of loss' and ultimately reinforce Hollywood's conservativism. S. Bruzzi (2005) *Bringing Up Daddy: Fatherhood and Masculinity in Post-War Hollywood* (London: British Film Institute), p. 191.

25. P. Grainge (2002) *Monochrome Memories: Nostalgia and Style in Retro America* (Westport, CT: Praeger), pp. 27, 6. See also P. Grainge (2002) 'Colouring the Past: *Pleasantville* and the Textuality of Media Memory' in Grainge (ed.) *Memory and Popular Film* (Manchester: Manchester University Press), pp. 202–19.
26. L. Spigel (2001) *Welcome to the Dreamhouse: Popular Media and Postwar Suburbs* (Durham, NC: Duke University Press), p. 394.
27. Bruzzi, *Bringing Up Daddy*, p. 191.
28. H. Ruitenbeek (1963) 'Men Alone: The Male Homosexual and the Disintegrated Family', *The Problem of Homosexuality in Modern Society* (New York: E.P. Dutton), p. 80. Cited in Ehrenreich, *The Hearts of Men*, p. 23.
29. For an extended discussion of the conflict between fatherhood and breadwinning in *The Best Years of Our Lives*, see L. Rotskoff (2002) *Love on the Rocks: Men, Women and Alcohol in Post-World War II America* (Chapel Hill, NC: University of North Carolina Press), pp. 92–104; for *The Seven Year Itch* and *The Man in the Gray Flannel Suit*, see Cohan, *Masked Men*, pp. 61–78.
30. Cohan, *Masked Men*, p. xi.
31. In 1998, Toni Morrison labelled Clinton the 'first black President' suggesting he exhibited 'almost every trope of blackness: single-parent household, born poor, working-class, saxophone-playing, McDonald's-and-junk-food-loving boy from Arkansas'. T. Morrison (1998) 'Clinton as the first black president', *The New Yorker* (October).
32. R. Dyer (1997) *White* (London: Routledge), pp. 2, 222–3. See also, G. A. Foster (2003) *Performing Whiteness: Postmodern Re/Constructions in the Cinema* (New York: State University of New York Press).
33. M. Marable (1995) *Beyond Black and White: Transforming African-American Politics* (New York: Verso), p. 6.
34. 'The Negro family: the case for national action' (1965) Office of Policy Planning and Research, United States Department of Labor (March).
35. Cited in L. B. Randolph (1990) 'What can we do about the most explosive problem in black America: the widening gap between the women who are making it and the men who aren't', *Ebony* 45 (10) (August), 52.
36. b. hooks (2004) *We Real Cool: Black Men and Masculinity* (New York: Routledge), pp. 104–5; See also, P. B. Harper (1996) *Are We Not Men? Masculine Anxiety and the Problem of African-American Identity* (Oxford: Oxford University Press); P. Gilroy (1992) 'It's a Family Affair' in G. Dent (ed.) *Black Popular Culture/a project by Michele Wallace* (Seattle: Bay), pp. 312–13; B. Herbert (1994) 'Who will help the black man?' *New York Times Magazine* (4 December), 72.
37. In a roundtable discussion of the poor state of black men in America, director John Singleton (*Boyz N the Hood*, 1991; *Poetic Justice*, 1993; *Higher Learning*, 1995) acknowledged the pressure he felt to move away from negative racial stereotyping in his films, saying: 'I try to have a strong black man in every picture that is responsible for other black men'. Cited in Herbert, Who will help the black man? 72. For an extended

discussion of the 'strong black man', see M. A. Neal (2006) *New Black Man* (New York: Routledge), pp. 21–8; also E. O. Hutchinson (1994) *The Assassination of the Black Male Image* (New York: Touchstone).

38. Cited in S. Waxman (2002) 'John Q. theme close to director's heart', *The Washington Post*, Arts and Life (19 February), D8.
39. M. Turner (2002) 'Doing it all for love', *The Advertiser*, Features (25 April), 30.
40. C. Rickey (2006) 'Real-life character an act of Will', *The Philadelphia Inquirer* (10 December), H01; J. T. Bennett (2007) 'Hollywood's hottest father/son duo', *Ebony* (January), 52.
41. See D. Carbado (1999) 'Introduction' in D. Carbado (ed.) *Black Men on Race, Gender and Sexuality: A Critical Reader* (New York: New York University Press), p. 6.
42. H. Gray (1995) 'Black Masculinity and Visual Culture', *Callaloo*, 18 (2), 403. *John Q.* is not entirely successful in its attempt to dispel myths about African American masculinity. John breaks the law in trying to protect his son although he receives a reduced sentence after winning over his hostages. While his crimes are validated as part of the 'greater good', the film still conforms to negative stereotypes associating African American men with crime and deviancy.
43. J. Stacey, cited in C. R. Smith (2002) 'Gender and Family Values in the Clinton Presidency and 1990s Hollywood Film' in P. J. Davies and P. Wells (eds) *American Film and Politics from Reagan to Bush Jr.* (Manchester: Manchester University Press), p. 81.
44. As Robert B. Ray has noted, the conflation of individual with society is a typical Hollywood strategy, particularly common in the western whereby 'the self-determining, morally detached outlaw hero came to represent America itself'. The self-determining, morally detached outlaw hero of the western is replaced with the morally upstanding yet untraditional father of *John Q.* and *The Pursuit of Happyness*, yet their individual solutions do little to challenge or counteract the wider cultural problems highlighted by their respective narratives. See R. B. Ray (1985) *A Certain Tendency of the Hollywood Cinema 1930–1980* (Princeton, NJ: Princeton University Press), pp. 91–2.
45. D. Marcus (2004) *Happy Days and Wonder Years: The Fifties and Sixties in Contemporary Cultural Politics* (New Brunswick, NJ: Rutgers University Press), p. 177.
46. J. Davies and C. R. Smith (1995) *Gender, Ethnicity and Sexuality in Contemporary American Film* (Edinburgh: Keele University Press), p. 5.

5   Aging Men: Viagra, Retiring Boomers and Jack Nicholson

1. See J. Hearn (1995) 'Imaging the Aging of Men' in M. Featherstone and A. Wernick (eds) *Images of Aging: Cultural Representations of Later Life* (London: Routledge), pp. 107–8; A. A. Fleming (1999) 'Older Men in Contemporary

Discourses on Ageing: Absent Bodies and Invisible Lives', *Nursing Inquiry* 6, 3–8; B. L. Marshall and S. Katz (2002) 'Forever Functional: Sexual Fitness and the Ageing Male Body', *Body and Society* 8 (December), 43–70; G. Spector-Mersel (2006) 'Never-aging Stories: Western Hegemonic Masculinity Scripts', *Journal of Gender Studies*, 15 (1) (March), 67–82.

2. M. Loe (2004) *The Rise of Viagra: How the Little Blue Pill Changed Sex in America* (New York: New York University Press), p. 173.

3. Manhood, in this case, takes on a dual meaning – describing both the masculine identity and the penis itself. For examples of Viagra's various marketing campaigns see www.viagra.com.

4. Loe, *The Rise of Viagra*, p. 90. See also E. Haiken (2000) 'Virtual Reality, or, Does Medicine Make the Man?' *Men and Masculinities* 2 (April), 388–409.

5. L. A. Weinbach (1995) 'Retirement crisis', *Chief Executive* 104 (June), 46–8; D. Cauchon and J. Waggoner (2004) 'The looming national benefit crisis', *USA Today* (3 October); K. Dychtwald (2003) 'The age wave is coming', *Public Management* 85 (6) (July), 6–10; R. J. Samuelson (1992) 'Perspective on a graying America', *Los Angeles Times*, Metro (26 November), B5; D. M. Walker (1997) 'The looming retirement crisis', *Employee Benefits Journal* 22 (2) (June), 17–24; R. Kuttner (2002) 'Retirement at risk', *The American Prospect* (3 September); K. M. Kristoff (1998) 'The real retirement crisis', *Los Angeles Times*, Business (11 January), D1; D. Wyss (2006) 'The gathering pensions storm', *Business Week* (5 June); K. Greene (2003) 'Many older workers to delay retirement until after age 70', *Wall Street Journal* (23 September), D2; P. Engardio (2005) 'Now, the geezer glut', *Business Week*, 3918 (31 January), 44.

6. B. Friedan (1993) *The Fountain of Age* (New York: Simon and Schuster), p. 165. Friedan was 72 at the time of writing.

7. C. Holmlund (2002) *Impossible Bodies: Femininity and Masculinity at the Movies* (New York: Routledge). See L. Dittmar (1997) 'Of Hags and Crones: Reclaiming Lesbian Desire for the Trouble Zone of Aging' in C. Holmlund and C. Fuchs (eds) *Between the Sheets: Queer, Lesbian, Gay Documentary* (Minneapolis, MN: University of Minnesota Press), pp. 71–90; V. Sobchack (1999) 'Scary Women: Cinema, Surgery and Special Effects', in K. Woodward (ed.) *Figuring Age: Women, Bodies, Generations* (Bloomington, IN: Indiana University Press), pp. 200–11; E. A. Kaplan (1999) 'Trauma and Aging: Marlene Dietrich, Melanie Klein and Marguerite Duras' in Woodward (ed.) *Figuring Age*, pp. 171–94; and P. Mellencamp (1999) 'From Anxiety to Equanimity: Crisis and Generational Continuity on TV, at the Movies, in Life, in Death' in Woodward (ed.) *Figuring Age*, pp. 310–28.

8. Holmlund, *Impossible Bodies*, pp. 144, 147, 246, 153.

9. M. Featherstone (1995) 'Post-bodies, Aging and Virtual Reality', in M. Featherstone and A. Wernick (eds) *Images of Aging: Cultural Representations of Later Life* (London New York: Routledge), p. 227; Hearn, Imaging the Aging of Men, pp. 107–8.

10. A. Breznican (2006) 'One last shot for a beloved bruiser', *USA Today* (18 December), 1A; P. Hartlaub (2006) 'Who you calling old?' *The San*

Francisco Chronicle (19 December), E1; A. Wallenstein (2007) 'Is Rambo just too old?' *Chicago Sun Times* (29 May), 32.

11. Featherstone, Post-bodies, Aging and Virtual Reality, p. 227.
12. Hearn, Imaging the Aging of Men, pp. 108–9.
13. Featherstone, Post-bodies, Aging and Virtual Reality, p. 227. See also M. Featherstone and M. Hepworth (1989) 'Ageing and Old Age: Reflections on the Postmodern Lifecourse' in B. Bytheway, T. Kiel and P. Allatt (eds) *Becoming and Being Old: Sociological Approaches to Later Life* (London: Sage Publications), pp. 143–57; and K. Woodward (1991) *Aging and Its Discontents: Freud and Other Fictions* (Bloomington: Indiana University Press).
14. Hearn, Imaging the Aging of Men, p. 110.
15. C. Russell (1993) *The Master Trend: How the Baby Boom Generation is Remaking America* (New York: Plenum Press); A. R. Hunt (1999) 'Fundamental shift in what it means to be senior: "third age" elderly begin to give new meaning to "retirement"', *Wall Street Journal* (11 March), A10; R. Gardyn (2000) 'Retirement redefined', *American Demographics* 22 (11) (November), 52–7; D. J. Macunovich (2002) *Birth Quake: The Baby Boom and Its Aftershocks* (Chicago: University of Chicago Press); L. M. Harris (2003) *After Fifty: How the Baby Boom will Redefine the Mature Market* (New York: PMP Books); L. M. Harris and M. Edelman (2006) *After Sixty: Marketing to Baby Boomers Reaching their BIG Transition Years* (New York: PMP Books).
16. Problematically, boomers are often discussed in the media and market journalism as a collective group. Such a generalisation, however, fails to take into account the possible diversity of this large demographic which comprises over 76 million Americans born during an 18-year period. The baby boomers featured in news stories about the looming 'retirement crisis' and revitalisation of aging refer to the early boomers – those boomers who came of age during the mid-1960s and early 1970s and who will reach or near the political retirement age of 65 in 2011. The latest boomers, however, will not reach 65 until nearly 2030. See, D. Cork (1996) *The Pig and the Python: How to Prosper from the Aging Baby Boom* (Toronto: Stoddart Books); M. Freedman (2000) *Prime Time: How Baby Boomers will Revolutionize Retirement and Transform America* (New York: Public Affairs); K. Dychtwald (2000) *Age Power: How the 21st Century Will Be Ruled by the New Old* (New York: Tarcher/Putnam).
17. M. Gobé (2001) *Emotional Branding: The New Paradigm for Connecting Brands to People* (Oxford: Windsor), p. 3.
18. P. Braus (1995) 'Vision in an aging America', *American Demographics* (June), 34; P. Diekmeyer (2002) 'The age of incontinence: boomers will force marketers to rebrand aging', *Strategy*, 13 (11) (28 January): 12; D. Berman (1998) 'Late-blooming scholars', *Business Week*, 3587 (20 July), 106; K. Doheny (2006) 'Golden years for gyms', *Forbes* (16 May); S. Dougherty (2003) 'Gadgets help baby boomers navigate old age', *USA Today* (17 November), 1A.
19. L. R. Williams and M. Hammond (eds) (2006) *Contemporary American Cinema* (London: McGraw Hill), p. 225.

20. According to Allen, the echo boom forms 'a demographic bulge almost as large and arguably as socially important as their baby boom parents' generation'. R. C. Allen (1999) 'Home Alone Together: Hollywood and the "Family Film"' in M. Stokes and R. Maltby (eds) *Identifying Hollywood's Cultural Audiences: Cultural Identity and the Movies* (London: The British Film Institute), p. 110. See also P. Krämer (2006) 'Disney and Family Entertainment' in L. R. Williams and M. Hammond (eds) *Contemporary American Cinema* (London: McGraw Hill), pp. 265–79.
21. E. Guider (2006) 'Boom times for showbiz', *Variety* (31 July), 5.
22. T. Austin (200) *Hollywood, Hype and Audiences: Selling and Watching Popular Films in the 1990s* (Manchester: Manchester University Press), p. 28.
23. D. Garrett (2006) 'Over-achievers get high marks: Studios stumped as DVD hits double (or triple) B.O. tally', *Variety* (31 July), 6.
24. M. Ryan and D. Kellner (1988) *Camera Politica: The Politics and Ideology of Contemporary Hollywood Film* (Bloomington: Indiana University Press), pp. 23, 83, 227.
25. M. Elias (2003) 'In *Something's Gotta Give*, boomers see themselves', *USA Today* (22 December), 10D.
26. D. Leigh (2003) 'Don't fence me in', *Sight and Sound*, 13 (5) (May), 13.
27. 'Jack Nicholson: the star with the killer smile' (1974) *Time* (17 August); S. Holden (2002) 'An uneasy rider on the road to self-discovery', *The New York Times* (27 September), E1.
28. D. Bingham (1991) *Acting Male: Masculinities in the Films of James Stewart, Jack Nicholson and Clint Eastwood* (New Brunswick: Rutgers University Press), p. 16; R. Dyer (1986) *Heavenly Bodies: Film Stars and Society* (London: British Film Institute), p. 11.
29. Despite being trained by Lee Strasberg and referring to himself a 'common method actor', Nicholson's excessiveness arguably goes against popular conceptions of The Method that associate the acting form with naturalness and authenticity. See B. Koltnow (2003) 'Being Jack is a day job', *Toronto Star* (6 January), E03; D. Kennedy (2002) 'Nicholson on age, acting and "being Jack"', *The New York Times*, Arts (22 September), 1.
30. S. Sontag (1972) 'The Double Standard of Aging', *Saturday Review of Literature* 39, 29–38. See also M. M. Lauzen and D. M. Dozier (2005) 'Maintaining the Double Standard: Portrayals of Age and Gender in Popular Films', *Sex Roles*, 52 (7/8) (April), 437–46. *The Witches of Eastwick* (1987) provides an earlier instance of the double standard of aging that favours men over women. In his discussion of the film, Dennis Bingham observes that Nicholson is allowed to 'let himself go' and still be a sex symbol whereas the female actors in the film, Susan Sarandon and Cher, have to 'work out and submit to tummy tucks' in order to retain their sexual attractiveness. 'If Cher and Sarandon put on weight', Bingham asserts, 'they would be playing supporting roles as Julia Roberts's or Marisa Tomei's mother before they knew it'. Bingham, *Acting Male*, 153.
31. R. Kelly (2001) 'Rough justice', *Sight and Sound*, 11 (10) (October).
32. P. Bradshaw (2001) 'Loneliness of a cop with a yearning for redemption', *Manchester Guardian Weekly* (24 October), 19.

33. Bradshaw, Loneliness of a cop, 19; J. Solomons (2001) 'You don't know Jack', *The Sunday Observer* (14 October), 9; M. Atkinson (2001) 'Wreckage and reckonings', *The Village Voice* (30 January), 122.
34. D. Ansen (2002) 'And one for the road', *Newsweek* (16 December), 64; Kennedy, Nicholson on age, acting and 'being Jack, 1; J. Morgenstern (2003) 'Keaton's autumnal lover turns formula into feeling in *Something's Gotta Give*; surprise: Nicholson is subtle', *Wall Street Journal* (12 December), W1; J. Giles (2002) 'About Jack', *Newsweek* (16 December), A60.
35. Ansen, And one for the road, 64.
36. For example, Erik Lundegaard for MSNBC news said recently that 'Jack' is 'The most ordinary of first names and he made it his own'. E. Lundegaard (2006) 'Top 10 Jack Nicholson scenes', MSNBC (6 October).
37. G. Whipp (2003) 'Jack Nicholson finally acts his age', *Los Angeles Daily News* (2 January), 3.
38. *About Schmidt* is not the first of Nicholson's films in which he 'acts his age'. In *Terms of Endearment* (1983), Nicholson/Garrett Breedlove embarks on a relationship with Shirley MacLaine/Aurora Greenway – a woman his own age. The relationship is short-lived, however, and Breedlove is all but absent from the sequel, *The Evening Star* (1997).
39. Of course, Nicholson has displayed a paunch since *Terms of Endearment*; it is thus more a marker of aging, and indeed 'aging well' since the paunch is often associated with prosperity and indulgence, than 'old' age.
40. K. Woodward (2006) 'Performing Age, Performing Gender', *NWSA Journal* 18 (1) (Spring), 165–7.
41. Keying, according to Goffman, refers to 'the set of conventions by which a given activity, one already meaningful in terms of some primary frame-work, is transformed into something patterned on this activity but seen by the participants to be something quite else'. E. Goffman (1986) *Frame Analysis: An Essay on the Organization of Experience* (Boston: Northeastern University Press), pp. 43–4.
42. B. Svetkey (2003) 'Jack on Jack: in a candid Q&A, the larger-than-life star of *About Schmidt* tells how he took on a 'small' role and started acting his age', *Entertainment Weekly* (3 January).
43. E. Hedegaard (2006) 'Jack Nicholson: a singular guy', *Rolling Stone* (20 September). In another nod to 'Jack', a deleted scene in a roadside diner saw Schmidt's unsuccessful attempt to order a sandwich the way he liked it to be told 'no substitutions' by the waitress, mimicking his more successful outburst in *Five Easy Pieces*. 'Since that famous scene so perfectly and succinctly distils the feeling of the times in which it was made', director Alexander Payne notes, 'I thought revisiting it with the same iconic actor would provide a commentary on how much we've lost since then and how conformist our current lives are, a conformism that produces empty, lost lives like Schmidt's'. *About Schmidt* DVD, New Line Cinema.
44. R. Weiskind (2003) 'The older Jack gives real charm to "Something"', *Pittsburgh Post-Gazette* (12 December), 17.

45. J. Naremore (1990) *Acting in the Cinema* (Berkeley, CA: University of California Press), p. 20.
46. On a film commentary, Nicholson describes how he wanted to look like a 'beached whale' when his character suffers a heart attack in order to be more realistic. Later in the film, when Harry is invigorated through his relationship with Erica (Diana Keaton), director Nancy Meyers admits to having Nicholson stand up in scenes where he is supposedly laying on a bed so that his neck sagged less from the gravity pulling his skin down.
47. Naremore, *Acting in the Cinema*, p. 20.
48. M. Wheeler (2005) 'The retiring brain boom', *Technology and Business Magazine* (5 September); M. Freudenheim (2004) 'To read the menu, baby boomers turn to eye treatments', *The New York Times* (11 September), 1; P. Peck (2003) 'Senior drinking/drug abuse often missed', *United Press International* (16 July); M. Tippett (2004) 'It's not over yet', *Times Colonist* (9 November), D1.
59. AARP Grownup Movie Awards. http://www.aarpmagazine.org/entertainment/ movies accessed November 2006.
50. According to the Recreational Vehicle Industry Association, baby boomers constitute the largest and fastest growing sector of RV ownership in America. In the 55–64 age group, a recent report found, one in ten households own at least one RV. 'New U-Mich study: RV ownership reaches all-time high' (2005) *RVIA News Release* (8 December).

Conclusion: Returns, Renewals, Departures

1. A. Klevan (2005) *Performance: From Achievement to Appreciation* (London: Wallflower), p. 103.
2. Klevan, *Performance*, pp. 7–8. Emphasis added.
3. Klevan, *Performance*, p. 104. Emphasis added.
4. Only Harry Sanborn in *Something's Gotta Give* moves closer towards a 'normative' masculinity by dating a woman closer to his own age, although it is important to note that Erica, in being pursued by the young doctor, is also defying her 'old' age.
5. M. Carlson (1996) *Performance: A Critical Introduction* (New York: Routledge), p. 189.

Filmography

About Schmidt (Alexander Payne, USA, 2002)
Absolute Power (Clint Eastwood, USA, 1997)
American Beauty (Sam Mendes, USA, 1999)
Any Given Sunday (Oliver Stone, USA, 1999)
As Good As It Gets (James L. Brooks, USA, 1997)
Bad Boys II (Michael Bay, USA, 2003)
Basic Instinct (Paul Verhoeven, USA/France, 1992)
Batman (Tim Burton, USA/UK, 1989)
Batman & Robin (Joel Schumacher, USA/UK, 1997)
The Best Years of Our Lives (William Wyler, USA, 1946)
Big (Penny Marshall, USA, 1988)
The Big Chill (Lawrence Kasdan, USA, 1983)
The Big Lebowski (Joel Coen, USA/UK, 1998)
Blood Work (Clint Eastwood, USA, 2002)
Bonnie and Clyde (Arthur Penn, USA, 1967)
Boogie Nights (Paul Thomas Anderson, USA, 1997)
Broken Flowers (Jim Jarmusch, USA/France, 2005)
The Browning Version (Mike Figgis, UK, 1994)
The Bucket List (Rob Reiner, USA, 2007)
Chinatown (Roman Polanski, USA, 1974)
Cocktail (Roger Donaldson, USA, 1988)
Collateral (Michael Mann, USA, 2004)
The Color of Money (Martin Scorsese, USA, 1986)
The Cooler (Wayne Kramer, USA, 2003)
Cruising (William Friedkin, USA/West Germany, 1980)
The Cry Baby Killer (Jus Addiss, USA, 1958)
The Curious Case of Benjamin Button (David Fincher, USA, 2008)
Dances with Wolves (Kevin Costner, USA/UK, 1990)
The Darjeeling Limited (Wes Anderson, USA, 2007)
Dead Reckoning (John Cromwell, USA, 1947)
Death of a Salesman (Laslo Benedek, USA, 1951)
Death of a Salesman (Volker Schlöndorff, USA/West Germany, 1985)
Detour (Edgar G. Ullmer, USA, 1945)
Die Hard (John McTiernan, USA, 1988)
Disclosure (Barry Levinson, USA, 1994)
Donnie Brasco (Mike Newell, USA, 1997)
Double Indemnity (Billy Wilder, USA, 1944)
Driving Miss Daisy (Bruce Beresford, USA, 1989)
Easy Rider (Dennis Hopper, USA, 1969)
Edmond (Stuart Gordon, USA, 2005)

The Evening Star (Robert Harling, USA, 1997)
Falling Down (Joel Schumacher, USA/UK/France, 1993)
Far from Heaven (Todd Haynes, USA, 2002)
Fargo (Joel Coen, USA, 1996)
Fatal Attraction (Adrian Lyne, USA, 1987)
Fight Club (David Fincher, USA/Germany, 1999)
The Fisher King (Terry Gilliam, USA, 1991)
Five Easy Pieces (Bob Rafelson, USA, 1970)
Flags of Our Fathers (Clint Eastwood, USA, 2006)
Forever Young (Steve Miner, USA, 1992)
The Game (David Fincher, USA, 1997)
Ghost World (Terry Zwigoff, USA/UK/Germany, 2001)
Gilda (Charles Vidor, USA, 1946)
Glengarry Glen Ross (James Foley, USA, 1992)
The Godfather (Francis Ford Coppola, USA, 1972)
The Godfather: Part II (Francis Ford Coppola, USA, 1974)
The Godfather: Part II (Francis Ford Coppola, USA, 1990)
The Graduate (Mike Nichols, USA, 1967)
Gran Torino (Clint Eastwood, USA/Germany, 2008)
Grizzly Man (Werner Herzog, USA, 2005)
Groundhog Day (Harold Ramis, USA, 1993)
Heist (David Mamet, USA/Canada, 2001)
Homicide (David Mamet, USA, 1991)
The Horse Whisperer (Robert Redford, USA, 1998)
Human Nature (Michel Gondry, France/USA, 2001)
The Human Stain (Robert Benton, USA/Germany/France, 2003)
I'm Not There (Todd Haynes, USA/Germany, 2007)
The Imaginarium of Doctor Parnassus (Terry Gilliam, UK/Canada, 2009)
In a Lonely Place (Nicholas Ray, USA, 1950)
Jerry Maguire (Cameron Crowe, USA, 1996)
John Q. (Nick Cassavetes, USA, 2002)
Junior (Ivan Reitman, USA, 1994)
Kindergarten Cop (Ivan Reitman, USA, 1990)
The Last Castle (Rod Lurie, USA, 2001)
Laura (Otto Preminger, USA, 1944)
Lean on Me (John G. Avildsen, USA, 1989)
Lethal Weapon (Richard Donner, USA, 1987)
Lethal Weapon 2 (Richard Donner, USA, 1989)
The Life Aquatic with Steve Zissou (Wes Anderson, USA, 2004)
Lions for Lambs (Robert Redford, USA, 2007)
Lost in Translation (Sofia Coppola, USA/Japan, 2003)
Mad Dog and Glory (John McNaughton, USA, 1993)
Magnolia (Paul Thomas Anderson, USA, 1999)
The Man in the Gray Flannel Suit (Nunnally Johnson, USA, 1956)
The Matrix Revolutions (Andy Wachowski/Larry Wachowski, USA/Australia, 2003)

Midnight Cowboy (John Schlesinger, USA, 1969)
Million Dollar Baby (Clint Eastwood, USA, 2004)
Minority Report (Steven Spielberg, USA, 2002)
Mission: Impossible (Brian De Palma, USA, 1996)
Mystic River (Clint Eastwood, USA/Australia, 2003)
North by Northwest (Alfred Hitchcock, USA, 1959)
The Notebook (Nick Cassavetes, USA, 2004)
Oleanna (David Mamet, USA/UK, 1994)
On the Waterfront (Elia Kazan, USA, 1955)
One Flew Over the Cuckoo's Nest (Milos Forman, USA, 1975)
A Perfect Murder (Andrew Davis, USA, 1998)
Pillow Talk (Michael Gordon, USA, 1959)
Pleasantville (Gary Ross, USA, 1998)
The Pledge (Sean Penn, USA, 2001)
Proof (John Madden, USA, 2005)
Psycho (Alfred Hitchcock, USA, 1960)
Psycho (Gus Van Sant, USA, 1998)
The Pursuit of Happyness (Gabriele Muccino, USA, 2006)
Quick Change (Howard Franklin/Bill Murray, USA, 1990)
Rambo (Sylvester Stallone, USA/Germany, 2008)
The Razor's Edge (John Byrum, USA, 1984)
Reds (Warren Beatty, USA, 1981)
Regarding Henry (Mike Nichols, USA, 1991)
The Remains of the Day (James Ivory, UK/USA, 1993)
Reservoir Dogs (Quentin Tarantino, USA, 1991)
Risky Business (Paul Brickman, USA, 1983)
Rocky Balboa (Sylvester Stallone, USA, 2006)
The Royal Tenenbaums (Wes Anderson, USA, 2001)
Rushmore (Wes Anderson, USA, 1998)
Save the Tiger (John G. Avildsen, USA, 1973)
Scarface (Brian De Palma, USA, 1983)
Scrooged (Richard Donner, USA, 1988)
The Secret of My Succe$s (Herbert Ross, USA, 1987)
Serpico (Sidney Lumet, USA/Italy, 1973)
The Seven Year Itch (Billy Wilder, USA, 1955)
Shadowlands (Richard Attenborough, UK, 1993)
The Shining (Stanley Kubrick, UK/USA, 1980)
Short Cuts (Robert Altman, USA, 1993)
Something's Gotta Give (Nancy Meyes, USA, 2003)
Space Cowboys (Clint Eastwood, USA/Australia, 2000)
Spy Game (Tony Scott, Germany/USA/France/Japan, 2001)
A Star is Born (William A. Wellman, USA, 1937)
A Star is Born (George Cukor, USA, 1954)
State and Main (David Mamet, USA/France, 2000)
A Streetcar Named Desire (Elia Kazan, USA, 1951)
Swimming with Sharks (George Huang, USA, 1994)

Tarzan (Chris Buck/Kevin Lima, USA, 1999)

The Terminator (James Cameron, USA/UK, 1984)

Terminator 2: Judgment Day (James Cameron, USA/France, 1991)

Terminator 3: Rise of the Machines (Jonathan Mostow, USA/Germany/UK, 2003)

Terms of Endearment (James L. Brooks, USA, 1983)

Top Gun (Tony Scott, USA, 1986)

Tropic Thunder (Ben Stiller, USA/UK/Germany, 2008)

Twins (Ivan Reitman, USA, 1988)

The Usual Suspects (Bryan Singer, USA/Germany, 1995)

Vanilla Sky (Cameron Crowe, USA, 2001)

Wall Street (Oliver Stone, USA, 1987)

The War of the Roses (Danny DeVito, USA, 1989)

War of the Worlds (Steven Spielberg, USA, 2005)

Witches of Eastwick (George Miller, USA, 1987)

Wonder Boys (Curtis Hanson, UK/Germany/USA/Japan, 2000)

X2: X-Men United (Bryan Singer, USA/Canada, 2003)

Bibliography

Adler, S. (1988) *The Technique of Acting*. New York: Bantam.

Affron, C. (1977) *Star Acting: Gish, Garbo, Davis* (New York: E. P. Dutton).

Allen, R. C. (1999) 'Home Alone Together: Hollywood and the "Family Film" ' in M. Stokes and R. Maltby (eds) *Identifying Hollywood's Cultural Audiences: Cultural Identity and the Movies* (London: The British Film Institute).

Arthur, E. (2004) 'Where Lester Burnham Falls Down: Exposing the Facade of Victimhood in *American Beauty*', *Men & Masculinities*, 7 (2) (October).

Ashcraft, K. L. and L. A. Flores (2003) '"Slaves with white collars": Persistent Performance of Masculinity in Crisis', *Text and Performance Quarterly*, 23 (1) (January).

Aubert, C. (2003 [1851]) *The Art of Pantomime*, trans. Edith Sears (Mineola, NY: Dover Publications).

Auslander, P. (1999) *Liveness: Performance in a Mediatised Culture*. London: Routledge.

Austin, J. L. (1955) 'How To Do Things With Words', The William James Lectures, Harvard University, reprinted in J. O. Urmson and M. Sbisà (eds) (1962) *How To Do Things With Words: J. L. Austin* (Cambridge, MA: Harvard University Press).

Austin, T. (2002) *Hollywood, Hype and Audiences: Selling and Watching Popular Films in the 1990s* (Manchester: Manchester University Press).

Austin, T. and M. Barker (eds) (2003) *Contemporary Hollywood Stardom* (Oxford: Hodder and Arnold).

Bainbridge, C. and C. Yates (2005) 'Cinematic Symptoms of Masculinity in Transition: Memory, History and Mythology in Contemporary Film', *Psychoanalysis, Culture and Society*, 10.

Baron, C. (2010) 'Film Noir: Gesture Under Pressure' in C. Cornea (ed.) *Genre and Performance: Film and Television* (Manchester: Manchester University Press).

Baron, C. (2007) 'Acting Choices/Filmic Choices: Rethinking Montage and Performance', *Journal of Film and Video*, 59 (2) (Summer).

Baron, C., D. Carson and F. P. Tomasulo (eds) (2004) *More Than a Method: Trends and Traditions in Contemporary Film Performance* (Detroit, MI: Wayne State University Press).

Barthes, R. (1977) 'The Grain of the Voice' in *Image, Music, Text*, trans. Stephen Heath (New York: Hill and Wang).

Barthes, R. (1972) 'The Face of Garbo' in *Mythologies*, trans. Annette Lavers (New York: Hill and Wang).

Bauman, R. (1977) *Verbal Art as Performance* (Rowley, MA: Newbury House).

Bean, K. (2001) 'A Few Good Men: Collusion and Violence in Oleanna' in C. Hudgins and L. Kane (eds) *Gender and Genre: Essays on David Mamet* (New York: St. Martin's).

Bechtel, R. (1996) 'PC Power Play: Language and Representation in David Mamet's *Oleanna'*, *Theatre Studies*, 41.

Bellinger, C. K. (2001) *The Genealogy of Violence: Reflections on Creation, Freedom, and Evil* (Oxford: Oxford University Press).

Bial, H. (2007) 'What is Performance?' in H. Bial (ed.) *The Performance Studies Reader*, Second Edition (Abingdon: Routledge).

Bial, H. (ed.) (2007) *The Performance Studies Reader*, Second Edition (Abingdon: Routledge).

Bigsby, C. (ed.) (2004) *The Cambridge Companion to David Mamet* (Cambridge: Cambridge University Press).

Bingham, D. (2004) 'Kidman, Cruise and Kubrick: A Brechtian Pastiche' in C. Baron, D. Carson and F. P. Tomasulo (eds) *More Than a Method: Trends and Traditions in Contemporary Film Performance* (Detroit: Wayne State University Press).

Bingham, D. (1994) *Acting Male: Masculinities in the Films of James Stewart, Jack Nicholson and Clint Eastwood* (New Brunswick, NJ: Rutgers University Press).

Bishop, C. (1958) 'The Great Stone Face', *Film Quarterly*, 12 (1) (Autumn).

Blankenhorn, D. (1995) *Fatherless America: Confronting Our Most Urgent Social Problem* (New York: Basic Books).

Bliss, S. (1987) 'Revisioning Masculinity', *In Context: A Quarterly of Humane Sustainable Culture*, 16 (Spring).

Bly, R. (1990) *Iron John: A Book About Men* (Shaftesbury: Element).

Bordwell, D. (2002) 'Intensified Continuity: Visual Style in Contemporary American Film', *Film Quarterly*, 55 (3).

Braudy, L. (1976) 'Film Acting: Some Critical Problems and Proposals', *Quarterly Review of Film Studies*, 1 (1).

Brod, H. (ed.) (1987) *The Making of Masculinities: The New Men's Studies* (Boston, MA: Unwin and Hyman).

Brokow, T. (1998) *The Greatest Generation* (New York: Random House).

Broude, G. J. (1990) 'Protest Masculinity: A Further Look at the Causes and the Concept', *Ethos*, 18 (1) (March).

Bruzzi, S. (2005) *Bringing Up Daddy: Fatherhood and Masculinity in Post-War Hollywood* (London: British Film Institute).

Buchbinder, D. (1998) *Performance Anxieties: Re-Producing Masculinity* (St. Leonards, NSW: Allen and Unwin).

Butler, J. (1999) *Gender Trouble: Feminism and the Subversion of Identity*, 10th Anniversary Edition (New York: Routledge).

Butler, J. (1999) 'From Interiority to Gender Performatives' in F. Cleto (ed.) *Camp: Queer Aesthetics and the Performing Subject: A Reader* (Edinburgh: Edinburgh University Press).

Butler, J. (1993) *Bodies that Matter: On the Discursive Limits of 'Sex'* (New York, Routledge).

Butler, J. (1990) *Gender Trouble: Feminism and the Subversion of Identity* (New York: Routledge).

Butler, J. G. (ed.) (1991) *Star Texts: Image and Performance in Film and Television* (Detroit: Wayne State University Press).

Bytheway, B., T. Kiel and P. Allatt (eds) (1989) *Becoming and Being Old: Sociological Approaches to Later Life* (London: Sage Publications).

Calasanti, T. and N. King (2005) 'Firming the Floppy Penis: Age, Class, and Gender Relations in the Lives of Old Men', *Men and Masculinities*, 8.

Carbado, D. (ed.) *Black Men on Race, Gender and Sexuality: A Critical Reader* (New York: New York University Press).

Carlson, M. (2007) 'What is Performance?' in H. Bial (ed.) *The Performance Studies Reader*, Second Edition (Abingdon: Routledge).

Carlson, M. (1996) *Performance: A Critical Introduction* (London: Routledge).

Carnicke, S. M. (2004) 'Screen Performance and Directors' Visions' in C. Baron, D. Carson and F. P. Tomasulo (eds) *More Than a Method: Trends and Traditions in Contemporary Film Performance* (Detroit, MI: Wayne State University Press).

Cavell, S. (2004) 'Reflections on the Ontology of Film' reprinted in P. R. Wojcik (ed.) *Movie Acting: The* Film *Reader* (Routledge: London and New York).

Chion, M. (1999 [1982]) *The Voice in Cinema*, trans. Claudia Gorbman (New York: Columbia University Press).

Chopra-Gant, M. (2006) *Hollywood Genres and Postwar America: Masculinity, Family and Nation in Popular Movies and Film Noir* (London: IB Tauris).

Clatterbaugh, K. (1990) 'The Mythopoetic Movement: Men in Search of Spiritual Growth', in *Contemporary Perspectives on Masculinity: Men, Women, and Politics in Modern Society* (Oxford: Westview Press).

Clover, C. (1993) 'White Noise', *Sight and Sound* (May).

Cohan, S. (1997) *Masked Men: Masculinity and the Movies in the Fifties* (Bloomington, IN: Indiana University Press).

Cohan, S. and I. R. Hark (eds) (1993) *Screening the Male: Exploring Masculinities in Hollywood Cinema* (New York: Routledge).

Connell, R. W. (2000) *The Men and the Boys* (St. Leonards, NSW: Allen and Unwin).

Connell, R. W. (1996) 'The Politics of Changing Men', *Arena*, 6.

Connell, R. W. (1995) *Masculinities* (Cambridge: Polity Press).

Connell, R. W. (1995) 'Men at Bay: The "Men's Movement" and its Newest Best-sellers' in M. Kimmel (ed.) *The Politics of Manhood: Profeminist Men Respond to the Mythopoetic Men's Movement (and the Mythopoetic Leaders Answer)* (Philadelphia: Temple University Press).

Connell, R. W. (1993) 'The Big Picture: Masculinities in Recent World History', *Theory and Society*, 22 (5), Special Issue: Masculinities (October).

Coontz, S. (1998) *The Way We Really Are: Coming to Terms with America's Changing Families* (New York: Basic Books).

Coontz, S. (1992) *The Way We Never Were: American Families and the Nostalgia Trap* (New York: Basic Books).

Cork, D. (1996) *The Pig and the Python: How to Prosper from the Aging Baby Boom* (Toronto: Stoddart Books).

Cornea, C. (ed.) (2010) *Genre and Performance: Film and Television* (Manchester: Manchester University Press).

Corner, J. (2002) 'Performing the Real: Documentary Diversions', *Television & New Media*, 3 (3).

Cosby, B. (1986) *Fatherhood* (New York: Doubleday).

Daniels, C. R. (ed.) (1998) *Lost Fathers: The Politics of Fatherlessness in America* (New York: St. Martin's Press).

Davidson, G. (2005) '"Contagious Relations": Simulation, Paranoia, and the Postmodern Condition in William Friedkin's *Cruising* and Felice Picano's *The Lure*', *GLQ: A Journal of Lesbian and Gay Studies*, 11(1).

Davies, J. (1995) 'Gender, Ethnicity and Cultural Crisis in *Falling Down* and *Groundhog Day*', *Screen*, 36 (3).

Davies, J. (1995) '"I'm the bad guy?" *Falling Down* and White Masculinity in 1990s Hollywood', *Journal of Gender Studies*, 4 (2).

Davies, J. and C. R. Smith (1995) *Gender, Ethnicity and Sexuality in Contemporary American Film* (Edinburgh: Keele University Press).

Dean, A. (1990) *Language as Dramatic Action* (London and Toronto: Associated University Presses).

De Cordova, R. (1986) 'Gender and Performance: An Overview', in B. K. Grant (ed.) *Film Genre Reader* (Austin, TX: University of Texas Press).

Deleyto, C. (1997) 'The Margins of Pleasure: Female Monstrosity and Male Paranoia in *Basic Instinct*', *Film Criticism*, 21 (3) (Spring).

Demos, E. V. (ed.) (1995) *Exploring Affect: The Selected Writings of Silvan S. Tomkins* (Cambridge: Cambridge University Press).

Dickinson, G. (2006) 'The Pleasantville Effect: Nostalgia and the Visual Framing of (White) Suburbia', *Western Journal of Communication* (1 July).

Dittmar, L. (1997) 'Of Hags and Crones: Reclaiming Lesbian Desire for the Trouble Zone of Aging' in C. Holmlund and C. Fuchs (eds) *Between the Sheets: Queer, Lesbian, Gay Documentary* (Minneapolis, MN: University of Minnesota Press).

Doane, M. A. (2004) 'Pathos and Pathology: The Cinema of Todd Haynes', *Camera Obscura*, 57, 19 (3).

Doane, M. A. (2003) 'The Close-Up: Scale and Detail in the Cinema', *Differences: A Journal of Feminist Cultural Studies*, 14 (3).

Doane, M. A. (1980) 'The Voice in the Cinema: The Articulation of Body and Space', *Yale French Studies*, 60, Cinema/Sound.

Drake, P. (2006) 'Reconceptualizing Screen Performance', special issue on Screen Performance, *Journal of Film and Video*, 58 (1–2) (Spring/Summer).

Dychtwald, K. (2000) *Age Power: How the 21st Century Will Be Ruled by the New Old* (New York: Tarcher/Putnam).

Dyer, R. (1997) *White* (London: Routledge).

Dyer, R. (1993) 'The Role of Stereotypes' in *The Matter of Images: Essays on Representation* (London: Routledge).

Dyer, R. (1986) *Heavenly Bodies: Film Stars and Society* (London: British Film Institute).

Dyer, R. (1979) *Stars* (London: British Film Institute).

Ehrenreich, B. (1983) *The Hearts of Men: American Dreams and the Flight from Commitment* (New York: Pluto Press).

Ellis, J. (1992) 'Stars as Cinematic Phenomenon' in *Visible Fictions: Cinema, Television, Fiction* (London: Routledge).

Faludi, S. (1999) *Stiffed: The Betrayal of the Modern Man* (London: Chatto and Windus).

Faludi, S. (1991) *Backlash: The Undeclared War Against Women* (London: Chatto and Windus).

Farrell, W. (1993) *The Myth of Male Power* (New York: Simon and Schuster).

Farrell, W. (1978) *The Liberated Man. Beyond Masculinity: Freeing Men and Their Relationship With Women* (New York: Bantam).

Featherstone, M. (1995) 'Post-bodies, Aging and Virtual Reality', in M. Featherstone and A. Wernick (eds) *Images of Aging: Cultural Representations of Later Life* (London New York: Routledge).

Featherstone, M. and A. Wernick (eds) (1995) *Images of Aging: Cultural Representations of Later Life* (London: Routledge).

Featherstone, M. and M. Hepworth (1989) 'Ageing and Old Age: Reflections on the Postmodern Lifecourse' in B. Bytheway, T. Kiel and P. Allatt (eds) *Becoming and Being Old: Sociological Approaches to Later Life* (London: Sage Publications).

Fleming, A. A. (1999) 'Older Men in Contemporary Discourses on Ageing: Absent Bodies and Invisible Lives', *Nursing Inquiry*, 6.

Foster, G. A. (2003) *Performing Whiteness: Postmodern Re/Constructions in the Cinema* (New York: State University of New York Press).

Frankenberg, R. (1993) *White Women, Race Matters: The Social Construction of Whiteness* (New York: Routledge).

Freedman, M. (2000) *Prime Time: How Baby Boomers will Revolutionize Retirement and Transform America* (New York: Public Affairs).

Friedan, B. (1993) *The Fountain of Age* (New York: Simon and Schuster).

Gabler, N. (1998) *Life: The Movie: How Entertainment Conquered Reality* (New York: Vintage).

Gabriel, J. (1996) 'What Do You Do When Minority Means You? *Falling Down* and the Construction of "Whiteness"', *Screen*, 37.

Garber, M. (1992) *Vested Interests: Cross-Dressing and Cultural Anxiety* (New York: Routledge).

Gardiner, J. K. (2002) 'Theorizing Age with Gender: Bly's Boys, Feminism, and Maturity Masculinity' in Gardiner (ed.) *Masculinity Studies and Feminist Theory: New Directions* (New York: Columbia University Press).

Gardyn, R. (2000) 'Retirement redefined', *American Demographics*, 22 (11) (November).

Gates, P. (2006) *Detecting Men: Masculinity and the Hollywood Detective Film* (New York: State University of New York Press).

Geraghty, C. (2000) 'Re-Examining Stardom: Questions of Texts, Bodies and Performance' in Christine Gledhill and Linda Williams (eds) *Reinventing Film Studies* (London: Arnold).

Gilbert, E. (2002) *The Last American Man* (New York: Penguin).

Gilroy, P. (1992) 'It's a Family Affair' in G. Dent (ed.) *Black Popular Culture/a project by Michele Wallace* (Seattle: Bay).

Ginsberg, E. K. (ed.) (1996) *Passing and the Fictions of Identity* (Durham, NC: Duke University Press).

Giroux, H. A. (1993) 'Living Dangerously: Identity Politics and the New Cultural Racism: Towards a Critical Pedagogy of Representation', *Cultural Studies*, 7 (1).

Gobé, M. (2001) *Emotional Branding: The New Paradigm for Connecting Brands to People* (Oxford: Windsor).

Goffman, E. (1986) *Frame Analysis: An Essay on the Organization of Experience* (Boston: Northeastern University Press).

Goffman, E. (1981) *Forms of Talk* (Philadelphia: University of Pennsylvania Press).

Goffman, E. (1959) *The Presentation of Self in Everyday Life* (New York: Anchor).

Gómez-Peña, G. (2007) 'Culturas-in-extremis: Performing Against the Cultural Backdrop of the Mainstream Bizarre' in H. Bial (ed.) *The Performance Studies Reader*, Second Edition (London: Routledge).

Gormley, P. (2005) *The New-Brutality Film: Race and Affect in Contemporary Hollywood Cinema* (Bristol: Intellect).

Grainge, P. (2002) *Monochrome Memories: Nostalgia and Style in Retro America* (Westport, CT: Praeger).

Grainge, P. (2002) 'Colouring the Past: *Pleasantville* and the Textuality of Media Memory' in P. Grainge (ed.) *Memory and Popular Film* (Manchester: Manchester University Press).

Gray, H. (1995) 'Black Masculinity and Visual Culture', *Callaloo*, 18 (2).

Gray, J. (2010) *Show Sold Separately: Promos, Spoilers and Other Media Paratexts* (New York: New York University Press).

Green, P. (1998) *Cracks in the Pedestal: Ideology and Gender in Hollywood* (Amherst, MA: University of Massachusetts Press).

Griswold, R. (1993) *Fatherhood in America: A History* (New York: Basic Books).

Gunning, T. (1997) 'In Your Face: Physiognomy, Photography and the Gnostic Mission in Early Sound Film', *Modernism/Modernity*, 4 (1).

Haiken, E. (2000) 'Virtual Reality, or, Does Medicine Make the Man?' *Men and Masculinities*, 2 (April).

Harper, P. B. (1996) *Are We Not Men? Masculine Anxiety and the Problem of African-American Identity* (Oxford: Oxford University Press).

Harris, L. M. (2003) *After Fifty: How the Baby Boom will Redefine the Mature Market* (New York: PMP Books).

Harris, L. M. and M. Edelman (2006) *After Sixty: Marketing to Baby Boomers Reaching their BIG Transition Years* (New York: PMP Books).

Hearn, J. (2004) 'From Hegemonic Masculinity to the Hegemony of Men', *Feminist Theory*, 5 (4).

Hearn, J. (1995) 'Imaging the Aging of Men' in M. Featherstone and A. Wernick (eds) *Images of Aging: Cultural Representations of Later Life* (London: Routledge).

Hewlett, S. A. and C. West (1998) *The War Against Parents: What Can We Do for America's Beleaguered Moms and Dad* (Boston and New York: Houghton Mifflin).

Higson, A. (1986) 'Film Acting and Independent Cinema', *Screen*, 27 (3).

Hill, M. (ed.) (1997) *Whiteness: A Critical Reader* (New York: New York University Press).

Hirsch, F. (1991) *Acting Hollywood Style* (New York: Harry N. Abrams Publishers/ AFI Press).

Hollinger, K. (2006) *The Actress: Hollywood Acting and the Female Star* (London and New York: Routledge).

Holmes, S. (2004) ' "All you've for to worry about is the task, having a cup of tea, and doing a bit of sunbathing": Approaching Celebrity in *Big Brother*' in S. Holmes and S. Redmond (eds) *Understanding Reality Television* (London: Routledge).

Holmlund, C. (2002) *Impossible Bodies: Femininity and Masculinity at the Movies* (New York: Routledge).

Holmlund, C. (1993) 'Masculinity as Multiple Masquerade: The "Mature" Stallone and the Stallone Clone', in S. Cohan and I. R. Hark (eds) *Screening the Male: Exploring Masculinities in Hollywood Cinema* (New York: Routledge).

hooks, b. (2004) *We Real Cool: Black Men and Masculinity* (New York: Routledge).

hooks, b. (1992) *Black Looks: Race and Representation* (London: Turnaround).

Hudgins, C. and L. Kane (eds) (2001) *Gender and Genre: Essays on David Mamet* (New York: St. Martin's).

Hutchinson, E. O. (1994) *The Assassination of the Black Male Image* (New York: Touchstone).

Hunter, J. D. (1991) *Culture Wars: The Struggle to Define America* (New York: Basic Books).

Jeffords, S. (1994) *Hard Bodies: Hollywood Masculinity in the Reagan Era* (New Brunswick, NJ: Rutgers University Press).

Jeffords, S. (1993) 'The Big Switch: Hollywood Masculinity in the Nineties' in J. Collins, H. Radner and A. P. Collins (eds) *Film Theory Goes to the Movies* (London: Routledge).

Jeffords, S. (1993) 'Can Masculinity be Terminated?' in S. Cohan and I. R. Hark (eds) *Screening the Male: Exploring Masculinities in Hollywood Cinema* (New York: Routledge).

Jeffords, S. (1989) *The Remasculinization of America: Gender, Genre and the Vietnam War* (Bloomington and Indianapolis: Indiana University Press).

Jenkins, H. (2006) *Convergence Culture: Where Old and New Media Collide* (New York: New York University Press).

Jones, J. P. (2004) *Entertaining Politics: New Political Television and Civic Culture* (Lanham, MD: Rowman and Littlefield).

Kaplan, E. A. (1999) 'Trauma and Aging: Marlene Dietrich, Melanie Klein and Marguerite Duras' in Woodward (ed.) *Figuring Age: Women, Bodies, Generations* (Bloomington, IN: Indiana University Press).

Keen, S. (1992) *Fire in the Belly: On Being a Man* (London: Piatkus).

Kelly, R. (2001) 'Rough justice', *Sight and Sound*, 11 (10) (October).

Kimmel, M. (1996) *Manhood in America: A Cultural History* (New York: Free Press).

Kimmel, M. (1996) 'Wimps, Whiners, and Weekend Warriors: The Contemporary Crisis of Masculinity and Beyond' in *Manhood in America* (New York: The Free Press).

Kimmel, M. (1987) 'The Contemporary "Crisis" of Masculinity in Historical Perspective' in H. Brod (ed.) *The Making of Masculinities: The New Men's Studies* (Boston, MA: Unwin and Hyman).

King, B. (2003) 'Embodying an Elastic Self' in T. Austin and M. Barker (eds) *Contemporary Hollywood Stardom* (Oxford: Hodder and Arnold).

King, B. (1985) 'Articulating Stardom', *Screen*, 26 (5).

King, G. (2010) *Lost in Translation* (Edinburgh: Edinburgh University Press).

Kirby, M. (1972) 'On Acting and Not Acting', *The Drama Review*, 16 (1) (March).

Kirkham, P. and J. Thumim (eds) (1995) *Me Jane: Masculinity, Movies and Women* (London: Lawrence and Wishart).

Kirkham, P. and J. Thumim (eds) (1993) *You Tarzan: Masculinity, Movies and Men* (London: Lawrence and Wishart).

Kirschenblatt-Gimblett, B. (2007) 'Performance Studies' in H. Bial (ed.) *The Performance Studies Reader*, Second Edition (Abingdon: Routledge).

Klevan, A. (2005) *Film Performance: From Achievement to Appreciation* (London: Wallflower Press).

Klevan, A. (2000) *Disclosure of the Everyday: Undramatic Achievement in Narrative Film* (Trowbridge, Wiltshire: Flicks Books).

Kozloff, S. (2000) *Overhearing Film Dialogue* (Berkeley: University of California Press).

Kozloff, S. (1988) *Invisible Storytellers: Voice-Over Narration in American Fiction Film* (Berkeley and Los Angeles: University of California Press).

Krämer, P. (2006) 'Disney and Family Entertainment' in L. R. Williams and M. Hammond (eds) *Contemporary American Cinema* (London: McGraw Hill).

Krämer, P. and A. Lovell (eds) (1999) *Screen Acting* (London and New York: Routledge).

Lauzen, M. M. and D. M. Dozier (2005) 'Maintaining the Double Standard: Portrayals of Age and Gender in Popular Films', *Sex Roles*, 52 (7/8) (April).

Lehman, P. (ed.) (2001) *Masculinity: Bodies, Movies, Culture* (London and New York: Routledge).

Leigh, D. (2003) 'Don't fence me in', *Sight and Sound*, 13 (5) (May).

Loe, M. (2004) *The Rise of Viagra: How the Little Blue Pill Changed Sex in America* (New York: New York University Press).

Lupton, D. and L. Barclay (1997) *Constructing Fatherhood: Discourses and Experiences* (London: Sage).

Macunovich, D. J. (2002) *Birth Quake: The Baby Boom and Its Aftershocks* (Chicago: University of Chicago Press).

Malin, B. (2005) *American Masculinity under Clinton: Popular Media and the Nineties 'Crisis of Masculinity'* (New York: Peter Lang).

Mamet, D. (1998) *True and False: Heresy and Common Sense for the Actor* (London: Faber and Faber).

Mamet, D. (1998) *3 Uses of the Knife: On the Nature and Purpose of Drama* (New York: Columbia University Press).

Mamet, D. (1996) *Make-Believe Town: Essays and Remembrances* (London: Faber and Faber).

Mamet, D. (1993) 'Realism' in *Oleanna* (London: Methuen Drama).

Mamet, D. (1991) *On Directing Film* (New York: Penguin).

Mamet, D. (1987) *Writing in Restaurants* (New York: Penguin).

Marable, M. (1995) *Beyond Black and White: Transforming African-American Politics* (New York: Verso).

Marcus, D. (2004) *Happy Days and Wonder Years: The Fifties and Sixties in Contemporary Cultural Politics* (New Brunswick, NJ: Rutgers University Press).

Marcus, G. (2000) *Double Trouble: Bill Clinton and Elvis Presley in a Land of No Alternatives* (New York: Picador).

Markson, E. W. and C. A. Taylor (2000) 'The Mirror Has Two Faces', *Ageing and Society*, 20 (2) (March).

Marshall, B. L. and S. Katz (2002) 'Forever Functional: Sexual Fitness and the Ageing Male Body', *Body and Society*, 8 (December).

Marshall, P. D. (1997) *Celebrity and Power: Fame in Contemporary Culture* (Minneapolis, MN: University of Minnesota Press).

Martin, J. (1991) *Voice in Modern Theatre* (London and New York: Routledge).

McDonald, P. (2004) 'Why Study Film Acting? Some Opening Reflections' in C. Baron, D. Carson and F. Tomasulo (eds) *More Than a Method: Trends and Traditions in Contemporary Film Performance* (Detroit: Wayne State University Press).

McDonald, P. (1998) 'The 'Unmanning' Word: Language, Masculinity and Political Correctness in the Work of David Mamet and Philip Roth', *Journal of American Studies of Turkey*, 7.

McDonough, C. (1997) *Staging Masculinity: Male Identity in Contemporary American Drama* (Jefferson, NC: McFarland).

Medved, M. (1992) *Hollywood vs. America: Popular Culture and the War on Traditional Values* (New York: HarperCollins).

Mellencamp, P. (1999) 'From Anxiety to Equanimity: Crisis and Generational Continuity on TV, at the Movies, in Life, in Death' in Woodward (ed.) *Figuring Age: Women, Bodies, Generations* (Bloomington, IN: Indiana University Press).

Modleski, T. (1991) *Feminism Without Women: Culture and Criticism in a 'Postfeminist' Age* (New York: Routledge).

Monteith, S. (2008) *American Culture in the 1960s* (Edinburgh: Edinburgh University Press).

Morrison, T. (1993) *Playing in the Dark: Whiteness and the Literary Imagination* (London: Pan).

Murphy, B. (2004) '*Oleanna*: Language and Power' in C. Bigsby (ed.) *The Cambridge Companion to David Mamet* (Cambridge: Cambridge University Press).

Naremore, J. (1990) *Acting in the Cinema* (Berkeley, CA: University of California Press).

Naremore, J. (1984) 'Film and the Performance Frame', *Film Quarterly*, 38 (2) (Winter).

Neal, M. A. (2006) *New Black Man* (New York: Routledge).

Neale, S. (1993) 'Masculinity as Spectacle: Reflections on Men and Mainstream Cinema', in S. Cohan and I. R. Hark (eds) *Screening the Male: Exploring Masculinities in Hollywood Cinema* (New York: Routledge).

Negra, D. and S. Holmes (2008) 'Introduction', *Genders*, 48, special issue: Going Cheap? Female Celebrity in Reality, Tabloid and Scandal Genres.

Pearson, R. (1999) 'A Star Performs: Mr March, Mr Mason and Mr Maine' in P. Krämer and A. Lovell (eds) *Screen Acting* (London: Routledge).

Pearson, R. (1992) *Eloquent Gestures: The Transformation of Performance Style in the Griffith Biograph Films* (Berkeley, CA: California University Press).

Peberdy, D. (2013) 'Acting and Performance in Film Noir' forthcoming in H. Hanson and A. Spicer (eds) *The Blackwell Companion to Film Noir* (Oxford: Blackwell).

Peberdy, D. (2013) 'Male Sounds and Speech Affectations: Voicing Masculinity' forthcoming in J. Jaeckle (ed.) *Film Dialogue* (London: Wallflower).

Peberdy, D. (2010) 'From Wimps to Wild Men: Bipolar Masculinity and the Paradoxical Performances of Tom Cruise', *Men & Masculinities*, 13 (2) (December).

Peberdy, D. (2007) 'Tongue-tied: Film and Theatre Voices in David Mamet's *Oleanna*', *Screening the Past*, Special Issue: Cinema/Theatre/Adaptation (Spring/Summer).

Pfeil, F. (1995) *White Guys: Studies in Postmodern Domination and Difference* (London: Verso).

Pomerance, M. (2004) 'A Royal Audience: Voyages of Involvement in David Fincher's *The Game*', *Quarterly Review of Film and Video*, 21 (3).

Pomerance, M. (ed.) (2001) *Ladies and Gentlemen, Boys and Girls: Gender in Film at the End of the Twentieth Century* (New York: State University of New York Press).

Popenoe, D. (1996) *Life Without Father* (New York: Free Press).

Powrie, P., A. Davis and B. Babington (eds) (2004) *The Trouble with Men: Masculinities in European and Hollywood Cinema* (London: Wallflower Press).

Prince, S. and W. E. Hensley (1992) 'The Kuleshov Effect: Recreating the Classic Experiment', *Cinema Journal*, 31 (2) (Winter).

Ray, R. B. (1985) *A Certain Tendency of the Hollywood Cinema 1930–1980* (Princeton, NJ: Princeton University Press).

Richardson, B. (2001) 'Voice and Narration in Postmodern Drama', *New Literary History*, 32.

Roberts, R. (2004) 'The Clinton Show: Notes on a Postmodern President' in T. G. Shields, J. M. Whayne and D. R. Kelley (eds) *The Clinton Riddle: Perspectives on the Forty-Second President* (Fayetteville: University of Arkansas Press).

Robinson, S. (2000) *Marked Men: White Masculinity in Crisis* (New York: Columbia University Press).

Roediger, D. (1994) *Towards the Abolition of Whiteness: Essays on Race, Class and Politics* (New York: Verso).

Rotskoff, L. (2002) *Love on the Rocks: Men, Women and Alcohol in Post-World War II America* (Chapel Hill, NC: University of North Carolina Press).

Ruitenbeek, H. (1963) 'Men Alone: The Male Homosexual and the Disintegrated Family', *The Problem of Homosexuality in Modern Society* (New York: E.P. Dutton).

Russell, C. (1993) *The Master Trend: How the Baby Boom Generation is Remaking America* (New York: Plenum Press).

Rutherford (1988) 'Who's That Man?' in R. Chapman and J. Rutherford (eds) *Male Order: Unwrapping Masculinity* (London: Lawrence and Wishart).

Ryan, M. and D. Kellner (1988) *Camera Politica: The Politics and Ideology of Contemporary Hollywood Film* (Bloomington: Indiana University Press).

Sanchez, M. C. and L. Schlossberg (2001) *Passing: Identity and Interpretation in Sexuality, Race and Religion* (New York: New York University Press).

Savran, D. (2001) *Taking It Like a Man: White Masculinity, Masochism, and Contemporary American Culture* (Princeton, NJ: Princeton University Press).

Savran, D. (1996) 'The Sadomasochist in the Closet: White Masculinity and the Culture of Victimization', *Differences*, 8 (2).

Schechner, R. (2007) 'Performance Studies: The Broad Spectrum Approach' in H. Bial (ed.) *The Performance Studies Reader*, Second Edition (Abingdon: Routledge).

Schechner, R. (2006) *Performance Studies*, Second Edition (New York: Routledge).

Schwalbe, M. (1996) *Unlocking the Iron Cage: The Men's Movement, Gender Politics, and American Culture* (Oxford: Oxford University Press).

Sconce, J. (2002) 'Irony, Nihilism and the New American "Smart" Film', *Screen*, 43 (4) (Winter).

Sedgwick, E. K. (1990) *Epistemology of the Closet* (Berkeley and Los Angeles: University of California Press).

Sedgwick, E. K. and A. Parker (eds) (1995) *Performativity and Performance* (New York: Routledge).

Segal, L. (1990) *Slow Motion: Changing Masculinities, Changing Men* (London: Virago Press).

Sergi, G. (1999) 'Actors and the Sound Gang' in P. Krämer and A. Lovell (eds) *Screen Acting* (London: Routledge).

Shaffer, L. (1977) 'Reflections on the Face in Film', *Film Quarterly*, 31 (2) (Winter).

Shields, T. G., J. M. Whayne and D. R. Kelley (eds) (2004) *The Clinton Riddle: Perspectives on the Forty-Second President* (Fayetteville: University of Arkansas Press).

Shingler, M. (2006) 'Fasten Your Seatbelts and Prick Up Your Ears: The Dramatic Human Voice in Film', *Scope: An Online Journal of Film Studies*, 5, Sound: Special Issue (June).

Silverman, K. (1992) *Male Subjectivity at the Margins* (New York: Routledge).

Sklar, R. (1992) *City Boys: Cagney, Bogart, Garfield* (Princeton, NJ: Princeton University Press).

Slotkin, R. (1992) *Gunfighter Nation: The Myth of the Frontier in Twentieth Century America* (New York: Atheneum).

Slotkin, R. (1985) *The Fatal Environment: The Myth of the Frontier in the Age of Industrialization 1800–1890* (New York: Atheneum).

Slotkin, R. (1973) *Regeneration through Violence: The Mythology of the American Frontier 1600–1860* (Norman: University of Oklahoma Press).

Smith, C. R. (2002) 'Gender and Family Values in the Clinton Presidency and 1990s Hollywood Film' in P. J. Davies and P. Wells (eds) *American Film and Politics from Reagan to Bush Jr.* (Manchester: Manchester University Press).

Smith, J. (2008) *Vocal Tracks: Performance and Sound Media* (Los Angeles, CA: University of California Press).

Smith, S. (2007) 'Voices in Film' in *Close-Up 02* (London: Wallflower).

Snead, J. (1994) *White Screens/Black Images: Hollywood from the Dark Side* (New York: Routledge).

Sobchack, V. (1999) 'Scary Women: Cinema, Surgery and Special Effects', in K. Woodward (ed.) *Figuring Age: Women, Bodies, Generations* (Bloomington, IN: Indiana University Press).

Solomon-Godeau, A. (1997) *Male Trouble: A Crisis in Representation* (London: Thames and Hudson).

Sonnenschein, D. (2001) *Sound Design: The Expressive Power of Music, Voice, and Sound Effects in Cinema* (Los Angeles: Michael Wiese Productions).

Sontag, S. (1972) 'The Double Standard of Aging', *Saturday Review of Literature*, 39.

Spector-Mersel, G. (2006) 'Never-aging Stories: Western Hegemonic Masculinity Scripts', *Journal of Gender Studies*, 15 (1) (March).

Spigel, L. (2001) *Welcome to the Dreamhouse: Popular Media and Postwar Suburbs* (Durham, NC: Duke University Press).

Stacey, J. (1996) *In the Name of the Family: Rethinking Family Values in the Postmodern Age* (Boston, MA: Beacon Press).

Staiger, J. (1985) ' "The eyes are really the focus": Photoplay Acting and Film Form and Style', *Wide Angle*, 6 (4).

Stern, L. and G. Kouvaros (eds) (1999) *Falling for You: Essays on Cinema and Performance* (Sydney: Power Publications).

Studlar, G. (2001) 'Cruise-ing into the Millennium: Performative Masculinity, Stardom, and the All-American Boy's Body' in M. Pomerance (ed.) *Ladies and Gentlemen, Boys and Girls: Gender in Film at the End of the Twentieth Century* (New York: State University of New York Press).

Tasker, Y. (1998) *Working Girls: Gender and Sexuality in Popular Cinema* (London: Routledge).

Tasker, Y. (1993) *Spectacular Bodies: Gender, Genre and the Action Cinema* (London: Routledge).

Thompson, J. O. (1978) 'Screen Acting and the Commutation Test', *Screen*, 19 (2).

Thompson, K. (1985) 'The "American" Style of Acting', in D. Bordwell, J. Staiger and K. Thompson (eds) *The Classical Hollywood Cinema: Film Style and Mode of Production to 1960* (New York: Routledge).

Tincknell, E. and D. Chambers (2002) 'Performing the Crisis: Fathering, Gender and Representation in Two 1990s Films', *Journal of Popular Film and Television*, 29 (4).

Tomkins, S. (1963) *Affect, Imagery, Consciousness: The Positive Affects (Vol. I)* (New York: Springer).

Tomkins, S. (1963) *Affect, Imagery, Consciousness: The Negative Affects (Vol. III)* (New York: Springer).

Turner, V. (1982) *From Ritual to Theatre: The Human Seriousness of Play* (New York: PAJ Publications).

Wald, G. (2000) *Crossing the Line: Racial Passing in Twentieth Century US Literature and Culture* (Durham, NC: Duke University Press).

Weis, L. (2006) 'Masculinity, Whiteness and the New Economy: An Exploration of Privilege and Loss', *Men & Masculinities*, 8 (3) (January).

West, C. (1993) *Race Matters* (Boston, MA: Beacon Press).

Wexman, V. W. (2004) 'Masculinity in Crisis: Method Acting in Hollywood' in P. R. Wojcik (ed.) *Movie Acting: The Film Reader* (London and New York: Routledge).

Wexman, V. W. (1993) *Creating the Couple: Love, Marriage, and Hollywood Performance* (Princeton, NJ: Princeton University Press).

Whitehead, S. (2002) *Men and Masculinities: Key Themes and New Directions* (Massachusetts: Polity).

Whitehead, S. and F. J. Barrett (eds) (2001) *The Masculinities Reader* (Cambridge: Polity).

Wicks, S. (1996) *Warriors and Wildmen: Men, Masculinity, and Gender* (Westport, CT: Bergin and Garvey).

Wierzbicka, A. (1999) *Emotions Across Languages and Cultures* (Cambridge: Cambridge University Press).

Williams, L. R. (2005) *The Erotic Thriller in Contemporary Cinema* (Edinburgh: Edinburgh University Press).

Williams, L. R. and M. Hammond (eds) (2006) *Contemporary American Cinema* (London: McGraw Hill).

Willis, S. (2003) 'The Politics of Disappointment: Todd Haynes Rewrites Douglas Sirk', *Camera Obscura*, 54, 18 (3).

Wilmeth, D. B. (2004) 'Mamet and the Actor' in C. Bigsby (ed.) *The Cambridge Companion to David Mamet* (Cambridge: Cambridge University Press).

Wojcik, P. R. (2006) 'The Sound of Film Acting', *Journal of Film and Video*, 58 (1–2) (Spring/Summer).

Wojcik, P. R. (2004) 'Typecasting' in P. R. Wojcik (ed.) *Movie Acting: The Film Reader* (New York: Routledge).

Wojcik, P. R. (ed.) (2004) *Movie Acting: The Film Reader* (New York: Routledge).

Woodward, K. (2006) 'Performing Age, Performing Gender', *NWSA Journal*, 18 (1) (Spring).

Woodward, K. (ed.) (1999) *Figuring Age: Women, Bodies, Generations* (Bloomington, IN: Indiana University Press).

Woodward, K. (1991) *Aging and Its Discontents: Freud and Other Fictions* (Bloomington: Indiana University Press).

Zinman, T. S. (1992) 'Jewish Aporia: The Rhythm of Talking in Mamet', *Theatre Journal*, 44 (2), American Scenes.

Index